STRATEGIC PLANNING
FOR
TECHNOLOGY INDUSTRIES

STRATEGIC PLANNING
FOR
TECHNOLOGY INDUSTRIES

PHILIP M. SHERMAN

Xerox Corporation

ADDISON-WESLEY PUBLISHING COMPANY
Reading, Massachusetts • Menlo Park, California
London • Amsterdam • Don Mills, Ontario • Sydney

Library of Congress Cataloging in Publication Data

Sherman, Philip M.
    Strategic planning for technology industries.
    Bibliography.
    Includes index.
    1. Corporate planning.   I. Title
HD30.28.S43   658.4'012   81-1446
ISBN 0-201-06664-5   AACR2

Reproduced by Addison-Wesley from camera-ready copy supplied by the author.

ISBN 0-201-06664-5
ABCDEFGHIJ-DO-8987654321

To my wife, Doris

PREFACE

The development of new technologies provides the management of technology-based corporations with the opportunity to offer products incorporating major advances over their predecessor products. At the same time, new technologies provide threats to such corporations as their competitors move ahead with their own advances.

Because of the opportunities and threats thus generated, the task of strategic planning in corporations is often difficult and complex. It involves gathering, analyzing, and interpreting a great deal of information. It involves identifying many possible activities and selecting from among them those which will best prepare the company for its future, however its management defines that future.

This book describes the strategic planning process as it applies to technology-based, profit-making corporations. Its goal is to explain the steps in this process, which is an essential procedure for all companies, technology-based or otherwise. The book describes the steps in planning in detail, offering a framework or structure for it. That process can be seen to be a logical sequence of tasks that answer this question for management: *"Where do we want to go and how should we get there?"*

The subject of strategic planning is large, comprehensive, and complex. This book does not attempt to cover all aspects of the process. Rather, it highlights major steps, giving some details. It emphasizes technology and the manner in which the planning process has to proceed to deal with it. Technology is, after all, the driving force in the companies under scrutiny; all other operations flow from its development and use.

The book has several features included to clarify and amplify the planning task. First, since implementing strategic planning is not without its problems, many that arise are discussed. In the first chapter, an overview of some problems is given, and after each of the steps of the strategic planning process is discussed, in subsequent chapters, comments are included on the problems associated with them. A summary of major problems and suggested solutions to them are given near the end of the book. Second, in order to illustrate the many steps in planning, a fictitious company, ConTronics Corporation, is introduced. As each step in planning is described, the actions taken by ConTronics management in carrying out that step are given. Third, the interrelationship among organizations and the flow of information among them are illustrated by the use of flow diagrams. Fourth, the timing of all steps is shown graphically in a sequence of calendar schedules.

The chapters of the book, in sequence, describe the steps in strategic planning. Chapter 1 provides an overview of both technology-based companies and the strategic planning process. Chapters 2 and 3, respectively, describe the process of gathering information about a company and its environment, activities undertaken to provide understanding of the current state of matters. Chapter 4 deals with projecting that state into the future. Chapter 5 describes the process of setting corporate objectives and goals.

Chapter 6 addresses many issues on technology that management must consider as it undertakes planning. Chapter 7, continuing the description of planning, describes the task of setting strategy, and Chapter 8 shows how that strategy is translated into a plan document. Chapter 9 describes how computers can be used to aid planning. Chapter 10 summarizes all of the steps in planning, thereby creating a theoretical planning framework, and describes how, in practice, changes to this framework must be made. Finally, Chapter 11 takes a brief look at the future. A glossary of the most important terms used appears near the end of the book.

Throughout the book, the point is made that, while a methodology is offered in a formal manner for the planning process, management must feel free to modify the method. All companies have their own problems, their own management styles, and their own philosophies of operation. The methodology here should be considered as a set of guidelines only.

In this book, the organizational units within a company, such as the research or the manufacturing organization, are identified by using capital letters. Thus, the term *Research* refers to the research division or group within a company. The term *research* refers to the activity that takes place in Research.

Strategic planning or *long-range planning*? These terms are often used interchangeably, and the former is currently more popular. Both refer to a corporation's planning that encompasses a rather long period, typically five to ten years. I personally favor the use of *long-range strategic planning* as more accurate than either in its connotation. *Strategic planning*, in my view, refers to the highest level of planning that corporate management undertakes; others are management control and operational control. It is concerned with formulating corporate philosophy and objectives, as opposed to detailed plans and budgets. *Long-range planning* implies planning that extends well into the future and encompasses what would be a "long range of time" for a particular company. The combined term reflects both the concepts of highest-level thinking and long term, though it is perhaps too lengthy to be used often.

Additional references given at the ends of chapters supplement those cited in the various chapters. They are listed in reverse chronological order. These have been selected as general references on strategic planning and as references for specific topics.

I wish to acknowledge the considerable assistance provided me by Professor William Hamilton of the Wharton School, University of Pennsylvania. He offered innumerable excellent suggestions for improvements of the material. Carolyn Tseou, of Xerox Corporation, identified many sources of information for planning. Joel E. Kocen, of Gleason Works, provided valuable help in financial areas. Many corporations, by answering my survey on strategic planning, provided insights into their approaches and their problems. Rima Zolina, of the Addison-Wesley editorial staff, was very helpful in improving the manuscript style and in the design of the book. Profound thanks must go to the management of Xerox Corporation, for its support of the writing of this book, which included the use of a computer-based document preparation system. This entire book was written and composed by using that system. Dale Green, of Xerox, provided the means for the computer printing of this book. Finally, I want to thank my wife, Doris, for her continuing encouragement during the writing of the book.

Philip M. Sherman

Rochester, New York
July, 1981

CONTENTS

1

STRATEGIC PLANNING

INTRODUCTION

Corporations, whatever their business, exist in markets where they must sell their products and services. Though they operate *today*, they by necessity must make plans to succeed *tomorrow*. This means they must make decisions today about what they will do in the future.

The future is unknown in its entirety. Much can be predicted — by examining historical trends and knowing about the "laws" of change — but there is also much that cannot be predicted. A corporation has to look both inward and outward to gather information for attempts at making such predictions.

With this knowledge and the knowledge of where it would like to be in the years ahead, the corporation can make decisions and set down a strategy for the future. With this done, it decides where and how to allocate its resources over time.

The task just described is *strategic planning*, and all corporations need to undertake it. Companies whose products are technology based have special needs in strategic planning, and they must use a special approach to the task.

1.1 TECHNOLOGY INDUSTRIES

Technology-Based Companies

Many corporations today sell products and services that rely upon applications of modern technologies. The technologies, in turn, draw heavily upon applied science and technical innovation. These corporations can generally be characterized as follows: they put to practice inventions described in patents, spend a significant proportion of their budget on research and development of new technologies, have large staffs of scientifically trained personnel, and sell products that are relatively new to the marketplace. They collectively comprise a number of industries that are known as the *technology industries.*

Technology is an elusive concept, and writers differ somewhat on its meaning. A reasonable definition is that technology is the systematic application of fundamental, scientific phenomena and principles in a device, process, or concept that performs a function useful to mankind. In the corporate milieux, the phrase *useful to mankind* would be replaced by *having commercial value.* Battelle Memorial Institute has defined *key technologies* as "those products, processes, systems, devices, and their applications which create geographically pervasive and significant effects on modes of conducting business, national behavior, production processes, recovery and utilization of resources, or the health and well being of mankind" [1].

The companies in technology industries are often called *technology-based, high-technology,* or simply *technology* companies. They share a number of characteristics, as noted above; the most frequently cited one is their relatively high ratio of research and development (R & D) expenditures to revenues. Table 1-1, extracted from *Business Week,* shows values of this ratio for several industries in the United States, listed as being "high" or "low" in technology [2]. (The overall ratio, for all the companies in the referenced article, representing $1,277 billion in sales, is 1.9%.) Clearly, the words *high* and *low* in this context are somewhat arbitrary. Several computer companies, generally small ones, spend over 10% of sales on R & D. Several companies in the drug, electronics, instrumentation, and semiconductor fields spend 7 to 10% of sales on R & D.

One must interpret such data with caution, since the ratio of R & D expenses to sales is not the only measure of technology level. Furthermore, R & D

Table 1-1.   R & D Expenditures in the United States, by Industry

Rates of R & D expenditures shown as a fraction of sales; 1980 data.

"High-technology industries"		"Low-technology industries"	
Industry	% of sales	Industry	% of sales
Computers	6.3	Tobacco	0.3
Semiconductors	6.0	Fuel	0.4
Drugs	4.9	Textiles and apparel	0.5
Aerospace	4.5	Steel	0.6
Office equipment	4.3	Foods	0.6
Instruments	4.2	Paper	0.8

expenditures are more logically related to future sales, several years into the future. Nonetheless, the table serves to illustrate the types of industries that are technology-based.

Particulars of Technology Industries

Examples of modern technologies that are of interest here include electronics, pharmaceuticals, optics, reprographics, lasers, computers, data processing, word processing, chemicals, instrumentation, and communications. There are many others, but these are among the technologies that are receiving the most attention and are developing the fastest.

Technology industries have the advantage of providing products that, by virtue of new technology embodiments, offer significant improvement over existing products in such areas as cost, quality, reliability, and product features. When a technology is developed that provides a quantum jump of improvement in one or more of these ways, the ensuing product may yield a fortune for its owner. The classic case of xerography and Xerox Corporation illustrates this. Xerography offered such a marked improvement in quality and convenience over its predecessor technology that it revolutionized an office function — making copies of a document — and created a new industry. Even when a new technology-based product cannot provide major improvements, it usually offers a better benefit-to-cost ratio. Sometimes it can offer both. (In order to simplify the text, when the term *products* is used in this book, *products and services* are intended.)

Along with such advantages, technology-based companies have problems peculiar to their class. Product lifetime tends to be short due to rapid technology advances. Because applications of new technologies can dramatically effect change, companies that develop them can be threatened by competitors whose technologies offer their own dramatic improvements. In recent years, technology advances have occurred so rapidly in many industries, that the threat is a real and serious one. For these reasons, planning for the future in high-technology companies is extremely important, must involve careful monitoring of the outside world, and must be flexible enough to allow sudden adaptation to new conditions.

There is often much risk associated with technology development. The cost of developing a new technology and putting it to practice in a new or improved product may be extremely high and the success it promises may be very uncertain. The cost can be high because ever-advancing frontiers force companies to attack ever more difficult problems. An example is provided by the technologies required to produce fuel. As natural energy resources dwindle in this country, more technology development and expenses are required to produce a given unit measure of fuel. Sudden breakthroughs that ease particular problems may be exceptions to this, but they cannot be planned. The uncertainty of success can be high because many efforts in technology development fail in the face of these difficulties. The element of risk is often very high and forces many an executive to assume a low-risk profile in guiding the company. This approach lessens the risk but also lessens the chances of technological breakthroughs.

It is evident that technology-based companies have their own particular advantages and disadvantages in trying to plan for the future. Planning in such firms must take these particular traits into account.

The primary motivation for companies to undertake development of technology-based products is to be able to offer important advantages in the products over competitive products. This should be evident from the preceding discussion. There are, however, other reasons for undertaking technology development programs. Companies sometimes do so to develop better versions of their own existing products. These are products that are more reliable, less costly to operate, and smaller; they also have more features, and so on. Some firms develop technology mainly to gain advantages in manufacturing cost, so as to be able to sell a product at lower cost.

Igor Ansoff and John Stewart express the view that management in technology-based companies must be concerned about four factors [3]: (a) There must be serious, continuous evaluation of technology alternatives, which may involve external acquisition of technologies and/or companies and the hiring or training of staff in new technology areas; (b) an adaptive organization is required because product and process development are relatively rapid; (c) management must plan for the ready substitution of products for one another, since the product market is very dynamic; (d) close supervision of technical efforts is required; senior managers must know a great deal about technical problems and performance.

The Customer's Point of View

With all the emphasis on technology in the minds of managers in high-technology companies and in this book, it is easy to overlook the fact that customers are not particularly excited by high technology. They respond more readily to the performance of the products they seek out and buy; cost, quality, reliability, and special features are important to them. Technology thus must be thought of as a means to achieve these ends. Customers do not usually care what is inside the "black box," as long as it works.

1.2 WHY STRATEGIC PLANNING IS NECESSARY

Planning for Survival

Management has an obligation to see that its corporation survives in a manner satisfactory to those who own it, its stockholders. A corporation operates continuously in an environment that both nurtures it and threatens it. The environment nurtures by providing a market for its products and it threatens by offering competition from other corporations in that same market. Because of this, management must understand that environment and the way it is likely to change in the future.

All corporations face both opportunities and threats; technology-based corporations face special kinds of opportunities and threats. There may be opportunities, for example, to improve profits by selling products in new areas of business or by improving existing ones, both such improvements resulting from technology advances. There may be threats from a new technology that could make current products obsolete, from competitors who announce competing products, or from a new government regulation that threatens products because of their environmental impact.

Consider a company that is operating acceptably today, making a satisfactory profit. If it could guarantee that this would remain true indefinitely by doing exactly what it is currently doing, there would be no reason for its management to make any changes. There would be no need to make any new decisions now or in the future. In other words, there would be no reason for its management to plan. In truth, of course, the company's environment will change, and new opportunities and threats, many unexpected, will be encountered. If the company does not or cannot respond satisfactorily to these changes, it almost certainly will fail eventually or at best exist in an ever-weakening state. Because of the inevitable change in a company's environment and its attendant uncertainty, its management must undertake formal planning for the future.

A corporation usually requires considerable time — often several years — to respond fully to an opportunity or a threat. Its management must make decisions today about the future. Since the company's environment will change in some ways not fully determinable today, certain other decisions must be postponed until some of that future is known.

What Planning Is

Planning involves making decisions today about what is to be done over a period of time in the future, in response to the expected nature of the company's environment, in order to attain certain desired objectives over that period. The period over which a company should plan depends on the nature of its products; more particularly, it depends on the development time of its technologies.

A corporation, at any given time, operates under some plan, explicitly or otherwise, as it carries out its operations day by day. The corporation's continued existence implies some method whereby it makes decisions; in the absence of such decisions, it would soon cease to exist. Since it expects to be around for some time in the future, it must make decisions that set its course of action into the future. The rate at which it must make decisions and the scope of those decisions will be different for other companies and will vary over time within the company. In any event, strategic planning is necessary for the proper making of decisions over time about the company's future. In summary, we can provide a useful, concise definition:

Strategic planning is a process whereby corporate objectives for the future are identified in response to perceived opportunities and threats and whereby activities are selected and resources are allocated to meet these objectives.

Some additional comments can be made about strategic planning: (a) it deals with the futurity of current decisions, rather than with future decisions; (b) it involves forecasting trends and events in the future, as a basis for taking action; (c) the forecasting entails an orderly, systematic approach to the gathering and analysis of external and internal information; (d) the planning does not eliminate risks; rather, it helps assess the risks that must be taken by a company.

Peter Drucker defines strategic planning as "the continuous process of making present entrepreneurial decisions systematically and with the greatest knowledge of their futurity; organizing the efforts needed to carry out these decisions; and measuring the results of these decisions against the expectations through organized, systematic feedback" [4]. This definition imparts its own flavor to the definition and includes the concept of monitoring a plan.

Strategic planning is an activity that is a major part of the management process; it is not distinct from it. It is a responsibility of all managers in a corporation, at all levels. Planning enables them to carry out all their responsibilities as managers, for it provides guidance for doing so. All the tasks that one associates with management − setting objectives, establishing policies, organizing, directing, motivating, controlling, and providing resources − are related in a direct way to the planning process. Strategic planning is actually tied strongly to all decision-making processes in management.

Though the process may seem complex and lengthy as developed in these chapters, it need not be. The extent of the task for a particular company will depend on its size, on the nature of its products, and on its management style. A company must develop its own planning procedures to meet its particular needs.

1.3 THE PROCESS OF STRATEGIC PLANNING

Basic Questions

One can summarize the strategic planning process by addressing three basic questions:

1. *Where are we today and where are we going?*

2. *Where do we want to go?*

3. *How do we get there?*

Once a plan is developed and is in use, it is appropriate to ask another question:

4. *Are we getting there satisfactorily?*

The balance of this section and indeed the balance of this book largely address these four questions.

Information Gathering and Analysis

Consider the first basic question: *Where are we today and where are we going?*

In order to proceed with planning, a company's managers must have information on the present and perceived future of the company and its environment. The question above should be broken down into five other questions:

Where are we today?

What are we planning to do?

What is our environment like?

What will our environment be like in the future?

Where are we going in that environment?

What these questions imply is that a projection of the company's future is obtained by an examination of its present status and its current plans as well as by a study of its environment and the environment's projected future. Then, the company's future — in that future environment — can be projected.

The information needed about the company is obtained from a *self-analysis*, which provides an analysis of the company's major problems, its strengths, its weaknesses, and its resources. The self-analysis addresses the major problems facing the company, its technological position, its present product line, its comparison with competitors, its staffing, its finances, its various other resources, and the trends of all these factors.

Management must also study its company's environment, undertaking an *environmental analysis*. It must consider the nature of the markets the company operates within and the competition's technologies and products. It may be affected by other technology developments, as those in universities or in government. It must also be concerned with the company's political, economic, sociological, demographic, legal, and regulatory environments. The current situation and the expected future in these areas must be examined.

The concern that a company must have for strengths, weaknesses, opportunities, and threats has prompted some authors to use the acronyms *SWOT* and *WOTS* for these factors.

The information gathered from studies of both the company and its environment includes *technology alternatives*, choices of current and future technologies that can be used in the company's products. These alternatives represent technological capabilities and limitations to be considered as new products are conceived and developed. They serve to set the bounds on the technically feasible and help define the economically feasible.

Forecasting

A company must attempt to predict the future of its environment, and forecasting technology developments is important to this task. There are several standard-ized, analytic methods for doing forecasting; all are based on extrapolating historical trends of the past and present. Whatever knowledge one has about specific events that are likely to occur in the future can be used to modify such extrapolations. By undertaking technology forecasting, management can gauge general trends in the environment and so be aided in planning its own technology programs.

Management then makes assumptions about what is expected to happen in its company's future environment. The assumptions are derived from forecasts of future events, and they relate to factors that will have measurable impact on the company. In a technology-based company, technological factors clearly play an important part. Among these factors are the evolution of major technologies, the announcement of competitors' technology products that seriously threaten the company's product line, and new government regulations that demand technological responses. The assumptions collectively provide a projection of the future environment, as perceived by the company. Finally, management forecasts the future of the company in that environment. It does so by determining what impacts on the company's operation future events will have. The information so gathered is used to identify opportunities for new products and to identify threats that management must address.

Setting Objectives

Consider the second basic question: *Where do we want to go?*

Management must define objectives which the company will strive to achieve in the future. These objectives define what management believes can and should be accomplished by the company in the future. They may also define the manner in which the accomplishments will be sought. Objectives are developed by a consideration of company strengths, weaknesses, opportunities, and threats, as well as management's perception of what broad accomplishments it wishes to make.

The setting of objectives is the actual starting point in strategic planning. Management plans the future course of its company by aiming at objectives to be achieved and then taking whatever actions it deems necessary for achieving them. Objectives must be carefully chosen. They must be well-defined and achievable in a reasonable time frame. They must be based upon management's best understanding of the company and its environment. They must be broadly based so as to encompass the entire corporation, yet they must be specific enough to avoid ambiguities in the planning process. They must be guides to action and provide aids to decision making.

The desired future of the company, as defined by its objectives, can be compared to the projected future. The difference in those futures defines a *gap*, and that gap helps drive the formulation of corporate strategy.

Setting Strategy

Consider the third basic question: *How do we get there?*

With objectives set, information about the company and its environment available, assumptions made, company strengths and weaknesses identified, opportunities and threats spelled out, and the futures gap defined, management can develop its strategy for the future. There are many factors that must play a role in the formulation of strategy. These include the current strategy (developed last year), the status of the company and its environment as revealed in the information analysis done, the futures gap, and the state of the competition. In formulating strategy, the company must address such matters as selection among possible alternative technology development programs, the allocation of resources, possible changes in the scope of products (which might involve diversification), shifts in budgets among its divisions, possible acquisitions and divestitures, and changes to the company's organizational structure. The purpose of the strategy is to set a course for the company that will aim to achieve corporate objectives.

Writing the Plan

The next task is that of actually writing the plan document. The statement of objectives and strategy are the preface to the plan. The heart of the plan comprises descriptions of activities to be undertaken, which include tabulations of resource allocations made to these activities. These descriptions are called *operational plans*. They include a budget, which provides a means for exercising control over a company's operation and performance. Decisions on allocation are among the most important made by management, for they determine the course of company operations. Associated with this task is that of deciding on policies for the acquisition, use, and disposition of those resources.

Monitoring Progress

Finally, consider the fourth basic question: *Are we getting there satisfactorily?*

The developed plan must be monitored as it is used, so that management can determine if the company is operating and succeeding as intended. To this end, it is important to identify milestones in the planning process, so that progress can be measured against them. During the time the plan is in effect, certain progress is planned and certain outside events are expected to occur. However, some events that occur are not expected. In any event, certain intermediate goals can be identified; these are milestones. Actual progress and events should be compared to milestones, so that an assessment can be made of progress.

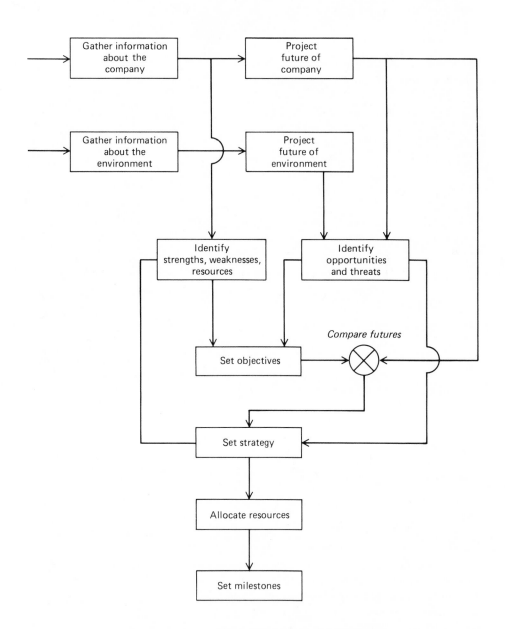

Fig. 1-1.   An outline of strategic planning.

Corrective action can then be taken as needed. When unexpected events take place, the company must respond. The response may be to consider changes either in the plan or in the milestones.

Divisional Planning

Not only must a corporation do strategic planning as a whole, but all divisions in the corporation must also plan. The planning in divisions is similar to that for the corporation, but there are these differences: (a) the divisions have charters whose boundaries have been prescribed by top management; (b) coordination of these plans with the other divisions' plans is essential; and (c) a section on matters beyond the control of specific divisions must be included.

If a corporation is organized along product-line divisions, it may be more appropriate for each of those divisions to have customized planning. There may be different sorts of objectives and strategies required. For example, if the product lines are very different from one another, the planning tasks may have to be done differently in each division. There should nonetheless be an overall coherence to the corporation's plan as a whole.

A Diagram of the Process

The strategic planning process can be shown as a flowchart (Fig. 1-1). This is a simplification of the planning process, but it portrays the essential steps and their manner of interconnection.

There is a danger inherent in the use of a diagram like this one. It implies a formalization and rigidity to the process that is, in truth, not always there. The steps are iterative and pathways are traveled many times, with loops back to earlier steps. The diagram can serve only to suggest the general sequence of steps and flow of information.

Periods for Planning and for the Plan

In this book, we assume that a new strategic plan is developed each year. The plan should be completed well ahead of the start of the period under consideration, in order that a budget can be drawn up for the first year or two of that period. We assume here that the plan is due August 1, five months prior to the plan period. Fig. 1-2 shows a calendar-year schedule of strategic planning activity; this year is termed the *planning year*. In general, the time during which planning is done is termed the *planning period*. Each of the steps discussed in this chapter is located in time in that chart. The actual times shown are approximate; they depend upon individual company characteristics and requirements. The schedule indicates that information gathering is a continuous process, but it is most intensive in the first quarter. Other tasks are more concentrated over time.

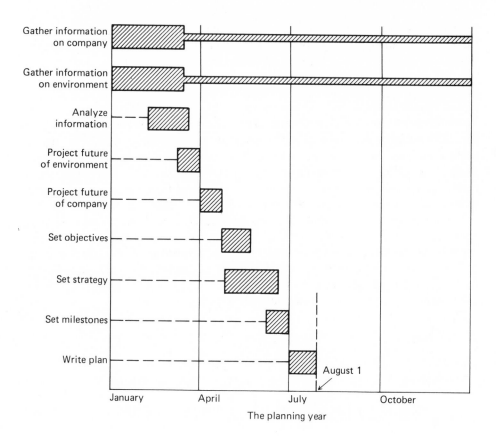

Fig. 1-2.   A schedule for planning.

The *plan period* is the time period for which planning is done. In this book, we assume a five-year plan period. The plan period in most corporations is in fact five years; most other corporations use longer periods. A company should use a period appropriate to its needs. The proper period of a strategic plan is largely a function of the "time constants" inherent in the company's products. Foremost among these is the product development time, from initial concept to commercialization. For example, if a product requires four years from its initial conception to its market introduction, at least four years must be addressed in the strategic plan, so that decisions affecting all phases of that product's development can be planned, if not made. In some instances, a portion of a company's plans may have to extend beyond the plan period. It is quite appropriate to include such longer-term activities into the strategic plan.

Other factors determining the plan period are times of planning and construction of new sites and buildings, acquisition times of certain supplies and equipment, and the recruitment time for key personnel. As another example, a company's products may require 18 months to develop from start to finish, but the company may need three years to build new plants and hire skilled engineers who are hard to find. These factors tend to apply pressure to lengthen the plan period. Countering this, the uncertainty of the future applies pressure to reduce the plan period. That uncertainty increases with the time out into the future under consideration.

In general, the plan period should be longer for technology-based companies than for other companies, because of the long time generally involved in technology development. A period of eight to ten years may be advisable. Since projections of both company performance and the external environment are extremely difficult to estimate so far out, management can feasibly forecast only a relatively few items. It is reasonable to undertake *component planning*, which involves further-out planning for those aspects of a business where long lead times are inherent and near-out planning for other areas. Individual companies' needs vary so much that no single approach can be universally used.

Operating Plans

Following the preparation of a strategic plan, management must draw up an *operating plan* for the upcoming year or two. The operating plan is similar to the strategic plan, but it covers a shorter period in more detail. Generally, this plan will include the tactics needed to implement a strategy. It includes more details and specifics for operating the company on a daily, weekly, or monthly basis.

Approaches to Planning

There are three basic approaches to planning, from the point of view of the forces that drive it and their origins. One is the *top-down* approach, where the chief executive officer or other top-level managers set guidelines. In a centralized company, the planning starts with the chief executive officer (CEO). In a decentralized company, it starts either with the CEO or the heads of divisions. This approach insures that top management will strongly influence the company's direction.

A second approach is termed *bottom-up*. Here, divisions receive no guidelines, and all levels of management submit plans upwards, starting with the lowest feasible units. An advantage of this approach is that lower management is sometimes in a better position to develop plans. Disadvantages are that there may be a lack of coordination among the resultant plans and that there may be little resemblance between these plans and what top management wants to accomplish. Further, they may collectively be beyond the company's capabilities.

A third approach is the combination of these two, wherein there is likely to be much dialogue among all levels of management. This is the approach advocated in this book. Here, top management provides guidance by generating objectives for the corporation, which are broad enough to allow divisions flexibility in developing their plans. Lower management, in turn, provides top management with data on technology advances made in the company and outside. In this way, plans take both corporate objectives and technological opportunities and limitations into account. Objectives are based on these limitations, while the opportunities suggest goals for the technologies.

A Planning Model

A *holistic* planning model can be designed to indicate the interaction of various parameters and forces in determining company results, in sales, cash flow, and related factors. A diagram of this model appears in Fig. 1-3; it is based on one offered by Laurence Liebson [5]. The model has two subsystems, each of which has both positive and negative feedback loops.

> Product–market subsystem. *The positive loop*: An increase in sales leads to an increase in investment, which results in an increase in R & D, manufacturing, and marketing expenses as well as improvements in new products and features, improved product performance and quality, production, and company image. These lead to increases in product availability, market share, and sales, in sequence. *The negative loop*: An increase in sales decreases product availability, which decreases sales. The feedback loop is in equilibrium when sales equals production capacity.

> Financial subsystem. *The positive loop*: An increase in investments ultimately increases sales, as shown above (in the product–market subsystem), which in turn directly increases investments and also increases earnings, proving increased internal cash flow and equity, both of which increase investments. *The negative loop*: An increase in investments leads to a decrease in internal cash flow, which causes the company to increase its debt financing, which in turn increases the level of debt outstanding and decreases the unused debt capacity. The lower unused debt capacity means that a lower supply of funds is available for future investments and so constrains the latter, completing the feedback loop.

Planning in Technology-Based Companies

Just as technology-based companies differ from other corporations, so do their strategic planning techniques. Surveillance of the environment, with special attention paid to the competition and technology developments in general, is vital to such companies. The components of the environment's future of concern to the company are relatively more unpredictable; there is more uncertainty so plans must be more flexible. Investment in R & D is a significant portion of such companies' total expense allocation, so a great deal of attention must be paid to planning R & D. In general, strategic planning for technology companies is more difficult and riskier than it is for other companies.

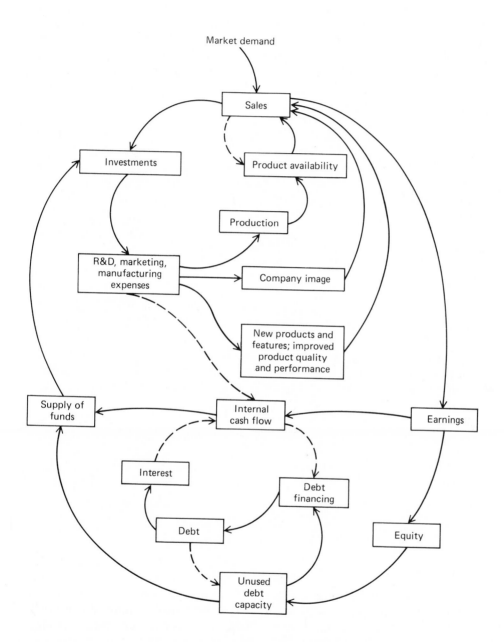

Fig. 1-3. A holistic planning model.

To a large extent, the strategic planning done in high-technology companies begins with research and development activities. These activities drive such companies; planning in manufacturing, sales, and service functions derive from those in R & D. Any technology advance or innovation has a ripple effect that impinges upon these other activities. The relatively small magnitude of the five or six percent of sales devoted to R & D belies its relative importance.

Specialized Types of Planning

The general term *planning* encompasses many different specialized kinds of planning activities. Many aspects of the running of a company involve their own planning processes. This book essentially addresses them all at once in what is best described as *corporate-wide planning*, but certain aspects of company operations merit some specialized attention. In Chapter 7, *Setting Strategy*, some of these processes — *business planning, product planning, resource planning*, and *project planning* — are discussed.

Technology within Companies

Technology plays a special role within corporations, whether they are technology-oriented or not, that is worthy of passing comment. Technology, most often computer-related, is used internally to allow companies to operate more efficiently; this is a strong trend that is continuing, with technology playing an ever-increasing role in internal operations. This phenomenon can be illustrated by some examples. Through the use of sophisticated laboratory equipment, complex testing and data collection and analysis proceed more efficiently and rapidly than previously. Computers are used in design and drafting processes, cutting costs and saving time. Numerically controlled machines save time and costs on routine manufacturing operations. Marketing studies can be scientifically planned and executed with the aid of computers. Planning is aided by the use of computer-based financial models that allow a variety of situations to be simulated and tested. Finally, a company's environment can be studied by means of computer data bases that contain hundreds of thousands of references to published material.

When Planning Is Less Useful

Even though much can be said in favor of strategic planning, there are situations where its value is very limited or is exceeded by its cost. If events that affect a company are frequent and occur with great, yet unpredictable, impact, necessary changes in strategy might be too frequent and too extensive to permit the use of a strategic plan. Since planning is basically an orderly process, it demands an orderliness within a company's internal operations as well as outside. Where the firm is highly susceptible to external forces that demand major shifts in strategy, plans that go out a few years may be scrapped after a few months. Conditions may exist that make strategic planning counterproductive, as, for example, volatile changes in a company's environment and great uncertainty in future trends as they affect the company. This is true, for example, in the electronics field.

Instead of planning for five years, such a firm's management should plan as far out as it can predict events with reasonable certainty. If markets change quickly, if costs and prices fluctuate rapidly, if innovations come rapidly, if new companies can easily enter the market, or if other events occur in short periods of time, planning very far out becomes unreasonable. As we shall see, such factors, and many others as well, influence the way planning is done. If they are volatile, so will the planning be, and long-range decision-making becomes impossible.

How does management decide not to plan in such situations? Probably the best way is to attempt strategic planning and to determine whether the information gathering and forecasting processes are reasonable. If they are not, a feasible alternative may be simply to do "short-range" planning, following the process discussed in this book, but looking ahead perhaps 12 or 18 months.

1.4 VALUES AND BENEFITS

A review of the steps just described should make it evident that planning offers clear advantages to managers practicing it. The importance of the strategic planning process is probably best illustrated by a list of the benefits a company is likely to receive as a result. Among the benefits are these:

a) <u>Answers to key questions</u>. Since strategic planning demands the setting of objectives and the collecting of information, management is forced to ask key questions about the company's future. These questions address all aspects of the company's operation and the environment within which it operates. Answers to these questions provide the basis for valid decisions.

b) <u>Responses to environment</u>. Because a company's success is highly dependent upon its environment, its strategic plan will by necessity deal with changes in that environment. As a result, the developed strategy comprises the best perceived approach for the company to achieve success in the future. The plan will enable a company to shape its future in that environment and to react to it as required. The company will be better able to deal with unexpected events, and it will be managed not by responses to crises but by decisions set down in a plan that looks well beyond short-term events.

c) <u>Decision guidelines</u>. A strategic plan provides the guidelines needed by management to conform short-range decisions to company objectives defined in the plan. The impact of decisions made against the plan's strategy can be better assessed. For example, technology breakthroughs may not bring about the sudden changes in strategy that they might otherwise seem to demand.

d) Expectations. A strategic plan provides expectations against which results can be compared, so that corrective action can be taken. It provides a measure of progress (or lack of it), so that any necessary changes in future activities are readily identifiable.

e) Responses to problems. The planning process puts problems in perspective, allowing management to address their long-term effects. Problems, which include company weaknesses and outside threats, can be viewed in the context of the full plan period.

f) Management evaluation. Because strategic planning involves serious thinking on the part of managers about all aspects of the company, it provides an excellent means of evaluating management.

The strategic planning document that the process yields is important, but the process itself is even more important. The process clarifies management thinking about the company. It stimulates creative thinking about the company. It forces management to consider and analyze many important and relevant factors that will influence the future course of the company. The result usually is that decisions are based on more comprehensive and well-considered information than would otherwise be available. As a result, management can do a better job of running the company.

Although the plan document may appear once a year, planning is a continuous activity that pervades all management actions, for those actions involve decision-making regarding alternative ways to expend resources.

1.5   INFORMATION

Information and Decision Making

The process of strategic planning is based on the making of decisions. Among the decisions made are selecting objectives for the company out of many that are applicable, making assumptions about the future of the company's environment and about its ability to react to that environment, identifying new products and markets, selecting areas for research and development, allocating resources, and establishing milestones for monitoring the plan. In short, every phase of planning involves decision making. Since decisions in the planning process take place at all management levels in all organizational units of a corporation, it follows that information must flow to and from all of these units. It must do so in a logical, well-planned manner.

Characteristics of Planning Information

The information that flows through a corporation for planning purposes generally can be characterized in several ways.

One characteristic of the information flow is its cyclic nature. Typically, a strategic plan is prepared once each year. The process consists of steps that occur somewhat in series after one another and somewhat in parallel, overlapping each other in time. In order for the entire process to be coordinated across a corporation, it is wise to establish a schedule of activities and to hold to it. In that way, information can be ready when needed.

A second characteristic of information flow is its iterativeness; i.e., it flows repeatedly back and forth. We have seen that the tasks of setting objectives and selection of technologies are interdependent and iterative. This trait pervades much of the planning process because all decisions made are tentative, good only until newer and/or improved information comes along. As discoveries are made outside the company or as environmental conditions change, corporate strategy may need to change in response. As technology advances are made in the company, new products may be conceived, and corporate strategy may have to be modified as a result.

A third characteristic is that certain information flows upward from lower to higher management, while other information flows downward from higher to lower management. Top management sends objectives, goals, and corporate strategy down to lower levels, while lower management sends technology alternatives and tentative strategies upwards. There is a hierarchical structure to this process. As information moves upward, it becomes less detailed and more broadly based; as it moves downward, it becomes more detailed and less broadly based. The chart in Fig. 1-4 provides an example of how information flows throughout levels of management over the planning year. The chart shows one calendar year. The solid boxes show the origins of information. The dotted boxes indicate that such information is received and modified by various levels of management. The process is the same each year, though there may be variations in timing due to special circumstances. This orderly flow is only a first approximation to actuality. Variations are discussed in later chapters.

Finally, a fourth characteristic is that the flow of information, although noncontinuous, occurs throughout the year. Ideally, all information generated at some point in the corporation is transmitted immediately to organizational units or managers requiring it. Practically speaking, however, much information proceeds periodically. Other information appears in reports as the need arises. To disseminate information around as soon as it is gathered would be to flood the company with many small, unstructured packets of information. Periodic reports, usually monthly or quarterly, generally suffice to keep management informed. Urgent information, however, must flow more rapidly.

Management of the Flow

Management of the flow of information is clearly a major task. There is much information that flows through the company. Once the strategic planning process

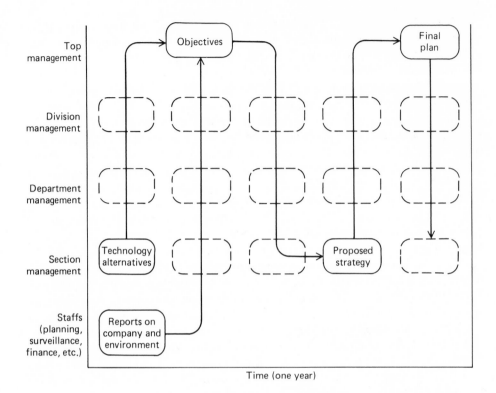

Fig. 1-4.   Flow of information.

is operational, however, management of this flow need not be an overpowering task. All managers, whatever their role in the process, issue and receive reports on a scheduled basis and so accommodate to this flow. Until this happens, though, management of the whole process is likely to be somewhat erratic and burdensome.

One problem with this extensive system of information flow is that it is like a large, complex machine. If a manager fails to meet a deadline for a report to be issued, the system may have a break in its operation. Whether or not this is serious depends on the importance of the report. Clearly, the proper way to accommodate such a situation is to avoid a strong dependence upon having everything working properly all the time. For example, there can be flexibility in the reporting of events. There can be a means for reporting urgent information that bypassses the routine method. Often, it is not particularly serious if a manager fails to meet a report deadline. The recipient of that report would assume that no new information is available and would proceed on that basis. It is important for the information system to be flexible enough to adapt to irregularities, for they will certainly occur.

1.6 ROLES OF ORGANIZATIONS

The responsibilities of every organization in the firm for planning purposes must be assigned and clearly understood. The flow of information from organization to organization must be equally well defined and understood. In this section, we review the organizations and the roles they each play in strategic planning.

The Planning Organization

The role of the planning organization in strategic planning is primarily to manage the process. Its role is not to do the planning; that responsibility belongs to line management. Managing the process involves several distinct responsibilities.

First, Planning has the responsibility for seeing that proper procedures for planning are set down and that they are carried out. This task may involve educating management in proper planning methodology. A "standard" approach is not appropriate, since companies vary so much, and it is Planning's job to to see that the established procedures are the best for the company at the time.

Second, Planning should coordinate the complex flow of information throughout the company. It must insure that the proper information about both the company itself and its environment is being gathered and properly analyzed and reported. The collection of all reports needed for strategic planning should pass through Planning, so that it can see that they are properly distributed. Planning should also monitor the issuance and distribution of all strategic planning documents.

Third, Planning must coordinate the plans of the company's divisions, insuring that they are consistent. This means that the strategy of Research, Engineering, Manufacturing, Marketing, and other organizations must be consistent with one another. The plans of these divisions must have consistent goals, so that, e.g., Research delivers what Engineering expects and needs.

Fourth, it must insure that all decisions made in evolving strategy are in support of corporate objectives and goals, as well as considering corporate strengths and weaknesses and environmental opportunities and threats. This task assures consistency in the planning process.

Fifth, Planning has the responsibility for compiling the strategic plan document itself. This task involves writing the document, utilizing the information sent it by the divisions and by top management.

Sixth, the planning organization should coordinate the monitoring of progress against plans with line organizations. The major responsibility for keeping the plan on schedule is line management's, as noted, but Planning can help by aiding in monitoring.

Seventh, Planning has the responsibility, in some corporations, for analyzing new businesses that the corporation is considering. This task involves analyzing the market (which may not yet exist), defining potential products in that market, assessing appropriate technologies both inside and outside the firm, assessing competition, and estimating resources and the time needed to develop and introduce the products.

Line Management

As stated above, the responsibility for planning is that of line management. Individuals responsible for implementing plans should be those who develop them. They perform the analyses for their organizations, they establish objectives and goals for their organizations, and they set the strategy. Thus they are in the best position to administer the plan, monitor it, and change it subsequently if need be. The responsibility for developing and executing the plan is shared among all managers. We shall look at several types of managers and organizations, examining their specific responsibilities in the planning process.

The Chief Executive Officer has, of course, overall responsibility for the strategic plan. Specifically, he or she must set down corporate objectives, in concurrence with the top level managers who report directly to that position and with the board of directors. Objectives setting must be coordinated with technology alternatives that are sent up by the technical organizations. And finally, general guidelines for strategy development must be set. Besides, the CEO has overall responsibility for seeing that each aspect of the plan is consistent with the rest. The budget-making process must be centrally coordinated to ensure that all resources are allocated with consistency and not in excess of corporate affordability.

The board of directors has the responsibility for approving corporate objectives. They should also be involved in setting them. The objectives represent the direction the corporation is planning to go in the immediate future, and so the board's approval is essential.

The top managers reporting to the CEO work with him or her in developing corporate objectives and goals. Division presidents have responsibilities similar to those of the CEO, with respect to their divisions. They share leadership in the information-gathering phase of planning, in the areas of their special responsibilities. They have an added responsibility, that of working with each other to insure coordination among the divisions' strategic plans. They have overall responsibility for the total plans of their respective divisions.

Line managers have the responsibility for translating corporate and divisional objectives and goals into their own and for setting specific plans of action, that is, of setting strategies for their own organizations. They must develop resource allocation budgets and submit these upward. It should be noted that, as a general rule, the higher a manager is in the organization, the greater is the portion of time that must be devoted to planning.

The managers of the research and development organizations have the added responsibility of providing technology alternatives regularly to top management. This means they must maintain an awareness of outside technology developments and report on both inside and outside developments. They must keep organizations that need to interact with theirs, primarily Manufacturing and Marketing, informed on developments. These divisions need such information for their own planning. Technical management also makes recommendations as to what technologies on the outside should be acquired or be investigated for acquisition.

The financial organization provides a number of services for planning purposes. It gathers and reports all financial information; it makes projections into the future as required in financial areas; it provides the means for required outside-source financing for long-term programs and facilities; it monitors the financial status of the company throughout the year to measure progress against plans; and it recommends changes in operations required to respond to financial deviations from the plans.

The marketing organization serves as a primary source of information on customer needs, desires, and expectations. It conducts market studies to determine the nature, scope, and size of current and potential future markets of interest to the company. It helps identify markets and their characteristics.

Because the R & D organization is the driving force in product development in high-technology companies, the interaction between R & D and marketing organizations is an important one. W. E. Souder has conducted a study of the interaction and collaboration between these organizations in a number of corporations [6]. Among his findings are these: (a) the degree of harmony and cooperation between R & D and Marketing is a significant factor in project success or failure; (b) these groups often fail to collaborate early enough during the life cycle of a product; (c) there are natural differences in the personalities, outlooks, and responsibilities of these groups that tend to separate them; and (d) nearly all companies have some incidence of problems in coordination between them. Finally, he found that, in general, ideas that originated within R & D organizations had lower commercial-success rates than those ideas which originated within marketing organizations.

Organization for Planning

If a corporation is to have an effective strategic planning activity, it is necessary for an organizational structure to exist that accommodates it, so that responsibility can be properly assigned. The key organizational issues to address with respect to a planning group are (a) where in the organization it shall be located, i.e., to whom it should report; (b) how large should it be; and (c) what kinds of skills its staff should have.

The location in the organization for the planning function should be carefully chosen. Ideally, the head of planning reports to top management, either the CEO or someone directly below that position. This is so because of the importance of strategic planning. The CEO, as noted, must spend a large amount of time involved in planning, and it is thus important that the planning staff be organizationally very close. In a corporation that has product-line divisions, it is probably best that each such division have its own planning organization, reporting to the top management of the division. In that event, the central or "corporate" planning staff acts as coordinator for the planning of all divisions, though the detailed work in planning is done by separate organizations. Careful allocation of responsibilities must be made here.

A potential problem in having separate planning groups, one per product-line division, is the strong possibility that they might plan in a manner inconsistent with the others. To the extent that their product lines are distinctly separate, such separateness may be all right. Very often, though, there are common aspects in their product lines or common dependencies on the environment; coordination among them is then essential.

Staff Organizations

The several staff organizations that provide services to the planning and line organizations for planning purposes must gather information and issue reports on analyses of both the company and its environment, on projections and forecasts of the future, and on progress within the company. There are several such organizations.

The *competitive surveillance staff* continuously monitors the external literature, collects information that is pertinent to the corporation, calls portions of it to the attention of management as appropriate, and makes selected portions of it available on request. The *government relations staff* watches governmental actions in federal and local jurisdictions, reporting political trends and changes in laws and regulations that may affect the company. The *socioeconomic development staff* monitors changes in the economy and in demography that may affect the company. Other special-purpose staffs may also be used. Clearly, not every corporation will need to or be able to support all such groups. It is important to note, however, that responsibilities of these listed are all worthy of serious consideration from a planning standpoint.

Often, top management will retain corporate staffs whose responsibilities are to monitor line operations and to act as liaison between top management and line organizations or between line organizations. They play a role in planning, which generally involves review of proposed strategic plans.

1.7 TECHNOLOGY ISSUES

Technology — its development, assessment, and utilization — poses special problems and raises certain issues for its managers. It is appropriate, therefore, in a discussion of strategic planning for technology, to identify these issues. Chapter 6, *Issues on Technology*, addresses a number of these; they are briefly described here.

The technology programs in a corporation must be intimately linked to its objectives, since it is by means of those programs that the objectives will be achieved.   Technology helps define objectives, while objectives guide management in making decisions on which technologies to pursue. The linkage between them does not readily come about, and management must make concerted efforts to see that it does.

The rapid changes that occur in technology and the resultant impact on new products are at times difficult to deal with and require particular effort by management. This characteristic of technology cuts two ways. It provides for breakthroughs by a company, allowing it to compete in its markets, but it also allows competitors to do the same.

Technology development involves the taking of risks. The risks vary among different technology programs and depend on their characteristics. Management cannot avoid taking risks and so must be aware of them and act accordingly.

Technology utilized in a corporation's products is acquired from two sources, the company itself and the outside world.   The internal development of technology has certain advantages, largely having to do with the proprietary and private nature of such technology. Acquisition of external technology is often a viable alternative. Its main advantage is that of saving development costs and time.   Management must weigh the choice between the two approaches.

A major driving force in the operation of a technology-based company is the development of technology and the flow of information about that development up through management levels. Technology development and top-management decision making must interact. As technology evolves, technology alternatives are sent up to top management to aid it in setting strategy and guiding operations. Conversely, when top management changes strategy, there may be shifts in emphasis on technology development in the R & D organizations.

An important aspect of the management of technology is its assessment on a regular basis by management. *Technology assessment* is undertaken to determine the utility of an internal technology to the company's products. It also helps management decide which of its own technologies can be utilized and which outside technologies ought to be acquired.

Most effort and expense in the funding of technology development involves ongoing technologies.   However, sometimes a company undertakes the development of a new technology or significantly increases its investment in one that it previously funded in a small way. In such instances, particular attention must be paid to the rationale for undertaking the new work and to the manner in which it will be funded and staffed.

Technology maturity is a parameter that management must consider. Some technologies that companies utilize have been under development for many years. Companies continue to fund development in these technologies to effect better and more competitive products. The technologies are relatively mature. Changes that result are typically *evolutionary*, and sudden breakthroughs are rare. Other technologies are relatively new and promise more dramatic changes in product performance.   The results are typically *revolutionary*.

The movement of technology advances from Research to Development, *technology transfer*, is a necessary step in the commercialization of a product, yet this transfer often does not occur successfully within a company. To assure success, it is necessary that Research and Development communicate well.

1.8 CAVEATS IN PLANNING

It may appear, from a cursory reading of this book, that strategic planning is a straightforward process that flows smoothly and effectively if the guidelines set down are followed. This is not the case, since companies vary considerably in style and structure and face situations uniquely their own, sometimes even unique within one company from time to time. These situations cannot all be foreseen by any planning methodology. It is important to note that no strategic planning process, however implemented, should be very formal and inflexible, for the reason that even within a given company circumstances change from one period to the next. All that can be set down are very general guidelines and planning steps. Management must be alert to this point, or else the planning process will tend to be ignored because it is inappropriate and bothersome to use.

Finally, management must be cognizant of the fact that planning is not an activity set apart from the managing process, but rather it is an integral part of it. Management's job is to make decisions about the firm's activities now and into the future, and the only way it can do this to is to plan. Truly, planning is managing to a very great degree, and a manager must be aware of this if he or she is to be successful.

1.9 PROBLEMS IN STRATEGIC PLANNING

Even though it may be obvious to managers that strategic planning is good for companies, it does not follow that its use is straightforward and trouble-free. Its purpose and processes are not universally understood or accepted by managers. There are potentially many problems and pitfalls in its implementation, and there is often resistance to its use. It is important for a manager, engaged in planning, to be aware of these difficulties. Some of the reasons for the problems associated with the strategic planning process and ways of addressing them are discussed here.

Strategic planning, as implemented in a corporation, must have the solid support of the chief executive officer, since a major part of the responsibility in this office is planning and since the officer's attitude on the subject will set the tone for all the management within the firm. Frequently, top management will spend so much time on current problems that it cannot devote enough time to planning. The process can become discredited as a result, because then these managers do not properly support it. This situation is very common and understandably so. If a major crisis arises that demands a solution from the top within two weeks, the CEO can hardly ignore it because corporate objectives are due that week. ("Strategic planning cannot help me with current problems.") Clearly, the CEO must devote much attention to the crisis and set the planning activity aside. The point is, though, that this kind of choice cannot be made frequently and regularly.

The attitude of all managers is an important factor in determining the success of strategic planning. There may be misconceptions about the purposes and methodologies of planning. There may be an insufficient understanding of the need for strategic planning. These situations can cause difficulties in the planning process. Top management must recognize and deal with them if they are present.

There are certain human tendencies that can diminish the effectiveness of strategic planning. First, managers are sometimes too optimistic about the future of their company, expecting substantially improved performance, even if this is unwarranted. This mitigates a sense of urgency about problems. Second, planning for the next year or even the next month is often taken much more seriously than for the years following. While this is understandable in the light of the future's uncertainty, the result can be weak planning for the long term. Third, people tend to avoid the most difficult issues facing their company, which can distort priorities and result in a less than optimal strategy. Fourth, people tend to resist change, so that their planning is usually done as extensions of the past. New initiatives and directions thus tend to be downplayed. Fifth, there is often a fear that control has to be relinquished when strategic planning is done.

In many corporations the reward system for managers runs counter to support for strategic planning. Most commonly, each manager's salary increase — and in fact that of each employee — is based on performance in the period since the last raise, typically twelve months earlier. The impact of strategic planning decisions will, for the most part, not be determinable for a few years. If a bad decision is made whose impact shows up years later, a current raise cannot reflect that. All this is not to say that one cannot reward good planning performance, but rather that there are built-in problems in the usual system.

Planning relies a great deal upon data about a company's environment today and in the future. Current data are often inaccurate, while forecasting the future is often very difficult.

The importance of decision-making in strategic planning has been discussed. Unfortunately, it often tends to be reactive rather than be based on planned events and activities. That is, managers often react to surprises and base decisions on them, more often than they should. This too is understandable and never totally avoidable. It is sometimes inconvenient or troublesome to review all the information one has or can get regarding a decision to be made. The greater and more accurate the information that one has, the better, but availability is relative, and often it is viewed as simply too much trouble to obtain that which is "available" on a subject.

We have already noted that technology-based companies have special problems in strategic planning. These originate from the fact that technological changes of a sudden and unpredictable nature occur. Management has an especially difficult task of monitoring external changes. Studying the environment, if done thoroughly, is expensive and time-consuming.

Throughout this book, many problems encountered in strategic planning are described. Most of these problems are collected and summarized in Chapter 10, *Theory and Practice*, and several solutions to them are offered.

1.10 A "STANDARD" CORPORATION

In order to clarify subsequent comments about corporations, we define a "standard" corporation. This corporation is typical of most, but it is not necessarily indicative of any particular one. Its definition here provides concepts and terms referred to throughout the book. No attempt has been made to propose the best organizational structure for a company with respect to strategic planning.

The *chief executive officer* may be the chairman of the board or the president. *Top management* comprises the CEO, the chief operations officer (if there is one), and all managers reporting to him or her or to the CEO.

The company is organized into into *divisions*; divisions comprise *departments*; departments are made up of *sections*. The divisions may be organized by product line (home appliances, aircraft engines, etc.) or by functions (R & D, Manufacturing, etc.).

The functional divisions of a corporation are termed *Research, Development, Planning, Finance, Manufacturing, Marketing, Sales*, and *Service. Engineering* is used synonymously with *Development*, as in industry, although sometimes a distinction is made. The term *Operations* is used to mean all organizations other than R & D, taken as a group.

Definitions of Activities

Definitions of R & D activities in a corporation based on those employed by the National Science Foundation are given here and are to be inferred in this book:

Basic research involves original investigations for the advancement of scientific knowledge that do not have specific commercial objectives but have a broad range of applications.

Applied research involves investigations directed to the discovery of new scientific knowledge about a particular problem or investigations with specific commercial objectives with respect to products or processes.

Development involves technical activities of a nonroutine nature concerned with translating research findings or other scientific knowledge into products or processes.

1.11 CONTRONICS CORPORATION

An understanding of most procedures is enhanced by illustration. So, as an aid to following the steps in the strategic planning process, we introduce an imaginary company and follow its strategic planning procedure. In this section, this company is described in some detail. Throughout most of the book, planning steps and concepts are illustrated by a reference to this company as it does its planning. The company is entirely fictional, bearing no intentional relationship to any existing firm.

ConTronics Corporation, based in New Haven, Connecticut, manufactures a line of electronic controllers. It sells primarily to corporations that use its components in their own products (two-thirds of its sales volume), an "original equipment manufacturer" (OEM) business, and also sells products for stand-alone applications, directly to business customers (one-third).

In its last fiscal year, calendar year 1980, its sales were $25,000,000. Its after-tax profits were $1,800,000; both of these figures represent 18% increases over 1979. It has 520 employees in five northeastern states.

ConTronics has its research and engineering group of 30 employees in New Haven, along with its main manufacturing plant with a staff of 155. It has other manufacturing plants in Plainfield, N. J. and Rochester, N. Y., totaling 270 workers. In addition, its sales offices, averaging staffs of five persons each, are located in 10 other northeastern cities.

The Company was founded in 1968, in response to the burgeoning markets in electronics. The founders saw a need for small electronic controllers of electronic systems that was not being met satisfactorily by suppliers at the time. Electronics manufacturers were designing and building their own controllers, usually at great expense. ConTronics developed a programmable controller that could be customized to meet a variety of needs. The founders began the Company with venture capital supplied by a consortium of businessmen and banks. Its capital requirements over the years have been met largely by these original sources, with an ever-decreasing proportion of total capital needs being so supplied. It began paying dividends at a small rate three years ago. Its revenues increased at an average rate of 25% and its profits at an average rate of 28% over the past five years. The growth in the past year, however, is markedly lower than in the few preceding years.

For some time, ConTronics' profit margin has been very high and, though its dividend payout has been only about 2.5%, its investors are pleased with its recent performance in growth. Investors today are optimistic about future growth, and the stock price has kept ahead of the market as a whole and has kept pace with electronics stocks.

Currently, the Company has two product lines. Its OEM product line comprises the Model 120, the Model 140, the Model 170, and the Model 210.

The Model 210 was new in 1980. These are four products in a family, with features increasing with model numbers. OEM prices for these products are $750, $950, $1200, and $1950, respectively. These units are used in equipment for television, video recording, film making, film showing, and communications.

The Company's retail product line comprises the System N5, the System N6, and the System N8, selling for $1400, $1750, and $2600, respectively. Sales are primarily to medium-sized businesses. The System N8 will be new in 1981. The products are sold through retail outlets for businesses and the more affluent homes. The Company's market shares range from approximately 10% to 25%; the lower ends of the product lines enjoy larger shares. These shares have not changed much during the past two years. ConTronics will emphasize its retail line more than its OEM line in the future.

Its research efforts, costing about $200,000 per year, are modest. Most work is focused on new automated circuit design methods and new computer software. These are planned for eventual use in a new line of miniaturized products, to supplant the present product lines. These are envisioned for the mid-1980's. They would have about one-half to two-thirds the selling prices of their predecessors (in today's dollars) and will have many new features. Another research effort focuses on special materials with interesting and useful properties for products in the late 1980's.

Its development efforts, costing about $1,500,000 per year, are split between (a) improvements in current products and the addition of new features and (b) development of two new products, the Model 110 and the System N4, planned for introduction in 1982. The latter activity consumes almost three-fourths of the current development budget.

The Company is also contemplating a totally new product line that would serve the products in the "office of the future". There is much uncertainty, however, about this market and about the Company's role in it.

ConTronics is planning the 1982–86 period and is doing its planning throughout the year 1981.

The material given in this chapter and the following chapters on ConTronics is intended to be representative of the procedure such a corporation would go through in doing its strategic planning. It is far from complete on the subject of planning, and the reader must bear this is mind. In general, its primary emphasis is on research, development, and technology, with emphasis also on the company's products.

SUMMARY

Strategic planning is an important activity for all corporations. It is especially vital for those corporations in the *technology industries*. These companies have special characteristics of their own, attributable to the nature of technology advances and their effect on the companies trying to develop and exploit them. Technology offers the possibility of sudden changes in product functions, with the result that costs can fall dramatically. Technology moves rapidly, and a company is sometimes hard-pressed to maintain its position. Furthermore, there is a great deal of uncertainty about technology development.

Strategic planning is important because it allows corporations to plan in an orderly way for the uncertainties of the future. It allows companies to make decisions today to best anticipate that future so as to respond rationally to it.

The process is orderly involving a series of reasonably well-defined steps that follow one another in logical fashion. The steps are the following:

* Gather information about the company today and project its future; identify strengths and weaknesses.

* Gather information about the environment; identify opportunities and threats.

* Forecast the future of the environment and make assumptions about it.

* Project the company's future in that environment.

* Establish objectives and thus define the desired future of the company.

* Set the strategy: identify the means of achieving the desired future in that environment.

* Develop operational plans and allocate resources.

* Set milestones.

Despite the formality of the procedure, there is much flexibility in it, and a particular company can and should tailor the procedures to its own needs. For example, planning can be done top-down, or bottom-up, or as a combination of the two. Several of the steps can be omitted in special instances where they do not apply. Further, there are situations when strategic planning is either hardly necessary or is inappropriate.

Many values and benefits derive from the undertaking of strategic planning. These both affect the manner in which the company operates and manages its operation as well as the way it deals with the forces outside. The process allows a company to be more responsive to its environment, to make decisions on a more timely rational basis, to allow short-term decisions to conform better to long-term plans, and to provide expectations against which results can be compared. Much value derives from the process of planning, often more than from the resultant document.

Information plays a major role in corporate decision-making and hence in strategic planning. The flow of planning information is complex. Planning information is cyclic, iterative, upward- and downward-flowing, and nearly continuous all year. Management of the flow is often a difficult problem.

The planning organization's responsibilities do not include actual planning;

that is done by line management. Its responsibilities do include insuring that proper procedures are carried out, coordinating the flow of planning information, coordinating all planning throughout divisions, insuring that strategy is developed in a manner consistent with corporate objectives, issuing the corporate strategic plan, and monitoring the company's progress against the plan. Line management has the responsibility for doing the actual planning. The CEO has overall responsibility for the planning, though all managers contribute to the process. A company should have several staff organizations that gather and disseminate information needed for planning, including financial, marketing, competitive, and other external information.

There are a number of special issues that relate to technology. These include linking technology programs to corporate objectives, dealing with the rapid pace of technology, risk taking with technology, technology acquisition, technology alternatives, technology assessment, new technology development, technology maturity, and technology transfer.

Strategic planning is not without its problems. There are many difficulties in a company's attempts to use it. The process, while orderly on paper, often proceeds in an erratic way, simply because it is a difficult activity to undertake. There are problems, e.g., when the CEO does not give it full support, when managers' attitudes run counter to good planning practice, when information obtained outside is inaccurate, when decision-making is reactive, and when technology surprises occur. There are other difficulties as well. Finally, strategy-setting is particularly troublesome because it involves making decisions of selection among many alternative courses of action (as, e.g., alternative technology development programs), without always having accurate data and certain needed forecasting results.

REFERENCES

1. Battelle Memorial Institute, private publication.

2. *Business Week*, "R & D Scoreboard", July 6, 1981, pp. 60–75.

3. Ansoff, H. Igor, and John M. Stewart, "Strategies for a Technology-Based Business", *Harvard Business Review*, vol. 45, no. 6, November/December 1967, pp. 78–79.

4. Drucker, Peter F., *Management: Tasks, Responsibilities, Practices*, Harper & Row, New York, 1974, p. 125.

5. Liebson, Laurence S., "Technology-Based Enterprises", M.S. Dissertation, Sloan School of Management, Massachusetts Institute of Technology, May 1979, p. 49.

6. Souder, W. E., "Exploratory Study of the Coordinating Mechanisms Between R & D and Marketing as an Influence on the Innovation Process", National Science Foundation, Report NSF/PRA 7517195/4/8, August 1977, Chapter 13. (Many of these results were published by the author in "Promoting an Effective R & D / Marketing Interface", *Research Management*, July 1980, vol. 23, no. 4, pp. 10–15.)

Additional References

Steiner, George A., *Strategic Planning: What Every Manager Must Know*, The Free Press, Macmillan Publishing Co., New York, 1979. (This is a very general, comprehensive book on the subject; cited in Chapters 5 and 10.)

Business International Corporation, *Strategic Planning for International Corporations*, New York, 1979. (This report addresses strategic planning in general terms, but stresses the influence of international operations on the process. Geographic planning is reviewed, for example.)

Lorange, Peter, and Richard F. Vancil, *Strategic Planning Systems*, Prentice-Hall, Inc., Englewood Cliffs, N. J., 1977. (This is an anthology of papers written on strategic planning; it provides a number of case studies.)

Rothschild, William E., *Putting it all Together: A Guide to Strategic Thinking*, Amacom, American Managements Association, New York, 1976. (This is a general book on the subject of strategic planning.)

Steele, Lowell W., *Innovation in Big Business*, American Elsevier Publishing Co., New York, 1975. (This book addresses the management of R & D in large corporations, addressing the role of R & D in strategic planning, among many other topics; cited in Chapters 6 and 7.)

Ewing, David E., editor, *Long-Range Planning for Management*, Harper & Row, New York, 1972. (This anthology covers many topics on long range planning, each in an introductory manner.)

Ewing, David W., *The Human Side of Planning*, Macmillan, New York, 1969. (This book addresses the human factors responsible for successes and failures of planning.)

Argenti, John, *Corporate Planning: A Practical Guide*, Dow Jones-Irwin, Inc., Homewood, Illinois, 1968. (This is a general book on planning; it focuses on the futures gap as the driver of strategy.)

Liebson, Laurence S., "Technology-Based Enterprises: Strategies, Structures, and Processes for Growth", M.S. Dissertation, Sloan School of Management, Massachusetts Institute of Technology, May 1979. (This dissertation discusses small, rapidly-growing technology-based companies; it addresses all aspects of strategic planning; cited in this chapter.)

Cleland, David Ira, "The Origin and Development of a Philosophy of Long-Range Planning in American Business", Ph.D. Dissertation, Ohio State University, 1962; also published by Arno Press, 1976. (This dissertation is one of the very first works on long range planning. It provides a history of the discipline and surveys the practices of many corporations.)

Quinn, James Brian, and Robert M. Cavanaugh, "Fundamental Research Can be Planned," *Harvard Business Review*, January-February 1964, vol. 42, no. 1, pp. 111-124. (This paper describes how a program of fundamental research can be planned and integrated into a company's total operation.)

Quinn, James Brian, "Long-Range Planning of Industrial Research", *Harvard Business Review*, July-August 1961, vol. 39, no. 4, pp. 88-102. (This paper is provides a comprehensive approach to planning for R & D and how to relate this to a company's overall planning process; cited in Chapters 5 and 7.)

The following journals are primarily devoted to long-range or strategic planning: *Long Range Planning* (Pergamon Press, Elmsford, N.Y.); *Planning Review* (North American Society for Corporate Planning, Dayton, Ohio). (There are many journals on management, and each occasionally has papers on the subject.)

2

ANALYSIS OF A COMPANY

Where are we today?

What are we planning to do?

INTRODUCTION

A major task early in the strategic planning process is studying the state of the company at the present time. This means understanding the company's strengths and weaknesses as well as its resources. It is vital also to understand where a company is headed, under present plans, so that its management can make decisions about how those plans ought to be changed in anticipation of the future. The best way to go about doing so is to answer questions about all aspects of the company's resources and operations. The areas of concern include technology, product lines, markets, manufacturing, marketing, sales, manpower, finances, and other company resources. The last strategic plan developed and the planning process used also need examination. A thorough analysis of the company involves asking many questions about its status and plans.

Answers to the questions should suggest both responses and tentative solutions to the problems they often imply. The answers should further suggest how the company's direction ought to be changed, once its strengths and weaknesses are identified. They ought to provide insight into new opportunities for as well as threats to the company. Finally, they ought to suggest the nature and structure of a strategy for the corporation's future undertakings.

2.1 THE ANALYSIS

The Purpose

Strategic planning usually begins with the undertaking of an analysis of a company and its environment. This analysis provides an understanding of the state of the company, so that management knows what major decisions it faces. The analysis has two phases, an analysis of the company, termed *self-analysis,* and an analysis of its environment. We deal with the first of these in this chapter and with the second in Chapter 3, *Analysis of the Environment.*

The purposes of a self-analysis are to determine what major problems face the company, to identify company strengths and weaknesses, and to identify the resources available for use in the future. The self-analysis not only addresses the current state of the company but also focuses on its future. Consequently, management must identify current plans for the future.

Since planning involves the future interaction of the company with its environment, it is necessary to project the environment's future over the strategic plan period. That projection is considered in Chapter 4, *Forecasting the Future.* Following that task, the company's future is projected.

In this and succeeding chapters, comments are made about trends and events. A *trend* is the sequence of values over time that some measurable entity experiences; examples are the profit margin of a corporation or the number of electric cars sold in California. Trends and rates of change of trends are both important. An *event* is an action that occurs at a definite point in time, such as the introduction of a new product or a breakthrough in a new technology.

Questions

In this chapter, key questions in each of the areas of concern are asked. A series of related, *auxiliary* questions is given in most of these cases in Appendix for Chapter 2. The auxiliary questions need not concern the reader at a first reading of this book. Their perusal can occur later, when the planning process is studied in depth. Listings of sources of information, useful in answering the questions, appear in that appendix under appropriate headings.

There are many questions in this and the next two chapters and many more in Appendixes for Chapters 2 through 4. Not all of these apply to every company, and those that do not apply should be ignored. Only those deemed important should be addressed. The aim is to motivate managers to ask questions and seek answers, thus stimulating creative thinking and causing new questions to be created and answered.

As each question is addressed, the following should be kept in mind:

1. *Determine whether the answer identifies either a strength or weakness of the company.*

2. *Determine whether the answer identifies either an opportunity for or a threat to the company.*

The next several sections deal with various resource and operations areas within a corporation. Section 2.2 addresses major problems and decisions facing a firm. Section 2.3 addresses technology. Section 2.4 addresses company products and markets. Section 2.5 addresses various other corporate resources. Sections 2.6 and 2.7 address planning within a company.

To whatever extent possible and where appropriate, management should formulate responses to the answers, representing actions that can be taken. Full responses must await an analysis of the company's environment, but tentative positions can be described here. In this way, addressing these questions results both in collecting information and in stimulating actions.

In order to supplement this formal approach to information-gathering, advantage should also be taken of informal sources. There generally are managers in various groups within a company who can offer knowledgeable opinions about all aspects of company operations. Much of this information does not appear in company reports, yet it can be very useful in rounding out the picture of the company's status. In addition, managers learn a great deal from informal communication and interaction with employees, customers, suppliers, and colleagues in other companies.

A Caution

In Chapters 2 through 4, there is a great deal of emphasis on questions and answers about a corporation and its environment in the past, present, and future. These questions are supplemented by dozens of others in the book's appendixes. The reader is strongly cautioned, however, to be aware that *equally important as are the answers to these questions is the use made of the information gathered.* The extrapolations formed, the conclusions drawn, the decisions made, and the ensuing planning following therefrom all represent driving forces behind the guidance of the company into the future. One must not let the mass of collected information obscure their true purpose: to enable management to devise sensible, meaningful, and effective plans.

2.2 MAJOR PROBLEMS AND DECISIONS

Major Problems

What major problems are we currently facing?

What major problems are we likely to face over the plan period?

Management should begin its analysis by identifying the major internal problems facing its company. Many of the major concerns management has involve both the company and its environment, and the two are not always separable. The breakdown into internal and external problems, with the latter addressed in Chapter 3, is somewhat artificial, but that is not important. Only problems that have or will have a major impact upon the company should be addressed here; generally, there are too many problems overall. An estimate of the seriousness of each candidate problem should be made, perhaps judged profits or market share, or by some other meaningful measure. It is useful to rank the problems by the seriousness of their impact, so that only the major ones can be addressed during planning.

These questions are general, designed to start management's thinking about its company's current and future situations. They address many aspects of technology, research, and development, particularly important in technology-based companies. Products and markets are thoroughly examined. Finally, company resources are analyzed. Responses to these questions should be used by way of introduction to the self-analysis. They serve to direct management's attention to the areas of operation most in need of help. As the self-analysis proceeds, these responses should be associated with that analysis, in the proper areas.

Major Decisions

What are the major decisions that management must make during the plan period?

A companion task to identifying major problems is that of identifying major decisions confronting the firm in the future. The question above can only be partially answered at this stage, because a full answer must also consider the results of an environmental analysis. The question is therefore addressed again later, in Chapter 7, *Setting Strategy*.

We have seen that many decisions must be deferred to the future. A complete list of such future decisions can be derived only when strategy is set. Nonetheless, it is reasonable to develop a preliminary list early in the analysis phase, to provide perspective for that analysis.

Forms for Analysis

It is very useful to utilize forms for structuring answers to the questions asked in Chapters 2 to 4. An example of such a form for answering the questions above is given in Fig. 2-1. The sections of the form have been designed to address the auxiliary questions given in the Appendix for Chapter 2. One copy of the form would be used for each major problem. Similar forms, with various structures, can be developed for each question articulated in these chapters. Even though such forms may not be ample enough to contain all the information needed for some, they are useful for summaries.

CURRENT MAJOR PROBLEM
Problem:
Likely consequences:
Previous experience with problem:
Possible solutions:
Costs:
Benefits:

Date:	Manager:

Fig. 2-1.   A form for self-analysis.

2.3 TECHNOLOGY

In a technology-based company, research and development are extremely valuable resources. Future products are developed in R & D organizations; they usually provide a high value added in the products eventually built and sold. It is appropriate for management to begin its analysis in this area.

The purpose of these questions is to understand R & D activities in the company and where those activities are leading it and to determine how and at what cost they can be improved. Management will, as a result of this review, develop an understanding of every major aspect of the R & D programs in the company.

(By convention, research activities are termed *projects*, while development activities are termed *programs*. In referring jointly to research and development efforts, the term *program* is used. This terminology is used throughout the book.)

Technologies

What is the status of our technologies?

As the key to the resources in a high-technology company, technologies must be carefully evaluated with regard to their utility today and their future prospects. As products and markets are defined for the future, the status of a company's technologies over the plan period must be projected, so that their capabilities can be made to match the product needs.

Research Projects

What are our research projects?

It is important to understand what research projects are under way, why they were undertaken, and toward what corporate and product objectives they are aimed. It is important also to know what future products would utilize the results of this research and what organizations within the company are the "customers" for it.

Research Activity

What is the quality of the research done in our company?

The research activity in a technology-based corporation is the origin of most products. It is most crucial, therefore, to focus much attention on this primal source of innovation. It is important for management to understand the quality of its research capability relative to its competitors, so that needed improvements can be identified.

Experience and Applications

What is our experience in various areas of technology? Where is it applicable?

Many corporations engage in technology development in a manner quite apart from product development. That is, they devote resources to *technology centers*, with the intention of applying developed technologies to several related products or across product lines. It is important to understand the relationship between a company's technology and its product lines, past, present, and future, for that relationship is crucial in setting a planning course.

Development Programs

What are our development programs?

As with research projects, it is important to know what development work currently exists and where it is headed. It is important also to identify the relationship of technologies to products, so that the relevance of development programs can be assessed.

New Programs

What new R & D programs are planned?

The analysis of current plans needs to be extended to the future, with a look at currently planned future research projects and development programs. Their relationship to future products must be understood. Work planned at present yet not under way should be addressed here.

R & D Spending

What is the pattern of our R & D spending?

In Chapter 1, the matter of R & D budgets as a fraction of revenues was discussed. It is useful to know how the company has been funding R & D, how it plans to continue doing so, and how it compares in its R & D spending with others in its industry.

Failures

Which R & D activities have failed to lead to products?

It obviously pays to learn from failures. Most research ventures will fail; many programs in development will never become products. Management should look at past failures and identify the events leading to them in order to understand them and benefit from the experience.

Technology Transfer

How effectively are research projects transferred to the development organizations?

Successful technology transfer is critical to eventual product commercialization. Nonetheless, there are many problems in the process, and many failures in programs can be traced to it. Management must understand the existing transfer process as it attempts to plan for its improvement. (This subject is addressed in some detail in Chapter 6, *Issues on Technology.*)

Responsibilities

The management of the research and development organizations is primarily responsible for addressing these questions on technology. The marketing organization can help evaluate the probable utility and success of technology as it moves to product commercialization. The relationship between technology development and product commercialization is an important one to analyze and understand. The technical and marketing organizations need to collaborate in this analysis. Technology transfer often is problematical, and the research and development organizations must jointly address this issue.

The salient points identified by ConTronics Corporation's management on its technology can be summarized:

* The materials research project is an investigation of totally new types of polymeric materials with very special properties. It appears that doping the materials with various additives and curing under various conditions yields many properties of great promise in future sensing devices for controllers. Results in the past year imply a greater chance of change than previously. There is, however, much risk in this work.

* The two other research projects – an automated circuit design system and new computer software methodology – together consume three-fourths of the current research budget. The work here is well along and will begin to find application in products by 1983.

* The electronics technology used in most of these products is of 1974 to 1976 vintage, except for that in the two newest products, which use 1979 technology. The company plans, in newer versions of products as well as newer products, to upgrade its technology.

* ConTronics' technologies are largely nonproprietary, though some research is being done to develop new ones.

* All development programs are aimed at current products and the 1982 products. There is no development activity that is not tied to specific products. This is perceived as a weakness in the development area.

2.4 PRODUCTS AND MARKETS

Consideration of a company's technology leads naturally to a study of its products. The markets within which those products must sell is an associated concern. The questions below deal with these areas.

With the questions answered, management will have a full understanding of its products. It will be in a position to determine whether changes in products are warranted and what these changes should be. If any changes are required, management will know what their costs and the benefits are likely to be.

Product Features

What new and improved features are being planned for our products, using our technology base?

In looking at technologies, we asked questions such as this one, so there is overlap. It is useful, however, to look at these again, this time from a product or business point of view. This dual approach stresses the important relationship between a company's technology and its products.

New Products

What new products are we planning to offer, based on our technology programs?

This question parallels that just above, now applied to new products. Generally, significantly more resources and technology advances will be required than for new product features, and much more thought is required to answer these questions. It is important to know where present development programs are leading. Both planned and potential products should be considered.

Current Products

How well are our current products doing in the marketplace?

There are several categories of concern regarding current products.

What are the sales of each current product?
What shares of their markets do our products have?
What are the component manufacturing costs of the product?
Which products now on the market are planned for withdrawal?

Sales. It is important to know not only the recent history of sales patterns but also to understand the forces determining that history and future sales.

Market share. Market share is critical to success in the marketplace; a dominant position, if maintained, virtually assures success. It is important for management to understand the dynamics of its particular markets so that it can understand what is involved in increasing its shares. This involves understanding all the significant forces in the marketplace. It is also necessary to know what resources would be required to maintain and to increase market share.

Product costs. One of the benefits of technology advancement is the potential for significant cost savings in new products. Management should determine when such advances would potentially be useful and when they would not. It is important to know the component manufacturing costs in order to control or reduce them.

Product withdrawals. In high-technology markets, products are sometimes removed from the market when other products, with improved technology, compete successfully with them. They are also removed when they are superceded by the company's own products.

Markets

What are the markets for our products?

What new markets are we planning to enter?

The need for detailed information on current and planned markets parallels the need for knowledge about geographical areas. In order to plan new products that are related to existing ones, it is necessary to understand as much of the markets as possible.

Geographical Areas

In what parts of the country or the world are our products now marketed?

It is important to delineate quite clearly in what parts of the world all company products are sold. Since these geographical areas have different characteristics and different kinds of futures, this delineation is an important part of the analysis for planning.

Responsibilities

Marketing and Product Planning are responsible for the responses to most of these questions. Customers can provide responses to questions about current products and, possibly, new products. Market surveys can provide valuable data. The technical staff of the company, jointly with product planners, can provide insight into uses of technology. Manufacturing has detailed data on product costs. Various budgets of divisions indicate costs of the several operations of the company, and the financial staff can also provide needed information.

ConTronics' management identified the following points on their products and markets as noteworthy for their planning:

* Relatively minor improvements are planned for the current OEM line, the Models 120, 140, 170, and 210. They have to do with improving manufacturing processes in order to lower manufacturing cost. The goal is an average 6% reduction per year.

* More significant improvements are sought for the Company's retail product line, the Systems N5, N6, and N8. The goals there include new features and a 10% reduction in manufacturing costs per year.

* New products at the low-cost end of the scale, Model 110 and Systems N3 and N4, are planned for mid- to late 1982. These will be "defeatured" products, aimed at markets less affluent than the present ones.

* Miniaturized versions of all products manufactured by using some new technologies are planned for the mid-1980s. These products will have all the features of their predecessors and will also provide new capabilities. The programs are called Program Hummingbird and Program Minnow, for the OEM and retail product lines, respectively.

* The Company is planning a new controller product line that would serve the "office of the future" with a variety of office functions. That market is not a well-defined one, and the Company's plans are indefinite at this time. Management is not certain just how to approach this market, but it feels confident that there are many opportunities for the Company in this market.

* The company plans new products in home electronics; this is to be its secondary new growth area. Devices under consideration include the following:

  • Electronic sensors of temperature, pressure, light, speed, etc., based on special proprietary materials, for use in controllers in many applications. Development money for this work is in the strategic plan for 1984–85.

  • A device to convert a telephone into a simple electronic message system, with automatic dialing, retention of distribution lists, retention of messages, etc. No development money is currently in the plan.

* Design and drafting costs for electronic components have been rising at about twice the rate of most other expenses. The company has identified an automated drafting system for possible purchase.

* The OEM markets are addressed by manufacturers that use ConTronics' systems as parts in large television, video recording, and motion picture studios and in communications systems. The retail market comprises small and medium-size manufacturing firms and households, mostly the former.

Most retail sales are through retail outlets. The Company plans to expand more in the household market. Its planned office products are aimed at small offices, a totally new market for them.

2.5 CORPORATE RESOURCES

The several components of corporate resources should be reviewed in detail, in order that the developed strategic plan be made consistent with the company's ability to achieve it. These components, other than its technologies and product lines which were already discussed, are reviewed here, each with a series of questions to be addressed.

Manufacturing and Facilities

What is the capacity of our manufacturing operations?

How flexible are our manufacturing operations?

What is the state of our manufacturing equipment?

What is the state of our other facilities?

What is the extent of the communication between Development and Manufacturing?

The manufacturing and other facilities that a company owns should be reviewed, so that plans for possible expansion can be included in the strategic plan. The addition of new facilities usually requires considerable time.

The purpose of the questions is to develop an understanding of manufacturing operations, so that means for increasing capacity to support new products and means for lowering costs can be identified. The ability of manufacturing operations to adapt readily to new technologies and their relationship to Development will be assessed. Manufacturing has major responsibility for the questions, but Development and Finance should aid in answering some of them.

The following items concerning ConTronics' manufacturing operations and facilities were identified:

* Manufacturing capacity is barely adequate for the next 12 months. As volume increases, it is expected that twice that space will be needed by late 1983.

* Manufacturing costs of the several products are as follows:

Model 120	$385	System N5	$400
Model 140	475	System N6	550
Model 170	600	System N8	800
Model 210	1000		

* Management feels that labor costs are too high and that automation can reduce them. One identified system should cut costs by one-fifth yet not reduce employment, due to expansion plans.

* Office and laboratory space is very crowded, because of recent staff expansion, yet much more staff is scheduled to be hired.

Marketing and Sales

What market studies have we recently done and are currently doing or planning?

Are all aspects of our company's markets adequately covered by our sales force?

In high-technology markets, an assessment of the future saleability of new products is often difficult, because of the uncertainty regarding technology advances. Since high-technology products often provide significant advances, customers frequently cannot know whether they will want such products. The purpose of the questions is to provide an understanding of the relationship of marketing and sales activities to sales of products, so that decisions on whether to increase them can be rationally made. Marketing and Sales have responsibility for the questions and Product Planning should provide support.

An analysis of ConTronics' marketing and sales operations yielded these results:

* Market studies in the new product areas need refining and expansion in coverage. ConTronics relies a great deal on published studies done by firms who sell such results, but management now feels it may be necessary to contract for special studies done for its own particular needs.

* Recent market studies have provided these results:
  • The total market containing the OEM line is expected to grow by about 15% per year for the next three years, then taper off to 10% six years from now.
  • The total market containing the retail line is expected to grow at about 35% per year for the next five years, then taper off to about 25% after that.
  • The market study for the planned office products provided mixed results, since the market is hard to define and the Company did not contract for its own study.

* Planned market studies are the following:
  • A segmentation of the office market, in line with the Company's specific strengths and plans, will be undertaken. Areas that appear feasible for ConTronics' controllers are office files storage and retrieval, word processing, and communications. These will be studied in depth.

An important task for ConTronics in this area is the identification of electronic parts and related subsystems that act as controlling, monitoring, and sensing components in such systems.

Service

What is the quality of service provided in the maintenance and repair of products, as perceived by customers?

What is the cost of maintenance and repair of each product?

It is necessary to understand what role service plays in customer satisfaction regarding a company's products and how, therefore, this relates to sales. Further, the questions should help management understand what constitutes the costs of service. Service has responsibility for the questions. Development may also be able to supply answers.

Manpower

What manpower skills and technical expertise exist now in our company?

What training programs do we currently have?

In technical areas — research, technology, and development — manpower is often in short supply. It is hard to find highly competent scientist and engineers, and planning for their recruitment and training those already employed are important parts of strategic planning for technology-based companies. Within most of the questions already reviewed, there are implicit manpower issues. These questions focus understanding of the current nature and weaknesses and strengths of manpower resources. Personnel, in conjunction with line management, is responsible for these questions.

The following point is the most important with regard to ConTronics' manpower: The Company has strong electronics skills, though that staff is small. Management plans to increase this staffing as quickly as it can. The engineering staff is weak in mechanical engineering talent. Because of expansion plans, all skills must be strengthened.

Finances

What has been our cash flow in recent years?

How consistent have our earnings been in recent years?

What has our record on revenues been in recent years?

What are our fixed charges?

What is our pricing structure?

What is our company's long-term and short-term debt?

What are our assets and liabilities?

What are our sources of additional financial resources?

What return are we getting on our investments and assets?

What is our investment policy?

What is our company's credit rating?

The financial status of the company is a crucial factor in strategic planning. An understanding of the company's cash flow, its consistency of earnings, its revenues, as well as the forces that drive and influence them, are essential to proper planning. The other financial data listed also play major roles in financial planning. Finance has responsibility for these questions. Top management must be involved as well.

High-Technology Equipment

What is the present state of our internal use of high-technology equipment?

What are our plans in this area?

We noted, in Chapter 1, that companies are generally using more and more modern technology within their operations, in order to operate more efficiently. Since this trend is currently accelerating and the options for technology-based equipment are increasing, companies must plan their use of such products.

Organization

How is the company organized?

Matters such as the extent of decentralization, the reporting relationships among organizations, the location of the planning organizations, and the relationship of R & D organizations to other parts of the company are important planning considerations for management. Top management, with the aid of management at all levels, has responsibility for addressing this question.

Management

What type of management does the company have?

What are the strengths and weaknesses of the company's management?

Consideration of the company's management is a major factor in planning. The answer to the first question will shape the strategy-setting process discussed later. Management's approach to running the company will influence the decisions it makes in response to the answers to the questions in these chapters. It may be difficult for top managers to answer the second question objectively, yet it is important for them to understand the impact of the way they operate on strategic planning. It might be best for an outside consultant to be brought in for the purpose.

2.6 THE LAST STRATEGIC PLAN

One of the most important sources of information for the planning process is the strategic plan developed for the last planning period and currently in use.

Objectives and Strategy

What are the objectives of the current plan?

What is its strategy?

The objectives and strategy, as well as the basis for setting them, will be useful in formulating the new objectives and strategy. This is discussed in Chapter 8, *Writing and Using the Plan.*

Budget

What is the budget in the current plan?

The budget data are valuable guides to the development of the budget in the new plan.

2.7 THE PLANNING PROCESS

The process of strategic planning that a company uses should also be reviewed. There are several questions that should be asked about this process.

Management Support

What kind of support does top management give strategic planning?

The attitudes of top management towards strategic planning — indeed, towards any internal enterprise — is crucial. It is important to evaluate and understand this and to modify it if necessary to assure success in this task.

Organization

What responsibilities do various organizations have in strategic planning?

To understand accurately how planning currently proceeds in the company, management must review the roles that all organizations play in the process.

Planning Successes

What successes can be attributed to strategic planning within the company?

The use of strategic planning offers no guarantee of corporate success, and management ought to know how well it has done with it in the past. It should review previous forecasts, decisions, and strategies, to see how they affected the rate of success.

Responsibilities

Top management and the planning organization share the responsibility in this area.

2.8 ANALYSIS OF THE INFORMATION

Answers

The previous sections list many questions, and the answers to them comprise a lengthy set of data. The tabulation of answers may appear unmanageable. It is not easy to take all this information and other information to be gathered and use it to formulate a strategy. However, not all of the answers are needed for that task. Management must examine the list carefully and identify those that are most important to the company. Some answers to questions will be of paramount importance, while others will be irrelevant; most will lie between these extremes. In any event, it is useful if as many questions as feasible are answered. Certainly, for some companies, the list omits questions that should be answered. Management must address this issue and provide its own questions.

The self-analysis of the company began with a tabulation of the major problems facing it, as perceived by management. It is important now to review that list and the answers to the other questions asked here, in order to compile a final list of such major concerns. After a complete review of internal issues, the original list may need revision. This final version can serve as a checklist against which the elements of a developed strategy can be verified. If the strategy does not satisfactorily address each of the problems on it, then the strategy must be revised.

Management, after tabulating the answers to the questions, should sort them on the basis of their potential impact on the company. It should focus on strengths, weaknesses, opportunities, and threats and compile a consensus analysis based on these issues. Generally, the self-analysis emphasizes strengths and weaknesses rather than opportunities and threats.

A company is not usually in a position to correct all or perhaps even a majority of its weaknesses. At this point in the planning process, however, it is important to have them identified, so that they can be improved. Similarly, a company is not usually in a position to capitalize on all of its strengths, because of time, money, or other constraints, but those too should be identified.

The Preplanning Analysis Report

Management should, at this point, prepare a report on information gathered. A suggested report is the *preplanning analysis report* (PAR), containing the results of the company's self-analysis.   It is structured as follows:

1. Major problems
2. Major decisions
3. Major sensitivities (to be supplied after an environmental analysis is done)
4. Company strengths
5. Company weaknesses
6. Opportunities for the company
7. Threats to the company
8. Responses to internal issues (a series of sections, one for each area of the company, summarizing the key responses to the answers supplied)

This report is a preliminary one.   After the environmental analysis is completed, it will be extended. Sections (1) through (7) may then be modified to accommodate new gathered information and to combine answers to questions on the company and its environment.

The sources of information used to supply all the needed answers are varied and widespread. Tables in the Appendix for Chapter 2 indicate many sources of information. In order to have all such information on hand, an extensive library of company reports must be maintained. It clearly would be helpful if this information was organized for planning uses. Unless specific direction from top management so dictates, it is likely that it will not be, because the reports are written primarily for other purposes. Each report format should be reviewed so that required planning information becomes readily extractable in the future. This would ease the information-gathering problem. It is probably necessary to prepare reports specifically for planning purposes.

The management of ConTronics Corporation prepared the following preplanning analysis report:

1. <u>Major problems</u>. Management identified the following as its major problems today and in the future:

    *   A need exists for the Company to enter new markets with new product lines, and the "office of the future" and home electronics have been identified for this purpose. Management's ideas and plans for the office area are far from adequate at this time, and it may take a long time to develop those plans.

* Much of the technology that the Company uses in its products is old for the electronics field. It must develop or acquire new technology to improve reliability and reduce the cost and size of its products.

* The Company's market shares in some areas are small and static, and management feels that unless strong efforts are made to increase them, the Company may cease to be a viable force in those market segments.

2. <u>Major decisions</u>. There is one overriding decision − or, really, set of decisions − that faces management:

* It must decide how to attack the rather ill-defined "office of the future" market, using its experience, skills, current products, and the new materials research effort as starting points. It must define the product it will sell in this market. Management must include these decisions in its current planning process.

4. <u>Company strengths</u>.

* ConTronics has an excellent staff of researchers and engineers in electronics fields.

* The Company has new proprietary materials which have a great deal of promise in a variety of applications.

* It has significant market shares in certain market segments.

* The company has a reputation for producing high-quality products.

* It has an excellent growth record in recent years, important for financing capital needs.

5. <u>Company weaknesses</u>.

* None of ConTronics' current products use the latest technologies, and so they are susceptible to being superceded by competitors.

* There is no general development activity, applicable across a whole product line.

* The Company lacks skills in mechanical engineering, which will be greatly needed in the future.

* It has very limited physical space and is already overcrowded, with much growth planned in staffing.

6. <u>Opportunities for the company</u>.

* ConTronics' new materials have promise in many areas of application.

* Its actual and planned markets are rapidly growing ones; this is particularly true of home markets.

7. <u>Threats to the company</u>.

* There are many technology developments outside that threaten the Company's own development.

* Competition is increasing in the Company's markets and will do so even more in the years ahead.

8. Responses to internal issues. The following actions should be taken, to the extent that they can be afforded:

* Develop new technologies.

* Invest heavily in materials research.

* Plan general development activities that apply across a product line.

* Continue to work on product improvements, in order to decrease manufacturing costs, improve reliability, reduce size, etc.

* Develop a miniaturized product line.

* Move into "office of the future" market with controllers; develop a plan for this.

* Move into home electronics market; develop a plan for this.

* Do cost-benefit analyses for the automated drafting and manufacturing automation systems, and acquire these if feasible.

* Monitor competition more thoroughly than at present.

* Buy more modern manufacturing equipment.

* Expand office, laboratory, and manufacturing facilities.

* Undertake better market studies, especially in new market areas.

* Develop a manpower plan and recruit needed staffing skills.

Current Strategic Plan

The following table is a brief form of the financial portion of the current strategic plan (1981–1985):

(Dollar amounts in millions; units in thousands)

Projections	1981	1982	1983	1984	1985
Revenues	$30	37	48	70	95
Net profit	$ 1.8	2.3	2.6	3.8	5.5
Margin	6.0%	6.2%	5.4%	5.4%	5.8%
Units sold	23	32	48	80	125
Revenue by divisions					
OEM	$20	22	25	35	40
Business	$10	15	21	30	35
Office	$ 0	0	0	0	10
Home	$ 0	0	2	5	10

Budget	1981	1982	1983	1984	1985
Research	$0.2	0.3	0.5	0.6	0.8
Materials	$0.05	0.08	0.2	0.2	0.2
Software	$0.075	0.12	0.2	0.1	0.1
Circuit design	$0.075	0.1	0.2	0.2	0.1
Other	$0	0	0	0.1	0.4
Development	$1.5	1.9	2.5	3.9	5.2
Current pdts	$0.2	0.3	0.3	0.2	0
New features	$0.2	0.2	0.3	0.4	0.4
New pdts (110, N4)	$1.1	1.4	1.2	0.5	0.3
Miniaturized pdts	$0	0	0.4	1.3	1.6
New matls tech	$0	0	0	0.3	0.7
Home cntlrs	$0	0	0.3	0.8	1.2
Office cntlrs	$0	0	0	0.2	1.0
Total R & D	$1.7	2.2	3.0	4.7	6.0

2.9   THE SCHEDULE

Information for strategic planning should be gathered the year round, as shown in the schedule in Fig. 2-2, but it should occur most intensively during the first quarter, at the start of the planning process. The schedule also shows that reports on certain phases of company operation are issued regularly, perhaps monthly. Analysis of the information begins at some point during the intensive phase of information gathering and proceeds as more information is gathered.

In specific instances, information can be gathered over a few weeks. The time involved depends upon the state of a company's reports on progress of its operations. With detailed, regular, up-to-date reports that are structured for the purpose, the questions can be answered rather quickly.

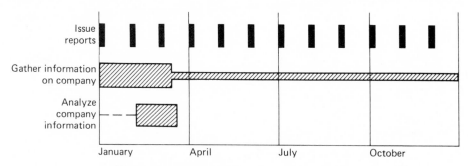

Fig. 2-2.   A schedule for self-analysis.

2.10   PROBLEMS IN SELF-ANALYSIS

There are many difficulties in doing strategic planning, and gathering information about a company is no exception. It might appear otherwise since, after all, management presumably controls all operations and therefore also the gathering of information about them. That is not entirely true, however. One reason is that, although there are many reports that a company prepares with data useful for planning purposes, their information is not generally organized for these purposes, and extraction and synthesis of the needed information can be tedious and time-consuming.

Perhaps the most difficult information to gather with reasonable accuracy is the nature and the extent of problems within the various operating divisions. Managers are loath to reveal problems to their bosses. There sometimes tends to be little incentive for managers of operating groups to report accurately on their work. As a matter of fact, there are forces that will tend to bias the information, as Richard Smallwood has pointed out [1]. Consider, e.g., a product development manager who has made a commitment to have a product ready by a certain date. He or she is asked to describe the uncertainty in the product's availability date. The manager will be reluctant to admit that the product will be available either before the commitment date (in which case the date will be moved up) or after the commitment date (in which case the manager admits missing a commitment).

SUMMARY

Self-analysis proceeds by addressing questions on all aspects of a company's resources and operations. It is useful to begin by addressing major problems that the company currently faces and major decisions that it will face in the plan period.   These set the tone for all succeeding questions.

It is then appropriate to address the major resources of a company:

*   Technology: research projects, research activity, experience and applications, development programs, new projects and programs, R & D spending, failures, technology transfer
*   Products and markets: product features, new products, current products, new markets, new geographical areas
*   Manufacturing: communication, flexibility and change, capacity, equipment resources
*   Marketing and sales
*   Service: quality, costs
*   Manpower: staffing, training
*   Finances: cash flow, consistency of earnings, revenues, fixed charges, prices, debt, assets and liabilities, return on assets, investments, credit

*   High-technology equipment

Next, management should consider aspects of the company's operations:

*   Organization
*   Management: style, strengths and weaknesses
*   Last strategic plan: objectives and strategy, budget
*   The planning process: management support, organization, planning successes

Once all the appropriate questions have been answered, management must organize its responses to them. It is useful, at this point, to prepare a *preplanning analysis report* (PAR), summarizing the results of the self-analysis. This PAR should include major problems and decisions, strengths, weaknesses, opportunities, and threats, as determined from the answers. It should further highlight the issues on company resources and operations that the question-answering provides. This report will be supplemented and revised after the next information-gathering phase takes place.

REFERENCES

1. Smallwood, Richard. Unpublished memorandum, 1977.

Additional references

Brown, James K., *This Business of Issues: Coping with the Company's Environments*, The Conference Board, New York, 1979. (This report addresses issues both inside and outside a company, considering classifying, identifying, scanning, monitoring, and responding to them; of value for Chapter 3 also.)

Bemelmans, Th., "Strategic Planning for Research and Development", *Long Range Planning*, vol. 12, no. 4, April 1979, pp. 33–44. (This paper contains an extensive checklist for analysis, with 150 questions on many subjects, including costs, markets, customers, and pricing.)

3

ANALYSIS OF THE ENVIRONMENT

What is the state of our environment?

INTRODUCTION

A companion task to studying the state of a company is studying the state of its environment. The environment plays such a major role in the fortunes of any corporation that management must understand what it comprises, what has driven it to its present state, what will drive it to change in the future, and how it will change. There are many sources of information on the environment, and they can be used to answer a broad range of questions about the environment. It takes a great deal of effort, however, to monitor them in a selective and appropriate manner.

Answers to the questions suggest responses, which delineate the opportunities for a company, which in turn help define strategy in technology and product development. The responses also indicate the threats that exist because of competitive and other pressures.

3.1 THE ANALYSIS

The Environment

The *environment* of a company comprises external factors that have had, now have, or may in the future have some measurable effect on the company. This definition excludes a great deal; clearly not everything out there has impact. Many factors have insignificant impact and can be ignored. The level of influence above which an external factor should be considered cannot be precisely identified; management must make its own judgments. It is clear that only *important* environmental factors need be monitored. What is not necessarily clear is which factors are important. There are no natural boundaries to a company's environment; any external event or information may be of some influence. The study and analysis of the environment is termed *environmental analysis* or *environmental scanning*. Philip Thomas has reviewed this activity [1].

The purposes of an environmental analysis are to determine what major problems face the company, to identify opportunities for and threats to the company, and to assess the status of all factors in the environment that have measurable impact on the company. The analysis addresses the future of the environment as well as the present. Chapter 4, *Forecasting the Future*, provides methods for doing this.

It is as important to study a firm's environment as it is to study the firm itself. No company operates without being influenced strongly by its environment, though the influence of that environment varies from company to company and from product line to product line within a company. Management must study the many forces in that environment, the interrelationships among them over time, and the effects those forces may have on the company.

The external factors that are likely to have impact and which must thus be analyzed include at least the following: the competition, technology developments, the market, the company's suppliers, its raw materials, economic and social developments, and government actions.

Questions

In this chapter, key questions on the environment are asked. Auxiliary questions appear in the Appendix for Chapter 3. As in Chapter 2, not all of the questions given here apply to all companies. Only those deemed important should be addressed. As each question is addressed, the two actions listed in Chapter 2 should be taken. They are repeated here.

1. *Determine whether the answer identifies either a strength or weakness of the company.*

2. *Determine whether the answer identifies either an opportunity for or a threat to the company.*

In addition, two questions should be kept in mind as the questions are addressed:

a) *How do we compare to other companies in our field, i.e., to the industry average?*

b) *What is the impact of external conditions on our internal operations?*

The next several sections deal with various aspects of a company's environment. Section 3.2 addresses major problems and factors in the environment to which the company is most sensitive. Sections 3.3 through 3.7 deal with factors in the environment. Appendix for Chapter 3 contains auxiliary questions that relate to those given here. The Appendix also contains a number of sources of information useful to answering the questions.

In addition to those sources, there are many informal outside sources of useful information, and these should not be overlooked. Personal contacts, for example, can be invaluable. Since individuals queried are usually well known, their expertise and bias can be taken into account in judging their information. Consultants too can be used who, if used often, know the company and its style and needs. There may be other sources that managers can draw upon.

3.2   MAJOR PROBLEMS AND SENSITIVITIES

Major Problems

What problems are we currently facing?

What major problems are we likely to face over the plan period?

Management should begin its analysis of the company's environment by identifying the major external problems facing it. As noted in Chapter 2, there are problems that involve both the environment and the company, and so external concerns may have been expressed in response to the questions in Section 2.2. The questions asked there about the company should be asked here about its environment. Note that we are here focusing on the present state of the environment; Chapter 4 probes its future.

The same rules apply to answering these questions as previously. A ranking of problems by "seriousness" should be undertaken. Probably the areas providing the greatest concern are the competition, technology developments, and the nature of markets and market trends.

Sensitivities

To what factors in the environment is our company most sensitive?

The answer to this question is tied closely to the answers to the questions above. It is highly likely that the areas of greatest sensitivity represent the greatest sources of problems. For example, a company may sell products that are purchased seasonally, in the summer and before Christmas. Another company's products may sell well at a time of large building construction expenditures and not otherwise. It is important to note the greatest of such sensitivities, to focus attention for the environmental analysis task.

3.3   THE COMPETITION

For most companies, competition has a major impact, so that understanding that competition is critical. Companies should, and usually do, expend a great time of time and money in attempts to understand both the nature and scope of their competition, as well as its expected future.

Companies

What companies are in competition with us, i.e., offer products that compete in the same markets?

The greatest threat in a company's environment is usually its competition. The more that it knows about its competitors, the better able is a company to anticipate their moves and to develop an appropriate strategy. To that end, a company must be diligent in competitive surveillance. The task involves careful monitoring of all public information about companies that are, or have prospects of becoming, competitors in the marketplace. Among the factors to consider are market share, product line, R & D spending, financial matters, key organizational and personnel changes, acquisitions, and divestments. This list should suggest other areas for surveillance to management, as befitting its needs. All these, and other indicators, tell something about a company's plans. Competitive surveillance systems are described in Chapter 4.

As a result of monitoring competition, it will become clear just which of a firm's competitors bear especially close watching. In response to this monitoring, a company may well decide to shift its priorities in company surveillance, to increase its surveillance budget, or take other actions.

Products

What are the products that compete with ours?

The most directly influential components of the competition are, of course, the families of products that compete with a company's own. All products that lie in the same markets as the company's should be examined. If funds are available, some of those products might be purchased and thoroughly scrutinized. However, once competitors' products are announced or are commercially available, it may be rather late for management to modify its plans in response. It is far better to try to anticipate those products, and the greater the time period of anticipation, the better. It is of course often difficult to do this, and the greater the time period the more difficult it is.

The more a company knows about its competitors' planned products, the better. It should attempt to predict features, costs, and embodied technologies of those products. It is also valuable to identify the markets that these products address and any "gaps" or missing markets that result. Management's response to this analysis could be to formulate product concepts for particular markets, though much more information is needed for true product planning.

Responsibilities

The responsibility for monitoring the competition is best handled by a staff assigned the task. The staff may gather all the necessary information itself; it may also make use of commercial services that do this. The information gathered can either be issued as reports on key competitors or markets or can be stored in files to be used upon demand. Computer-based systems are valuable in this process; Chapter 9, *Computers in Planning*, discusses this use of computers.

The following items concerning ConTronics' manufacturing operations and facilities were identified:

* ConTronics' competition in their two extreme OEM product markets consists of the companies shown in the table, with indicated market shares:

OEM Market

	Mod. 120 mkt.	Mod. 210 mkt.
ConTronics	25%	10%
Purple Electronics	30	10
Cactus Controllers	15	15
Sunflower Electronics	10	5
Blue Controllers	5	10
Green-tronics	5	30

* Purple Electronics, ConTronics' major competitor, recently announced two new products that will compete very strongly with the OEM line.

* Cactus Controllers, a smaller competitor, has doubled its revenue each of the last two years with products that also compete strongly.

* The following product "gaps" exist in the markets for potential ConTronics products: the low end of the both product lines, needed for penetration into home markets, and in miniature sensors and controllers.

* Purple Electronics, Cactus Controllers, and Green-tronics each have a significant number of patents to support their technical development in areas directly competitive to ConTronics. These technologies pose a threat to ConTronics' products.

* A company called Popeye Manufacturing Co. is a potential acquisition for ConTronics. Their sales last year were $7,000,000, and their profits were $758,000. Their product line would provide need mechanical subassemblies. The acquisition cost would be $18,000,000.

3.4   TECHNOLOGY

Technology-based companies are naturally interested in the development of technology outside, particularly within competitor firms. Questions should be asked about external technologies of concern to the company today and in the future.

Competitive Research

What research is being undertaken by our competitors that is of concern to us?

Information about research at competitive firms is often available in technical literature. it is important to learn as much as possible about such research, since this provides an indication of future product plans. Management should try to ascertain research goals, assess the nature and quality of competitive research activity, and identify R & D spending in those companies.

Competitive Technology

What is the status of technologies under development in competitive firms?

Knowledge of competitive technology also provides indications of product plans as does research information, but it is harder to obtain. The patent position and proprietary status of this activity are also valuable for judging overall competitive technological expertise. Furthermore, such information may be useful in judging whether a technology can and should be acquired by the company.

Other Research and Technology

What is the status of research and technology at universities and government agencies?

Information about university and government R & D activities is generally readily available. Such knowledge allows a company to consider acquisitions, which are discussed below. Their status and potential value should be assessed.

Acquisition

Are there any technologies outside the company that we should consider acquiring?

A company may wish to acquire the technology of another firm by outright purchase or by licensing. Alternately, R & D work at universities is often readily available for acquisition. A company that needs a particular technology, but is not a leader in the field, must determine whether it is better to develop or to acquire a capability in that area.   Management must determine where technologies of interest to the firm are to be found, whether they can be acquired, and what the costs and benefits of such acquisition are likely to be. Such tabulations of internal and external technologies provide the technology alternatives which figure heavily in management's strategy development. The questions asked in Section 2.3 on potential benefits realizable through a company's own technologies can now be asked here of outside technologies. Technology acquisition is discussed in more detail in Chapter 6, *Issues on Technology*.

Sources and Responsibilities

The best sources, in many instances, of technology information are the patents that companies obtain. A company will at times withhold patent applications for a while, but in so doing it risks losing patent protection; it relies on trade secrets in such cases. Other useful sources are the scientific and technical literature, though a large fraction of these does not relate to the use of technology. It is particularly valuable to monitor the progress of a technology, for that reveals trends over time.

Technology watching is best done by the technical staff or by a special staff charged with the responsibility, provided this staff uses technical experts as advisors. Patent attorneys can interpret the patent literature. The matter of acquisition of other companies goes beyond the responsibility of the staff just described, for top management must be involved in such issues. Sometimes, a corporation establishes a specialized staff to study the matter of outside acquisition and, for that matter, divestment.

> The major issues on technology in the ConTronics' environment are the following:
>
> * Green-tronics is a major threat in the area of the research planned for miniaturization efforts; its products are already smaller and management expects further miniaturization.
>
> * ConTronics is considering the purchase or outright acquisition of a new circuit design and fabrication process from a company, Auto-Electronics, Inc., that offers a system for fabricating very inexpensive, highly reliable circuits.

3.5 MARKETS

In order for a company to work out its plans for product development, it must define its markets and understand their characteristics. The company must also be able to define new potential markets in which it may be able to sell new products.

Present Markets

What are the markets in which our company competes?

The more precisely that a market can be defined, the better is management able to define the characteristics of the products it should design and the technologies it should invest in for those products. Those characteristics include potential size (in number of units), type of customer, geography, and price sensitivity. Management can determine the extent to which its portfolio of technologies can supply those characteristics. It is sometimes difficult, however, to define a company's markets, especially when those markets are planned for future entry. Often, of course, the products of several companies define the market, and if so the trends in the market are direct functions of its products' characteristics.

Potential New Markets

In what ways can our present markets be extended?

This question follows logically from that above; it is concerned with extensions of present markets and the creation of new ones. The issue here is that of shaping markets by new technology embodiments rather than determining if technologies meet market needs.

Customers

Who are the customers for our present products?

In a market, products are matched with customers, i.e., product characteristics and prices are matched with customer needs and wants. Consequently, it is important to understand actual and potential customers, i.e., to characterize them, by size, type, geography, and so on. It helps also to know why they acquire products of the type the company sells and what kinds of features they want. A major task is developing a technology portfolio to meet the needs and wants of these customers.

Noteworthy on ConTronics' markets are these points:

* Present markets that the Company is active in are the electronics segments of the following:
  * The OEM industrial electronics market
  * The retail market for small businesses
  * The affluent home market
* New electronics markets for the Company are the following:
  * The whole home electronics market (not just the affluent portion)
  * The office electronics market

These markets are not well enough defined for ConTronics' management. It needs to know more about sizes, customers, and pricing, and the trends of these factors.

* ConTronics believes that the home market is one of the most rapidly growing ones. For that reason, it is attracting many manufacturers and will be highly competitive.

3.6 SUPPLY FACTORS

A corporation often depends heavily upon raw materials and on component parts from suppliers.

Raw materials

What is the availability today of the raw materials upon which we depend?

Raw materials that are natural resources are of limited supply. Management must know their costs and availabilities. If, at projected future rates of consumption, shortages can be expected, it is obviously necessary to plan for this. Management's response can be to try to reduce the need, to seek more abundant substitutes, or to develop new technologies that do not use these materials. Technology development can play an important role in materials substitution.

Suppliers

What suppliers is our company dependent upon?

The more sources of supplies a company has, the better are its prospects for continuing to obtain them. Those suppliers should be identified, and alternatives should be considered.

Energy

Is our company especially vulnerable to energy shortages?

The recent dramatic increases in the cost of energy may cause serious problems in the future for a firm, requiring serious reassessments of technology development. Alternate ways of doing business and of designing products may be required. New technology development may be needed.

Responsibilities

Manufacturing would have the major responsibility for monitoring the supplies factors. Technologists would address energy issues.

3.7 SOCIOECONOMIC FACTORS

A corporation also operates within subenvironments of a socioeconomic nature. These influence its operations and thus the products it offers. They include economic, social, demographic, legal, and political factors. Changes in these factors may result in new opportunities for and threats to a company's technology efforts and products.

Economic Factors

What is the current state of the economy in the geographical areas in which our company operates?

The purposes for addressing this question are to aid in making decisions about expanding the existing plants and starting new ones and to aid in making decisions on financing. It is also important to consider how susceptible the company is to the prices of labor, energy, and materials, as well as to economic cycles.

Social Factors

What social factors today have impact on our company?

Social factors, as the term is used here, are factors that relate to the way in which individuals and families view their work, their education, their place of employment, their home, their leisure time, and their lives in general. Corporations often seek to have their objectives match "national objectives" that which the country as a whole attempts to achieve, which in a sense derive from the collective views of individuals. These currently include, e.g., pollution abatement and control, unemployment reduction, reduced energy dependence, and inflation reduction. The public's attitude towards technology has impact on all technology-based companies.

Demographic Factors

What is the distribution of population that is of concern in our markets?

The distribution of population helps define markets to which a company sells its products.   Factors include age, population, and economic distribution. Management should decide which of these have significance for its own products.

Legal Factors

What laws and regulations today affect our company?

Such issues as interstate commerce, price controls, health, safety, and governmental concern with monopolies are all potentially of importance to a corporation. It is necessary for a company to monitor laws and regulations closely, since many have potential impact upon it.

Political Factors

What are the political conditions in the states and countries in which we operate?

The issues of foreign markets, tariffs, international monetary stability, and the political atmospheres in various countries are also of potential concern. The extent of defense R & D spending is a major factor in technology development. These factors also demand careful monitoring.

Responsibilities

The areas of concern here are very diverse, and the responsibility would be shared among several persons and organizations. Most likely, a staff of experts in economic, social, and political factors would address many of the issues.

The following are important socioeconomic points for ConTronics:

* There is a growing acceptance of electronic home systems. This is due to lowering costs and an increasing variety of available services.

* The apparent trend to less business travel (because of higher transportation costs) and the trend to the greater use of the home as a place of business indicate the greater need for information in offices and at home.

* The age distribution in the U.S. population, with a large marriage-age cohort (ages 21-35), suggests a rapidly growing market for the Company's products. This group will be establishing new households in the 1980's.

* The only legal issue that would appear to affect ConTronics is the gradual deregulation of the communications industry, causing it to be more competitive.

3.8 ANALYSIS OF THE INFORMATION

Formal Analysis

The information needed for responding to the questions raised in this chapter is broad, far-reaching, and multifaceted. It must be obtained from a variety of sources. To be useful, the information so gathered should be comprehensive, timely, and accurate. Sources of information are tabulated in the Appendix for Chapter 3. There are other sources as well, and each company can identify those meeting its needs. In addition, a company can perform in-depth studies, or have consulting firms do so, on special subjects.

Because of the importance of this information to the company, a formal system of information gathering is highly desirable. The size and scope of the system that a company needs depends upon its particular requirements. If a company is large, its informational needs are large as well, and it probably should have its own surveillance organization for the gathering and analysis of information. Such an organization can make use of commercial computer-based data bases or can develop specialized data bases itself. The information within these data bases must be properly indexed (i.e., accompanied by terms that describe it) so that selective retrieval can be accomplished; such indexing can be done either commercially or internally. Searching of the data bases is performed by the company's surveillance staff in response to company needs. Finally, analysis of the retrieved information by staff members within the company is performed. More detail on information monitoring, with respect to the competition, is given in Chapter 4.

The information gathered must be analyzed so that it can be used by those who do planning. These users are top management, the planning organization, and line management. Each organization acts at its own level and in its own manner, using its own type of decision-making. Top management is concerned with a long view and broad objectives; planners are concerned with product lines; line management addresses strategy and schedules. Consequently, the information analysis done must be tailored to the needs of particular users.

The manner in which the analysis is done is critical. For example, it is impractical for all information gathered on a subject, such as the problems in the management of office paperwork, to be transmitted to a product planner of office automation products. The planner does not have the time to sort through all such information, determining what is important and how it all interrelates. It may be important for such information to be sent to the head of R & D, so that needed technologies can be identified; that manager also is probably too busy to sort it all out. So it is necessary for the analyst, who is experienced in sorting through information, to extract its important parts and coalesce these into a coherent body of information.

The Environment

The environmental analysis began with a tabulation of the major problems facing the company. It is important to review that list and the answers to other questions asked here. The strategy developed later must address each of these concerns.

The answers should be sorted in order of importance to the company. Focus should be on strengths, weaknesses, opportunities, and threats. Most commonly, the environmental analysis emphasizes opportunities and threats more than strengths and weaknesses.

A company is not usually in a position to respond to all of the opportunities and all the threats facing it or perhaps even to a majority of these. Nonetheless, it is important to identify them at this point. The task of scanning the environment is not complete at this point, because the future must be projected. That task, however, is deferred to Chapter 4, following a discussion of forecasting.

Monitoring and analyzing a company's entire environment is a time-consuming, expensive process if the company is large and diverse. It may be more useful for such a firm to scan the environment in a more selective manner, concentrating primarily on those factors of greatest significance. The rest of the environment would be monitored in a less intense fashion. Special studies, as deemed necessary, would be undertaken, e.g., on markets in China, a particular reprographics marking technology, or the electronics typewriter market. If a company chooses to scan and analyze the environment selectively, its staff should regularly review all external factors to identify those of continuing relevance to its needs.

3.9 THE SCHEDULE

Information gathering on the environment is best done on a year-round basis, since much of the required information is available in external monthly or quarterly reports. Competitive surveillance must be continual, as must technology surveillance. Some data can be gathered just once a year, since it changes relatively infrequently. Among these are the data on socioeconomic factors. Other data should perhaps be gathered quarterly, as, e.g., political and legislative information. In addition, some needed reports on special subjects are published from time to time or are commissioned, as noted earlier. A schedule for environmental analysis is given in Fig. 3-1. That schedule, by the manner in which it is drawn, indicates the irregular nature of the gathering and use of reports on the environment. The reports shown refer to any of the types described above.

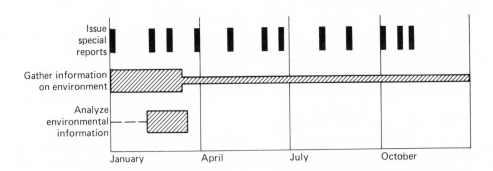

Fig. 3-1. A schedule for environmental analysis.

3.10   PROBLEMS IN ENVIRONMENT ANALYSIS

As in the case of self-analysis, there are problems in obtaining information about a company's environment. This is understandable, especially with regard to the competition, which is trying to remain as secretive about its plans as are the companies watching it.

The main problem area is the competition. While there are many sources of information about competitors, totally accurate information cannot be obtained. The patent trail that companies leave is usually the most revealing about their technology developments, but it is not foolproof. A company may abandon a technology after it has obtained patents in the area, or it may invest heavily in a technology prior to filing patents or to their being granted. Because of the long time to patent issuance, much work can be hidden prior to that time. A company may choose not to patent a process in order to keep it secret. Finally, it is not always totally clear just how the methodologies in granted patents are to be used in products.

The difficulties in understanding what markets exist and how they might be extended has been discussed. The problem is often one of defining what a market really is. Market studies are sometimes accomplished by surveying actual and potential customers, who are asked about their needs and desires. If a company is contemplating the development of a new product that differs significantly from a product currently on the market, it may be difficult for a customer to describe his or her envisioned use of that product. It may offer features that are not perceived as valuable, when in fact they later turn out to be, or the reverse may be true. Furthermore, though the concept of a "market" appears clear enough, it really is a vague concept when applied to a particular product family. For example, the size of a market is often price-dependent, so one can double a "market" by cutting price.

Understanding the impact of socioeconomic factors on company sales and profits is often difficult. The effects of changes in the economy are not always obvious. One company's fortunes may depend on the actions taken in certain industries, and these may be unpredictable. Some industries are more subject to recessions than others. Sales of products that are labor-intensive in their use may suffer badly as unemployment increases. Cutbacks in spending may shift customers' priorities from some products to others, benefiting some companies while hurting others. Social and demographic factors are sometimes the hardest to fathom. Many questions can be asked. What does it mean, e.g., when there is a strong shift of population from the suburbs back to the cities? What effect will sharply higher gasoline prices have on product sales? What if people keep having smaller and smaller families? Although some of these trends will result in fewer sales of certain products, can a corporation provide new products that sell better under such circumstances? These questions cannot always be easily answered.

There are many uncertainties in world politics that can drastically affect a company's sales, depending upon the nature of its products. Many of these events are unpredictable, but what seems to be true is that world events have an ever-increasing influence on the way U.S. companies do business.

SUMMARY

Environmental analysis proceeds by the addressing of questions on all aspects of a company's environment. As with self-analysis, it is best to begin by identifying the major problems that the company faces externally; these are usually competitive concerns. It is also helpful to delineate those factors in the environment to which the company is most sensitive.

Next, management should address the several factors in the environment:

* The competition: companies, products
* Technology: status, acquisition
* Markets: present markets, potential new markets, customers
* Supply factors: raw materials, suppliers, energy
* Socioeconomic factors: economic, social, demographic, legal, political factors

With the questions answered, management must develop responses to them. The preplanning analysis report developed earlier should now be expanded to incorporate new material and to combine material of an internal and external nature.

Because of the diversity of information sources, as regards their detail, timeliness, and accuracy, it is best to formalize the process of monitoring and using information about the environment. Computer data bases are valuable in this task. An important task here is that of analyzing the information for particular users.

REFERENCES

1. Thomas, Philip S., "Environmental Scanning — the State of the Art," *Long Range Planning*, February 1980, vol. 13, no. 2, pp. 20–28. (This paper describes the process of environmental scanning and provides examples of the methods used by several companies.)

Additional reference

Segev, Eli, "Analysis of the Business Environment", *Management Review*, August 1979, vol. 68, no. 8, pp. 58–61. (This paper discusses environmental analysis in general terms — its characteristics, how it should be accomplished, and problems.)

4

FORECASTING THE FUTURE

What will our environment be like in the future?

Where are we going in that environment?

INTRODUCTION

Strategic planning involves the futurity of current decision-making, and so it is essential to attempt to forecast the future. Forecasting involves identifying possible and probable future events. It is a vital stage in planning, for it requires that the management of a corporation react to its forecast by allocating resources to carry out its objectives, in the light of what it expects the future to be. Technology-based companies are particularly concerned with technology forecasting, but their interests extend across the entire spectrum of external events.

A company must project the future of its environment and its own future in that environment. It must address the factors considered during an analysis of the present state of the company and its environment. It must then make a set of assumptions about the future, against which its strategic plans will then be set.

4.1 FORECASTING AND ITS NATURE

Forecasts

In Chapter 3 we considered several factors in a company's environment. Management must next forecast the future of that environment and the future of the company in that environment, which are more difficult tasks. The projection into the future is accomplished by addressing the issues in the questions of Chapter 3, but directed ahead in time. This procedure is discussed in Sections 4.3 and 4.4. Management sometimes ignores the distinction between forecasting and planning, looking at forecasts as generating plans. Forecasting merely provides some of the information about a company's future environment that is needed for planning.

The interaction between a company and its environment is mutual. The company's technology advances and new products will influence the development of external technologies and competing products. We shall ignore this effect at this stage, so that internal and external factors can be treated independently. Their interaction is discussed later. The larger the company, the more likely is its environment affected by the company itself. If, for example, the company develops a product far superior to anything on the market at the same price as existing products, that product would likely replace the others.

All forecasting is an attempt to infer future events on the basis of what has occurred in the past, which is our only source of factual data. Thus, all forecasting methods are based on the analysis of trends, with consideration given to a variety of other factors. The accuracy of a forecast depends on the accuracy and completeness of the data used and on the type of data sought. It is interesting and useful to consider the following kinds of questions, to stimulate thinking about the future; they are based on suggested questions offered by Robert Ayres [1]:

1. Will event A occur?

2. Will event A occur before the year 19XX?

3. When will event A occur?

4. Will event A precede event B?

5. If event A occurs by year 19XX, when will event B occur?

6. By when will both event A and event B occur?

7. What does event A's occurrence depend upon?

8. In what order will events A, B, and C occur?

Some of these questions can be answered by simple extrapolation; others require more knowledge of the environment and the interaction of events than others.

How far ahead a company should forecast technology developments depends upon the particular technologies involved and the extent to which their futures can be predicted with reasonable accuracy. Forecasting should extend at least over the company's entire plan period, wherever feasible. In some instances, as where major facilities expansion is required, forecasting may have to go beyond this period. In other cases, it may not be possible to go this far. Although it is not possible to forecast very precisely several years into the future, management decisions for strategic planning generally do not require high precision; a forecast of the probable ranges of future events and trends usually suffices. As the future evolves, predictions can be corrected or reinforced.

Simon Ramo points out that many technology developments are viewed as surprises, yet by hindsight they can often be seen as extensions of past trends [2]. The trick, of course, is to see and understand such future extensions today. At least, one ought to be able to identify some of these surprises as likely possibilities. The art of understanding current trends and the forces behind them and extending this knowledge to the future with reasonable accuracy is hard to cultivate.

Technological Forecasting

Forecasting deals with the construction of models of possible futures, with possible activities occurring within those futures and with probabilistic assessments of their taking place. *Technological forecasting* deals with forecasting the future of technologies.

The process involves determining the trends in the technologies of concern to a corporation and the impact that these trends will have on its future. The impact works in two opposite ways. Technology advances offer opportunities for the company to exploit in the development of its own products. They also offer threats when embodied in competing products.

(Technology forecasting is also used to refer to the opportunities and threats that nontechnology events offer a company regarding its development of technology. This concept is explored in Section 4.4.)

The capabilities required to do technological forecasting properly include an appreciation of the developments as they unfold relative to the company's own activities and planned products, an appreciation for the economic aspects of science and technology, and broad access to all pertinent sources of information. Human judgment is far more valuable here than mathematical processes of analysis. This task must be the responsibility of both top management and technical management, aided by corporate planners and the staff of literature searchers in the company library.

Valid Forecasts

A predicted event should have a date associated with it; a prediction without a time for its occurrence is of little value. Timing of events is critical in planning. If one predicts the trend of a factor, the value of the factor should be specified as a function of time. The prediction should also indicate what the values are expected to be at particular times in the future. Since such accuracy is usually beyond most forecasting capabilities, a probabilistic distribution of expected events is useful. In summary, forecasts should include dates, values, and probabilities, wherever possible.

Examples of structurally valid forecasts are: "The cost of computer memory will be 40 cents or less per million bits by 1986, with a probability of 80%", "The price of iron ore, delivered to the factory, will rise 10% each year for the next five years, with a probability of 95% or more", and "With probabilities of 25%, 50%, and 25%, respectively, home computers will be found in a majority of homes before 1985, from 1985 through 1990, and after 1990."

Information Sources

Many sources of information for use in technological forecasting are listed in the Appendix for Chapter 3. These sources report on advances in science and technology and, in some cases, point the way to the next stages of advancement. Knowledgeable scientists and technologists can often predict reasonably well what the state of various technologies will be in the next several years. It is valuable to forecast the future of scientific advances and where these are heading, for they form the basis of tomorrow's technologies. Much of the literature only describes the past and present, but some publications make predictions of the future. They are concerned with science, technology, energy, societal attitudes, demography, government regulations, and so on. A list of such sources is given in the Appendix for Chapter 4.

In some instances, where its needs are specialized, a company may wish to undertake its own in-depth forecasts. For example, it may wish to assess future demand for automated factory machines or changes in consumer values regarding electronic filing systems. In such cases, it may contract with a firm that specializes in such forecasts or undertake the task with its own staff.

Judging the Factors

The many factors in a company's environment have various impacts on the company's future. The attention, time, and money spent on each should vary with its importance to the company. Its management should identify those of greatest importance to the firm. That task, deciding which external factors are most important to the company's future, is not always an easy one. Careful judgment is required.

4.2 METHODOLOGY OF TECHNOLOGICAL FORECASTING

Causes of Technological Change

There are two approaches to looking at technological change, termed *exploratory* and *normative*. The exploratory view is that invention and innovation are self-generating activities with lives of their own, that technology evolves in response to technological opportunities and challenges, and that technological change occurs without consideration of the marketplace. This approach to forecasting starts from today's base of knowledge and predicts what is likely to become technically feasible. The approach is sometimes called the "push" theory of technological change and results in what is called *supply-pushed* innovation. In this view, customers' needs change slowly, and it is reasonable to forecast change as though technology developments were based on challenges. In other words, in this approach, R & D organizations tend to "push" in directions opened up by scientific discovery.

The normative view is that invention and innovation are processes determined by existing needs or by economic demand. This is referred to as the "pull" theory of technological change and results in what is called *demand-induced* innovation. In this view, the individual inventor is not important. ("If Bell had not invented the telephone, someone else would have.") This viewpoint suggests that technological change can be forecast as a consequence of demands or requirements imposed by the marketplace or by operations groups within the company. Thus, if a need is recognized, a technological response might be determined. The approach in this type of forecasting is to define specific future objectives and then work backwards to determine how, if at all, they can be attained by technology developments. Investigation of feasible means for fulfilling such needs is deemed reasonable.

One can ask two basically different kinds of questions that exemplify the exploratory and normative approaches, respectively, as stated by Ayres [3]:

1. *Where can we go from here? What are the opportunities and dangers (threats) involved?*

2. *Where do we want to go from here, i.e., toward which objectives? How do we get there?*

In actuality, both views are correct and apply in different circumstances; technological change occurs as a result of both forces. Products are developed for a particular market as a result of the interaction between customers and producers. For example, if office managers want high-quality, fast computer printers, companies will in all probability provide them; if they want low-quality, slow printers that are inexpensive, they will get them. There are factors that affect the timing — e.g., the rate of technology advancement, the cost of R & D, and product manufacturability — but, ultimately, technology is driven to fulfill the needs and wants of customers in the market, wherever feasible.

The probability of a breakthrough in a particular technological area depends on how different it is from technologies that have already been proven. In a totally new area of science or technology, the possibilities for breakthroughs are relatively small. As the area matures, the possibilities increase, since more is known and more advances in different directions — from which yet newer advances can be made — then exist. Finally, as the technology ages, breakthroughs become less likely once again, since most paths for exploration have already been traveled. In mature technologies, management must be content with evolutionary changes which, nonetheless, may hold promise for commercial potential. This is in direct contrast with young technologies, where revolutionary changes that may yield dramatically improved or totally new products may occur.

The several methods that have been developed for technological forecasting all involve analysis of the past, as well as study and interpretation of the data gathered for the purpose. Forecasting techniques can be divided into five categories, as described by James C. Van Pelt: trend extrapolation, intuitive methods, trend correlation, analogy, and dynamic predictive methods [4]. The first two of these are considered here in some detail; the others are briefly described.

Trend Extrapolation

The simplest type of forecast is *trend extrapolation*, where the assumption is made that the environment does not change or changes very little and that whatever has occurred in the recent past will continue in the future. Obviously, in certain realms and for certain, generally short time periods into the future, this is valid. The longer into the future one predicts, the less likely are the predictions to be accurate.

For forecasting by trend extrapolation, the trend involved must be quantifiable. There should be sufficient historic data available for the extension into the future. The forecaster should be able to go back in time about as far as he or she wishes to predict forward. The method involves extending the trend line into the future by using a best-fit curve.

There are several ways to fit curves to past data in order to predict future trends. The simplest curve is obviously a straight line. Most likely, such a line should be placed on a semi-log plot of the trend value as a function of time. If the historical trend line is curved, extension of the curve by mimicking its shape forward in time is probably reasonable. Often such a fitting by eye is as effective as one analytically calculated. Very often, if one plots a trend where a sequence of different underlying technologies have existed, an *envelope* can be discerned that identifies the trend. As an example, one can plot maximum speeds for several types of aircraft propulsion systems — reciprocating engine, subsonic turbojet, supersonic turbojet, etc. — as a function of time. The result would be a series of distinct curves forming an envelope, the trend line of which would then be extended. This approach is illustrated in Fig. 4-1, which is provided by Ayres [5].

It should be noted, however, that this approach fails to take into account any reasons for the trend, as well as any constraints that may exist on it. Referring again to the aircraft example, if the trend of maximum aircraft speed were being predicted five years out by trend extrapolation, consideration would not be given to the type of propulsion that might be used nor to the limitations imposed on the airplane's skin by frictional forces.

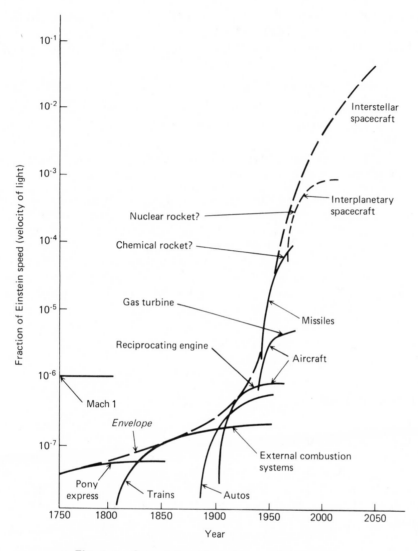

Fig. 4-1. Speed trend curves and envelope.

In extending curves into the future, one must consider constraints. Some constraints comprise inherent natural limits: input-to-output ratios (energy conversion efficiencies, efficiency of recovery of metals from ore, etc.), absolute natural limits (the speed of light, absolute zero temperature, etc.), and other limitations (maximum acceleration tolerable by humans, maximum traffic flow, maximum velocity in atmosphere, etc.). Other constraints may be present because of capabilities existing at a particular time but changing over time. Examples are maximum DC magnetic-field intensity, resolution of cameras, laser coherence, and computer CPU speed. If such constraints are considered, one must modify the extrapolation accordingly.

Several types of trend curves that describe parameters as a function of time have been identified. They include the following:

a) A linear increase with flattening, due to approaches to certain limits;

b) An S-shaped curve, which characterizes many technologies; the curve approaches an asymptote when few further economic advances seems possible;

c) A double-exponential curve with subsequent flattening, which, e.g., characterizes the operating energy in particle accelerators.

There are other specialized trend curves that apply in particular situations.

In a variation of the extrapolation approach, one environmental factor is assumed to change. The approach first involves identifying several factors that have particularly strong influences on the firm. Then, likely changes in these factors are postulated. Finally, with consideration given to a change in one factor at a time, the trend extrapolation procedure described above is repeated.

A more elaborate approach is to allow two factors to change simultaneously. One has to be concerned in this case with the possible interaction between them. As a result, the process is much more complex. It is possible to carry this process too far, however. The more factors that are assumed to change, the less valid is the extrapolation approach.

Intuitive Methods

The intuitive method is widely used for forecasting. It is accomplished, in its basic form, by having an expert in a technology field, who is well-versed in its underlying scientific and engineering principles, predict future events and trends in that field. There are, however, limitations in this approach. These can be somewhat overcome by querying a group of experts in the field, where, hopefully, errors in judgment by individuals may be eliminated by the collective judgment of others.

One form of such interaction among a group was developed by Olaf Helmer et al [6,7]. It is known as the *Delphi method*. Experts in a field are questioned individually (usually by questionnaire) about their expectations for a number of possible future events. Their collective responses provide the basis for forecasting. A typical question might be: "In what year do you expect that 50 percent of the automobiles in the United States will be battery-powered?" The experts may also be asked to indicate their familiarity with each field as follows: "expert in the area," "generally familiar with it," "casually acquainted," "unfamiliar in general," and "totally unacquainted."

When the set of questionnaires is collected, the answers are stated in terms of means and percentiles (e.g., deciles or quartiles), along with comments made by the participants. The consensus response to the question above might be that the mean fell in 1986, with 20% of the responses being dated prior to 1983 and 20% after 1990. The participants are given these results, along with any reasons given for the predictions. They then submit revised predictions, with reasons for or against supporting the consensus. This process repeats perhaps one or two more times and generally converges, with a narrowing of differences. The results of this process become the predictions.

There are a few variations on this approach. The experts might be asked to indicate whether the occurrence of a stated event depends on the occurrence of any other event. They may be asked to explain why they changed their positions from one set of responses to the next. They may be asked to judge what technological and other changes are likely to follow from the stated events.

There are inherent problems with the Delphi method. Foremost is the possible negative effect of interpersonal influences on participants' ultimate responses. Some participants may not ignore others' responses in forming opinions. Secondly, it is hard to select participants who are at once equally well qualified to make predictions in a given discipline and who are from as diverse a background as possible to provide different perspectives. Finally, personal biases, due to individuals' field of work and other experiences, are hard to eschew.

Other Approaches

The trend of a factor which is complex and difficult to predict by itself may be more easily expressed as a result of a relationship between two or more other trends, by a method termed *trend correlation*. To use two or more trends to determine a third, the forecaster must know the technical interrelationship among all trends involved. The trend of the better known and understood variables is predicted, and from that the trend of direct concern is predicted.

Technology progress can be viewed by *analogy* to growth situations, as biological growth or the growth of technical publications. As an example, consider Table 4-1, offered by R. C. Lenz, that shows the analogy between biological growth and technological improvement [8].

Table 4-1. An Analogy in Growth

Biological growth	Technological improvement
Initial cell	Initial idea or invention
Cell division	Inventive process
Second-generation cell	New idea and invention
Cell division period	Time to stimulate an invention
Nutrient media	Economic support for invention
Cell lifetime	Useful life of invention
Cell death	Obsolescence of invention

Another forecasting approach is to use a model of a market, the economy, or other portions of the environment. A model is a mechanism for predicting the performance of a process or system; in particular, it is useful for predicting the changes that will occur as the result of certain conditions. *Dynamic predictive modeling* uses this approach. As an example, one can assume as inputs to a model such factors as numbers of technically trained people, distribution of skills among them, and the capacities of available R & D facilities. Such factors as external R & D funding, government constraints, and markets are taken into account. The outputs are technological knowledge and progress.

Probabilities and Uncertainties

All forecasts have some measure of uncertainty; the extent of the uncertainty varies considerably over the many possible forecasts. In all cases, forecasts provide ranges of possibilities of future trends and events and can be described as distributions of values. Probabilities can be plotted against the time of an event or the value of a factor. Such curves will often be bell-shaped, and if so their peaks represents the most likely values. For trends and events that can be predicted with high accuracy, the "bell" will be narrow, i.e., the distribution will have a small standard deviation. For others, the "bell" will be broader. As time passes and an event gets closer to happening, uncertainty diminishes.

When a forecast is made a short time into the future − e.g., three months − the predicted future will likely be rather accurate. On the other hand, where a forecast is made far into the future − e.g., four years − the prediction is likely

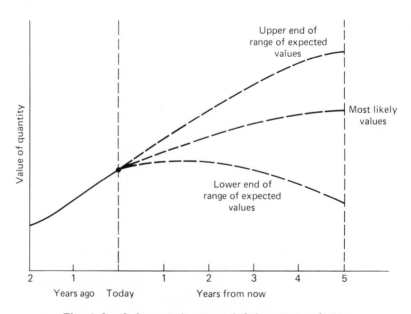

Fig. 4-2. A forecast; uncertainty over values.

to be rather inaccurate, although some factors can be accurately predicted that far ahead. Clearly the accuracy in a particular case depends upon its circumstances.

An example of a range of future values of a quantity of interest is given in Fig. 4-2. The projected values of the quantity are plotted as a function of time. Lines are shown that represent the upper and lower bounds of its expected range of values at each future point in time. Strictly, this means that the probability of having values outside those lines is very small, say 1.0%. The set of the most likely values for the quantity over time is also shown. Other lines, representing specific probabilities, can be drawn. This uncertainty of values is usually associated with trends, and the graph shows a probability distribution over time.

In another situation, an event may be certain to occur but only with a probability distribution of time of occurrence known, as shown in Fig. 4-3. The most likely time of occurrence is t_b; the range of expected times of occurrence is from t_a to t_c. This uncertainty of time is usually associated with events. The same data can be plotted over time, with cumulative probability of occurrence plotted against time, as shown in Fig. 4-4. In this case, the event will certainly occur, by the time t_c. Another event that has a chance of not ever occurring would appear on such a graph with a curve (an *asymptote*) that levels out below the 100% line. The data for such curves may be obtained from one or more of the methods described earlier. The Delphi method usually yields such results directly.

Dealing with uncertainty is not always easy. Michael Menke proposes the following course of action [9]:

> The key to coping with uncertainty in strategy formulation is for managers to discriminate among alternatives whose consequences have widely different degrees of uncertainty, allowing them to search for the most profitable plan where uncertainty is low and to 'pay' for a suitable degree of flexibility where uncertainty is high.

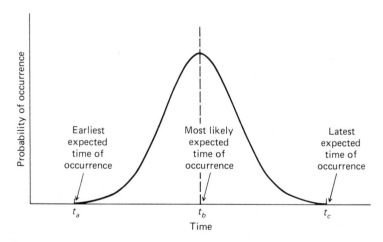

Fig. 4-3. A forecast; uncertainty over times of occurrence.

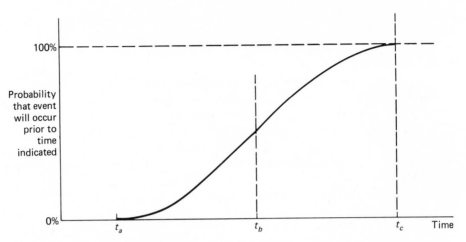

Fig. 4-4. A forecast; probability of an event occurring over a period of time.

Generality of Methods

Although this section addresses technological forecasting, the methods described largely apply to nontechnology areas. Most of them can be used to forecast markets, customer trends, and socioeconomic factors. This should be kept in mind as the questions in these areas are addressed.

4.3 COMPETITION AND TECHNOLOGY

The major factors in the environment, for a technology-based company, are the company's competition and outside developments in technology, so it is appropriate to start there. The questions listed below are all concerned with the future over the plan period. These questions are phrased to ask what various future events *will be*, though they are actually queries on what future events *are likely to be*. That is all that one can truly expect to address. As with previous chapters, auxiliary questions appear in the back of the book, in the Appendix for Chapter 4.

Competition

Which companies will compete in our company's markets?

Knowing one's future competition is as important, if not more so, as knowing one's present competition. Companies may begin to compete in new markets, and new companies may arise; both situations can provide competitive threats. In the former case, most likely a company will begin competing in a market related to its current products. It will be drawn to do so if that market is attractive and it feels it has enough resources to compete effectively. Both indicators can be appraised and the likelihood of such new initiatives estimated. In the latter case, one can only look at markets themselves, judging whether they show potential for growth and/or whether new technology would allow new, highly competitive markets from new firms.

Competitive Products

What new products will be introduced that will compete with us?

Difficult as it is to know precisely what a competitor is doing today, it is more difficult to predict its future products. One can infer them from its current indicators — its patents, technical papers, etc. It is very important to try to predict the features that characterize those products, for such knowledge is a critical factor in planning.

Future Technologies

What is the expected progress of the technologies of concern to our company?

Technology must be monitored closely, so that future trends can be predicted. It is important to know of such trends both to predict competitive technology-based products and to be aware of possible acquisitions.

Technology Acquisition

What new technologies will be available for our acquisition?

Technological forecasting done by the company will be useful here. It is important, in evaluating candidate acquisitions, to understand the potential costs, benefits, and uses of each. Availability depends on the companies' and universities' willingness to sell or license their technologies. The cost and benefits of acquisition must be assessed.

The management of ConTronics Corporation identified the following as the major future competitive issues:

* <u>Competition</u>: Of the Company's competitors listed, all but Blue Controllers are likely to remain competitive beyond the next two years or so. In addition, the Company expects two or three other companies to become competitive by 1984; one promises to be a threat as early as late 1982.

* <u>Competitive products</u>: The Company expects very stiff competition in the office products area. It already has competition in the home market, where it only has a very small share, and it expects that to become very strong also.

* <u>Technologies</u>: There are a number of materials advances at universities and at a few companies that are directly competitive. ConTronics believes it has the edge in its materials work, however.

A Competitive Surveillance System

A large corporation having strong competition probably should have a formalized competitive surveillance system. Its purposes would be to monitor competitive activity, to maintain information files or computer data bases on such activity, and to report on the activity to those who need the information. The system would attempt to answer such questions as these:

What are our competitors going to do?

How do they intend to do it?

When will they do it?

What will be the impact on our company?

It should be noted that, though these questions address future events, they can be modified to refer to the present. The future is more important in planning than is the present, of course, but the surveillance system can also be used to help answer the questions of Chapter 3.

The system, to be fully functional and provide comprehensive services, shall include the following:

1. A means of determining what sources are to be monitored and what information is to be collected and saved;

2. A means of deciding upon which competitors, industries, and markets to monitor;

3. A means for combining gathered information in a structured manner, to reduce redundancies, omissions, and inconsistencies;

4. A system of reporting on gathered information to assure its proper distribution to organizations requiring it; and

5. Analysis of the gathered, combined information by the using organizations for evaluation of the competitive activity studied.

Management, upon receiving information from this system, must respond to it. It must determine how the information will be used in setting strategy. A major task here is to determine, as part of that strategy, how to proceed so as to minimize the negative impacts of any competitive actions.

The benefit of using such a system is in having much relevant data quickly and easily available. This should result in an in-depth analysis of competitive activity, a better understanding of market penetration by competitors, and the specification of technologies that should receive more attention internally. These benefits are even more likely to accrue if the surveillance system is computer-based. Chapter 9, *Computers in Planning*, has details on such an approach.

4.4 PREDICTING TECHNOLOGY NEEDS

To this point, we have concentrated on forecasting competition and technology advances of the future. It is necessary to examine other, nontechnological elements in the environment for information that will indicate what demands for future technology needs are likely to be made. (As mentioned earlier, the term *technological forecasting* is also used for this task.) Forecast data gathered about the markets of interest to the company, the company's present and prospective customers, its materials and supplies, the state of the economy, and various sociological factors can all potentially provide such information about the future. Each of these factors was addressed in Chapter 3. The next task is to identify the requisite technologies for fulfilling those needs.

Markets

How are our company's markets going to change?

Markets change: they evolve, they grow, and they shrink; they also spawn other, new markets. A company must attempt to predict any such changes in its markets. Changes are caused by technology advances in products, by price shifts, by changes in relevant population sizes and locations, and by changes in the law and political situations. It is necessary to know of projected changes and, just as importantly, to know the reasons for these projections.

Customers

Who will be the customers for our future products?

Just as markets change, so do customers. Their wants and needs should be monitored continuously, since their tastes, budgets, and priorities evolve over time. New customers for current products and customers for new products should be identified.

Raw materials

What will the availability be of raw materials we require?

Raw materials often constitute a major source of concern for corporations, since most such materials exist in but finite amounts on earth. Identification of alternative materials can be critical, and strategic planning may be especially important here.

Socioeconomic Factors

Economic, social, demographic, legal, and political factors play major roles in the marketplace. These factors have had and will continue to have everincreasing influence on companies' products and therefore on companies' plans. The issues can be summarized by the following questions:

* *What will the state of the economy be in the geographical areas in which our company will be doing business in the future?*

* *What social factors will be critical in determining our future products?*

* *What will the distribution of population be that will be of concern to us?*

* *What new laws and regulations will take place that impact our company?*

* *What changes will occur in the political situation in states and countries of interest to our company?*

Determining the Technology Gaps

An analysis of these various factors will indicate what product advances will be required in the future. These advances can be translated into technology needs, i.e., technologies that would meet the needs of those products. Management's task is to identify the gaps between the forecast technology future and the forecast of future technology needs. These gaps are the shortfalls by which the known and forecast technologies will fail to meet future needs.

It is necessary to identify the research and development information needed to fill these gaps. Having done this, management's next step is to forecast when, if, and how the information needed will be found. A study of the company's extrapolated future, covered in Chapter 2, and the forecast future of the environment will help. The final step in attempts to close the gaps come about when management decides how its company will seek this information, i.e., how it will set its R & D strategy.

The following are the salient points regarding those factors in the ConTronics' environment that help determine technology needs:

* Markets – how they will grow:
  * Home and office markets are expected to grow rapidly in control systems, communications, information retrieval, and word processing.
  * Number of end products utilizing controllers in the Company's markets:

	Industrial/business	Home	Office
1982	50,000	200,000	10,000
1985	100,000	1,000,000	40,000
1990	300,000	5,000,000	500,000

* Customers are the following:
  * Businesses, small to medium, transaction- and information-storage-and-retrieval-oriented, with need for broad dissemination of information;

- Homes, oriented toward obtaining information and/or using control systems;
- Offices utilizing word processing and other automated equipment

* Socioeconomic factors:
   - There will be continued greater dependence on communication and less on travel.

* Demographic factors:
   - The population is aging; demand for leisure products will increase.
   - The need for more advanced home control systems will increase.

* Technology gap:

   These drivers of technology were identified:
   - New features, especially in home products, will be in demand.
   - Miniaturization will be very important.
   - Cost will be crucial (especially for the home market).
   - New materials will be needed that are cheaper, more rugged, and less expensive.
   - More reliability will be needed; servicing in homes is costly.

The Preplanning Analysis Report

The preplanning analysis report prepared after the self-analysis was done should now be expanded.   It is now structured as follows:

1. Major problems
2. Major decisions
3. Major sensitivities
4. Company strengths
5. Company weaknesses
6. Opportunities for the company
7. Threats to the company
8. Responses to internal issues (a series of sections, one for each area of the company, summarizing the key responses to the answers supplied)
9. Responses to external issues (a series of sections, one per environmental area, summarizing the key responses to the answers supplied)

Sections (1) through (7), as previously written, should be modified to accommodate the results of the environmental analysis. To whatever extent possible, the information gathered from the two analyses should be combined. At this point, the PAR is complete.

The material below is *added to* ConTronics' Preplanning Analysis Report, initially prepared in Chapter 2.

1. Major problems
   * Technology advances are generally very rapid in electronics, the Company's main technology area, and this requires a strong effort to keep pace.

3. Major sensitivities
   * The Company is sensitive to the rapid electronics technology advances outside, to the state of the economy (since the products tend to be nonnecessities), and to the rate of growth of electronics markets.

6. Opportunities for the company
   * There are product niches at the low ends of markets and in miniaturized sensors and controllers.

7. Threats to the company
   * Competition is increasing in the Company's markets, particularly in the rapidly growing office products area.

9. Responses to external issues

   These actions should be taken, to the extent that they can be afforded:
   * Concentrate most heavily on the low end of the markets.
   * Acquire Popeye Manufacturing Company and the circuit design and fabrication process from Auto-Electronics, Inc.
   * Study socioeconomic trends in the future more carefully in the areas of direct concern to the Company.

4.5 ANALYSIS OF FORECASTS

What has been the record of our company in making forecasts in the past?

The record of a company's use of forecasting methods and its forecasts should themselves be subject to scrutiny. If the company has not been particularly successful in this endeavor in the past, it is worth the company's efforts to modify its approach. If it has been successful, that is worth noting as well.

It is very helpful, as management prepares to forecast the future, to evaluate previous forecasts. The methods used should also be evaluated, and other methods considered if those have proven inadequate. The sources of information used and the method of analyzing it should also be examined. For this analysis to be properly done, management should regularly record its predictions, so that they can be compared to actual events. Attempts should be made to understand why any errors occurred. This should lead to improvement in future forecasting.

4.6   ASSUMPTIONS

Assumptions must be made about a company's future environment. Its management must assume that specific trends and events will occur over the plan period, so that a strategy can be developed in preparation for them. Only with specific trends and events identified can a unique picture of the future be derived. For a strategic plan, a future should be defined so that planning can proceed, even though that future is only an approximation. (As pointed out in Chapter 8, *Writing and Using the Plan*, some uncertainty can be built into the plan.)

If all projections of the future could be accurately made, assumptions would not be necessary, for the future would be known. If projections were made with reasonable accuracy, where the probability distribution of values is known, assumptions could easily be made. They would simply be the expected or most likely values of the significant trends and events, as shown in Figs. 4-2 and 4-3. In many cases, however, even the probability distribution of values or over time is not known. In such a situation, the management of a firm must make assumptions about the expected values of trends or times of events. These are what management perceives as the likeliest occurrences. The most important assumptions made are those that address the areas of greatest uncertainty.

In a technology-based corporation, key assumptions involve research and development activities. Technical management must make assumptions, e.g., as to when (and if) research projects will be successful. If a particular project involves developing a key technology, the assumptions about its completion are critical. Other assumptions may relate to research breakthroughs, the company's ability to improve product reliability through new technologies, and technology advancements by competitors and others on the outside.

Because of the uncertainties of forecasting, actual trends and events are likely to be different from predicted ones. It is wise therefore to make secondary assumptions, of other outcomes, where it is felt that the forecasts are least accurate. This does not mean that management should consider all likely variations from the expected future in all possible combinations. Rather, other outcomes can be noted for the major factors felt to be the least accurately predicted. In other words, management should develop contingent assumptions, which derive from a different set of events than initially projected. This approach leads to *contingency planning*, which is discussed in Chapter 7, *Setting Strategy*.

ConTronics management has made these assumptions about the future, based on its analysis of the future environment:

* Internal R & D efforts will produce the following results:
  * A cost reduction of at least 6% per year over the next five years in the OEM line and at least 10% per year in the retail line will be achieved.

- Miniaturization of product size and cost by 20% over two years and 40% over five years will be achieved, with products retaining the same functions.
- The materials research and development efforts will succeed and yield a useful technology by 1984 or so.
- The other two research projects will be successful.

* The proprietary materials that the Company is working on will have direct competition in the future, giving the Company about two years' lead time.

* The markets for its type of products in businesses, homes, and offices will grow rapidly in the 1980s. The number of such products in 1985 will be four times that of 1980; the number in 1990 will be 20 times that of 1980. These numbers refer to the total number of products that comprise the markets that ConTronics is now in and expects to be in through the 1980's.

* There will be many more competitors ten years from now than at present, so the Company's market shares, on average, will shrink. The shares in some market segments will increase, however.

* Word processors will be pervasive and be used in offices by 1990 as commonly as typewriters are in 1980.

* Price erosion in electronics products will continue at about 20% per year (in real dollars) throughout the 1980's.

* There will be a hundredfold increase in the on-line usage of information in the home by 1990, compared to 1980.

Inflation will be in the 7 to 10% range, on average.

4.7 THE EXTRAPOLATED FUTURE IN THE ENVIRONMENT

Extrapolation of the Company's Future

In Chapter 2 we examined the current status of a company and its plans for the future. In this chapter, we looked at the projected future of a company's environment. Now, we must attempt to project the future of a company in its future environment.

What we are trying to achieve to describe a company's future by taking into account events and trends that are likely to occur in its environment. We do this under the assumption that no decisions within the company have been changed. (That assumption will be removed when strategy is developed as described in Chapter 7.) The result is a projection that is an extrapolation within a changing environment, itself changing in response to that environment.

To yield this view of its company's extrapolated future, management must review its responses to the questions on the environment's future to see how they are likely to affect the company's operation and performance. The process consists of reviewing each response to see if it might impact the company. Since comparing every response to every trend in the company can be extremely tedious, the process must be shortened. Only the most critical interactions of company and environment future trends and events need be so compared.

One useful way to quantify the effect of the company's future environment is to take the current strategic plan and modify it to reflect new information recently gathered about the future of the environment. It is very helpful to modify the strategic plan revenue and profit projections and budget over the period of the current plan and extend these at least one year into the future.

Sales Forecasting

An important aspect of forecasting the future of a company is forecasting the sales of its products. If management can accomplish good sales forecasting, it can derive these benefits from it: better identification of proper products for the company to make and sell, improved scheduling of production and inventory control, better scheduling of capital improvements, and improved adaptation to business cycles, customers, and competitors. If production could respond instantly to changes in market demand, sales forecasting would not be necessary. However, since decisions on the allocation of resources must be made well in advance of market developments and product sales, the forecasting is needed.

ConTronics management has projected that revenues in the 1982–1985 period will not rise as quickly as thought when the current plan was developed. Profits are now also projected to be lower than in the plan. These changes in views are due to greater competition than had been expected.

Projections of Revenues and Profits

(Dollar amounts in millions; units in thousands)

	1981	1982	1983	1984	1985	1986
Revenue	$30	35	45	65	90	120
Net profit	$ 1.8	2.0	2.0	3.0	5.0	6.5
Margin	6.0%	5.7%	4.4%	5.0%	6.0%	7.2%
Units sold	23	30	45	75	120	200
Revenues by divisions						
OEM	$20	22	25	30	40	45
Business	$10	13	18	23	30	35
Office	$ 0	0	0	2	10	20
Home	$ 0	0	2	5	10	20

Conjectures

A useful way to formulate questions on future events is to ask questions of the form "What if . . . ?" The purpose here is to conjecture that a particular event will take place or that a particular trend will occur and to ask what will happen to certain plans as a result. The list of such conjectures, coupled with the plans that each can bear upon, can yield an almost endless set of questions. Management must be highly selective and consider only the most likely events and trends which have a meaningful potential impact upon the firm.

The task is begun by examining the questions raised about the future and imagining the occurrence of events not projected to take place. As examples, one can ask: "What if our technology development programs X and Y prove to be failures?" "What if our program ABC is completed one year behind schedule?" "What if our strongest competitor introduces a product that undercuts ours in price by 20%?" Management clearly must be selective in this task and limit itself to perhaps two or three dozen questions.

Another approach is to examine the assumptions made by management and conjecture that each may not happen or that some variation of the assumption will instead occur.

Each conjecture ought to be made with consideration of the probability of occurrence and its potential impact on the company. It does little good to conjecture an event that has a 5% change of happening that will affect revenues by 3%. It is best if management sets cut-off limits on these two factors, below which conjectures are discarded. Note that if either the probability of occurrence or the impact is high while the other is low, the conjecture should be considered.

The conjectures developed will generally fall into two categories, those that are *positive* and those that are *negative*. Quite simply, the positive conjectures address events that are better for the company, in terms of profitability, market share, or other situations, while the negative conjectures address events that are worse for the company.

In any event, management, at this stage of planning, need not attempt to answer the conjectures. It need only state them for response after the strategy-setting process. Once a strategy is set, the conjectures and management's respones to them should be addressed.

The following conjectures have been posed by ConTronics' management:

Positive

* What if a breakthrough in materials research were achieved in 1982?
* What if we achieve 50% greater sales increase than we are aiming for through 1984?
* What if we achieve twice the annual cost reduction we project?
* What if our major competitor suddenly had severe financial problems and became much less competitive?

Negative

* What if inflation were to be in the 12 to 15% range?
* What if there is a severe recession?
* What if our efforts in materials research were to yield no useful results?
* What if the home electronics market were to increase only 10% each year?
* What if a competitor achieves a major breakthrough directly threatening our plans in the office automation and/or home areas?

Other questions can be asked which relate to management decisions about internal operations.   Consider the following:

What are the effects of decreasing and of increasing the several budgets (R & D, marketing, advertising, etc.) on revenues and profits in the future?

Such questions are intended to provide management with information to make budgetary trade-off decisions.   They are distinct from other conjecture questions because they deal with internal matters and with decisions management can make.   These questions involve both the company and its environment — i.e., the interaction between them — and so are different from other questions in this respect also.

4.8 THE SCHEDULE

The tasks in forecasting the future are three in number. First, the future plans of the company are identified; this is part of the self-analysis. Second, the future of the environment is projected. These are independent tasks, each utilizing no data from the other; they can be done simultaneously.   Third, the future of the company is extrapolated, now considering the impact of the environment's projected future. This task must follow the other two. Fig. 4-5 provides a schedule for these tasks.

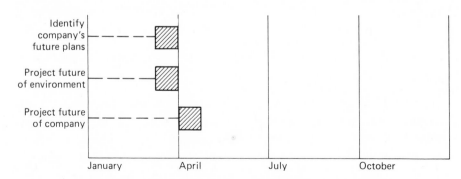

Fig. 4-5. A schedule for forecasting the future.

4.9 PROBLEMS IN FORECASTING

There are two categories of problems to consider in doing forecasting; one relates to the information gathered and the other two the use made of it by people.

First, since predicting the future is impossible, all projections are just guesses. Estimating the future becomes more difficult and accuracy diminishes as one goes out in time. We have seen that the best one can hope for is to estimate a range of possible and probable values for both the times of events and the values of trends over time. No matter how careful one is, surprises will always occur. Managers can be sure of that, but they cannot know where the surprises will come from.

The data gathered about the past and present, on which extrapolations are based, are at best incomplete and inaccurate. Moreover, certain data gathered will be more accurate than other. For example, information on one's own company is likely to be rather accurate, while information gathered about competitors is bound to be less so. Projections of the future of the latter become particularly hard to undertake. Data gathering can be costly, particularly if high accuracy is sought.

Second, there are human factors that cause problems in technological forecasting, such as wishful or emotional thinking, personal bias, preconceived ideas, and the problem of forcing "facts" into such ideas. In addition, the following may be true: (a) forecasters may lack imagination in conceiving the possible technologies that may evolve in the future; (b) they may fail to recognize forces acting upon technology development that come into play; an example is the negative reaction the public has felt to nuclear-power plants as the result of accidents that have occurred; (c) there may be overemphasis of specific technologies and insufficient attention to the "whole picture", a problem similar to focusing on the "electronics business" rather than the "entertainment business". Forecasters should be aware of these difficulties in order to account for them.

SUMMARY

The tasks of forecasting the future environment of a company and its future in that environment are difficult tasks. It is best to accomplish this in two separate stages, forecasting the environment's future and then forecasting the company's future. Technology-based companies focus primarily on technology forecasting, but they must undertake forecasting in general. Technology forecasting focuses on technologies that concern the company. There are many sources of information on the future of technologies and other matters, though sometimes a company may need to undertake its own, specialized forecasting study.

There are two basic views on the manner in which technological change comes about, *exploratory* and *normative*. In the former view, invention and innovation are self-generating. In the latter view, these processes are determined by needs and demands. These two approaches are exemplified, respectively, by these questions: "Where *can* we go from here?" and "Where do we *want* to go from here?"

There are several approaches to technological forecasting. *Trend extrapolation* involves extending the past into the future, assuming that nothing in the environment changes. This approach does not take into account any of the reasons for trends and changes, and it ignores the fact that the environment will change and keep changing over time. *Intuitive methods* involve having experts express their views on what they expect will happen in the future. The *Delphi* method, which is based on a collective approach to event prediction among experts, is widely used. There are other methods: *trend correlation*, involving the correlation of several trends; *analogy*, wherein technology progress is likened to the growth of other systems; and *dynamic predictive modeling*, where the market or other part of the environment is modeled.

It is necessary to address and analyze various factors in the environment and attempt to answers questions about their future. The major environmental factors are competition and technology advances. It is very important for companies in highly competitive situations to have formalized competitive surveillance systems.

To predict technology needs, a company should examine nontechnology elements in its environment, such as the competition, markets, customers, supplies, and several socioeconomic factors. Analyzing these factors will indicate what product advances and what technological capabilities will be required. When these are compared to projected technological development, gaps can be identified that a company can try to fill with R & D advances.

Management must make assumptions, based on its forecasts, about the future it expects to see. With those assumptions made, it must then extrapolate the future of its company, subject to those assumptions. This is done by combining the analyses of the company's current situation and future plans with the projected environment. A useful way to speculate about the future is to ask several "What if . . . ?" questions.

REFERENCES

1. Ayres, Robert U., *Technological Forecasting and Long-Range Planning*, McGraw-Hill Book Company, New York, 1969, pp. 41–42.

2. Ramo, Simon, "Toward Scientific Anticipation of Change," *Managerial Planning*, Sept–Oct. 1970, vol. 19, no. 2, pp. 9–13, 28.

3. Ayres, *op cit*, p. 34.

4. Van Pelt, James C., "Technological Forecasting: Approaches, Techniques, and Theory", *Long-Range Planning for Management* (ed. by David W. Ewing), Harper & Row, New York, 1972, pp. 347–361.

5. Ayres, Robert U., *op cit*, p. 21.

6. Olaf Helmer and T. J. Gordon, *Report on a Long-Range Forecasting Study*, RAND Corporation, Santa Monica, Calif., Paper P-2982, September 1964.

7. Olaf Helmer, *Social Technology*, Basic Books, New York & London, 1966.

8. Lenz, R. C., Jr., "Technological Forecasting", ASD-TDR-62-414, Aeronautical Systems Division, Air Forces Systems Command, June, 1962.

9. Menke, Michael M., "Strategic Planning in an Age of Uncertainty", *Long Range Planning*, August 1979, vol. 12, no. 8, p. 28. (This is a useful paper on the subject of strategic planning in uncertain situations.)

Additional References

Van Pelt, James C., "Technological Forecasting: Approaches, Techniques, and Theory", *Long Range Planning for Management* (ed. by David W. Ewing), Chapter 3, Harper & Row, New York, 1972. (This chapter of the book, listed in Chapter 1, is a useful, nontechnical introduction to technological forecasting; cited in this chapter.)

Lippitt, Vernon G., *Statistical Sales Forecasting*, Financial Executives Research Foundation, New York, 1969. (This book provides an in-depth review of all aspects of the subject.)

Ayres, Robert U., *Technological Forecasting and Long-Range Planning*, McGraw-Hill Book Company, New York, 1969. (This book provides an in-depth treatment of technological forecasting; cited in this chapter.)

Jantsch, Erich, *Technological Forecasting in Perspective*, Organization for Economic Cooperation and Development, Paris, 1967. (This book is a standard reference on the subject.)

Bittner, F. H., and H. W. Lanford, "Technology Forecasting: Determining What to Forecast", *Industrial Marketing Management*, July 1980, vol. 9, no. 3, pp. 187–199. (This paper provides a methodology for determining what factors to forecast.)

Lippitt, Vernon G., *Statistical Sales Forecasting*, Financial Executives Research Foundation, New York, 1969. (This book addresses all aspects of sales forecasting, including its relationship to strategic planning.)

Hubbard, Charles L., and N. Carroll Mohn, "How to Reduce Uncertainty in Sales Forecasting", *Management Review*, June 1978, vol. 67, no. 6. (This paper shows how decision analysis can be applied to new product sales forecasting.)

5

OBJECTIVES AND GOALS

Where do we want to go?

INTRODUCTION

The starting point for the preparation of the strategic plan document is the set of objectives that a corporation establishes for its future attainments. Everything else in the plan evolves from these objectives. The information gathered about a firm's own operation and about its environment represent the most useful body of data for the development of objectives, along with management's views on where the firm ought to go. It is essential that management understand what objectives are, what their purposes are, how they are derived, and how they are used. Because they represent guidelines for all decisions and actions, the nature and contents of corporate objectives are very important to the company's operations.

5.1 CORPORATE OBJECTIVES

The "True Objective"

Corporations exist to make a profit satisfactory to their owners, the stockholders. Owners often look to the long term and may accept relatively low profits for a while if they expect significant long-term appreciation of principal. As John Argenti points out, the only true objective for a corporation is to combine a satisfactory profit yield with a satisfactory long-term growth [1].   This primary objective is a strong motivator for a corporation's managers because for them to ignore it would be to invite stockholder displeasure and, inevitably, the corporation's demise.

Strategic planning is undertaken to provide guidance to the task of accomplishing satisfactory corporate performance.   This task is achieved by identifying objectives, setting a strategy, allocating resources, and carrying out plans. The "true objective" cited above offers no guidance in this process, so management must set down "corporate objectives" which more precisely define the direction and manner in which the company is to move. These are objectives that will be sought for the purpose of achieving the primary objective of the corporation, that of obtaining a satisfactory combination of profit and growth over the long term.

What Objectives Are

For a corporation, an *objective* is a description of what it wishes to strive for and achieve in the future.   Objectives generally define the future state of the corporation over the plan period, as management intends it to develop.   They may also describe the manner by which the company attains that future state.

In a description of the intended future state, objectives refer to desired results.   They provide the motivation to plan a strategy for achieving that intended future. They provide coordination for the development and execution of a strategic plan and as such are directed at major issues facing a corporation. Properly addressed in a strategic plan, the objectives will offer guidance for management decisions on all matters and at all levels.

It should be noted that the term "objective" has a variety of meanings, and corporations attribute the term to different kinds of statements as guides to corporate action. The term is used here in a sense that seems to be consistent with most writers' and managers' usage of the term.

Questions to Ask

There are basic questions that management should ask when setting corporate objectives:

1. *What business should our company be in?*
2. *What are acceptable rates of profit and revenue growth?*
3. *By what method shall the company grow?*

Question 1 can be answered in many ways and levels of detail.   The answer can range from a narrow description like "the 10- to 100-kilowatt transformer business" to a broad description like "the electronics business".   For a large company, there may be several such answers, one for each major division. The answer defines the markets of the company (though perhaps only in a vague way), provides guidance for the technologies of concern, and sets the tone for strategy development. Yet it does not do any of these things directly. More detailed objectives are needed to achieve those ends.

Management often inappropriately stresses the *means* whereby its company will provide products rather than the *nature* of the products themselves. For example, a company may state that it is in "the electronics business" or "the railroad business", while it might be better to state that it is in "the home communications business" or "the transportation business". In other words, management should look at the *functions* that their products perform rather than the *techniques* by which they perform them. This approach provides leadership in a technology-based company by focusing R & D plans on their eventual purposes. Technologies can be better related to products and therefore to the company's business by this functional approach.

Question 2 relates to the primary objective discussed earlier. It might be supplemented by such questions as these:

2a. *What market shares shall the company strive for?*

2b. *What productivity levels are acceptable?*

2c. *What level of assets is desirable after five years?*

A company must determine a growth rate that it can feasibly achieve, taking into account its technological, financial, and marketing capabilities. Where necessary, it must be able to develop these capabilities sufficiently to support the planned growth rate.

Question 3 relates to the strategy that will eventually be developed during strategic planning, for that strategy will address various means of attaining the desired future. It is concerned with the markets to be entered, the products to be designed, and the technologies to be developed. It deals with such alternatives as vertical versus horizontal development, movement into new product lines versus increased penetration of existing markets, and acquisition versus internal development. These choices will directly affect the nature and scope of the R & D programs of the company. Of particular concern is the choice between technology acquisition and internal development, which affects the size and orientation of R & D programs.

All three questions are important to high-technology companies, but question 3 relates particularly to technology and its role in such companies. In general, setting technology-related objectives is more difficult than setting other objectives, because the alternatives are more numerous and the relationships between technologies and objectives is sometimes obscure. Establishing these relationships is a subsequent step and is discussed in Chapter 7, *Setting Strategy*.

A fourth question, which addresses the manner of operation, can be asked:

4. *How should we conduct our business?*

This question relates to the mission of the corporation and its philosophy of operation, addressed in the next section.

ConTronics' management answered the first three basic questions as follows:

1. The Company is to be in the business of selling electronics control devices for various markets.

2. Growth rates sought in revenues and profits over the 1981–1986 period are approximately 30% and 40% compounded annually, respectively.

3. The Company will grow by these means:

   * Almost entirely by internal growth;

   * By expanding present markets by improving products – in cost, reliability, size, and features;

   * By growing new markets closely allied to present ones;

   * By developing products primarily based on proprietary technologies;

   * By occasional acquisition of technologies that cannot be developed internally, because of cost and time, though no more than one-fourth of the technologies shall be so acquired;   and

   * By increasing productivity in engineering and manufacturing operations.

Areas of Concern

In technology-based companies, growth by means of advances in research and development is crucial, and a company must reflect this in setting its objectives. The long-term effectiveness and stability of its R & D program depend upon management's commitment to development of new technology, as embodied in its corporate objectives. Thus, a corporation's objectives must take advantage of the possibilities offered by technology advancement as well as take into account the limits of technology.

There are many other areas of concern to which management can direct the company's objectives. Among these are product development, productivity, new geographical markets, response to the competition, structure of organization, manager and employee performance, minority hiring, social responsibilities, and public image (including the technology image). In selecting corporate objectives, management must consider these and other areas that relate particularly to its company. The major problems identified in Chapters 2 and 3 are of great help in this task. Further, the many areas identified in those chapters are all worthy subjects for corporate objectives. Peter Drucker identified the following subjects as those to address in setting objectives: profitability, innovation, physical and financial resources, productivity, market standing, manager performance and development, worker performance and attitude, and public responsibility [2].

5.2 MISSIONS AND PHILOSOPHY OF OPERATION

Corporate Missions

Before objectives are examined at length, we consider other, related concepts that corporations often address.

Corporations sometimes identify missions. A *mission* can be defined, in general terms, as *the business with which an organization is charged.* A more aggressive definition is, *the responsibility that an organization is assigned or assumes.* Peter Drucker states that management must answer the question: "What is our business and what should it be? [3]" Some writers view the answer to this question as a mission; others view it as an objective. (This writer has viewed it as an objective in Section 5.1.)

Another motivating drive for a corporation is a statement of its philosophy of operation. This philosophy explains why the company is in business and the manner in which it plans to operate. It may also address such matters as product quality, efficiency of internal operations, treatment of employees, social responsibilities, and a code of conduct; in short, it generally addresses the company's creed.

Generally, *objectives* represent what the corporation is trying to accomplish, *missions* provide guidance on the general rationale for existence, and a *philosophy of operation* tells how the business is to operate. The distinction among these concepts must be kept clearly in mind.

An example of a major technology-based corporation's objective is the following, Texas Instruments' Corporate Objective [4]:

> Texas Instruments exists to create, make, and market useful products and services to satisfy the needs of our customers throughout the world. Because economic wealth is essential to the development of our society, we measure ourselves by the extent to which we contribute to that economic wealth — as expressed by sales growth and asset return. We believe our effectiveness in serving our customers and contributing to the economic wealth of society will be determined by our innovative skills.

By the definitions in this chapter, this statement is a combination of corporate objectives and a mission.

An example of a set of corporate objectives is the following (from the Monsanto Company) [5]:

> Shareowner objective. We will manage Monsanto to optimize shareowner value through consistently superior long-term performance in growth of earnings per share and return on equity.

Social responsibility objective. We will conduct our business at all times in an ethical, lawful, and socially responsible manner.

Employee relations objective. We will provide a climate in which our employees can realize their full potential and in which employment with Monsanto can be a rewarding experience for the individual as well as for the company.

This is a statement of philosophy of operation, as that term is defined in this book.

Clearly, what is a set of objectives to one corporation is a statement of mission to another and a philosophy of operation to a third. All approaches are appropriate if they serve the corporations well. Whatever terms they use, however, all have objectives, missions, and philosophies of operation, whether those are explicitly stated or not.

It is clear that a company's philosophy of operation imposes certain constraints on that operation. If that it is true, management must decide on its hierarchy of aims, i.e., in what order they are to take precedence. Certainly, moral attitudes on the part of top management will help establish such priorities, as they should. The point is that management should be aware of the role that its philosophy plays in the setting of missions and objectives.

George Steiner has suggested that there exists, in general, a network of business aims in a corporation [6]. The network varies from company to company, with no uniformity among them, but it generally has a pyramid-like structure. The layers of the pyramid are *basic socioeconomic purposes, personal aims and values of top managers, missions, long-range objectives,* and *short-range goals and targets.* The lower a layer is located in the pyramid, the lengthier are the statements for the aims and the more specific and concrete they become. This concept is useful; it shows that one can look at generalized aims for a corporation in a hierarchical manner, to varying degrees of depth and detail. The degree of detail can be selected to suit management's purposes.

Divisional Missions

The distinction between objectives and missions at the divisional level is noteworthy. Divisions are assigned responsibilities (and sometimes assume them) which, in the interests of corporate-wide consistency and coordination, should be quite specific in content. James B. Quinn addresses this point with respect to research and defines what he called the "research mission" [7]:

The research organization can support any given strategy in a variety of ways. And it is up to top management to specify which types of support it expects from research. Is research to be the dominant source of new product and process ideas, or is this the function of sales or operating managers? To what extent should research simply serve present products and processes? Is research to be the technological arm of management consulting on all aspects of the company's technological situation?

The same kind of questions should be asked of all divisions in a company. In identifying a division's mission, it is certainly neither appropriate nor necessary to consider the fine details of assignment of responsibilities; they are too numerous. Only major responsibilities should comprise what is termed the mission of the organization.

The statement of a division's *mission* describes the nature of the tasks or the kinds of work to be undertaken by the organization, while an *objective* delineates a specific goal toward which the organization works. The mission is essentially the division's share of the total task that the corporation has undertaken. A research mission might be to publish widely and to generate patents. A research objective might be to explore low-temperature properties of a newly derived substance in order to determine its utility in specific planned products.

5.3 THE NATURE OF CORPORATE OBJECTIVES

Traits

Corporate objectives should be based on the company's present state, on a projection of the future of the company's environment, on technological possibilities and limitations, and on the company's collective resources. We consider what the characteristics of objectives ought to be.

Objectives should be consistent with the corporation's fundamental mission; in fact, they really should be a reflection of that mission, stated in more specific terms. Each objective, if achieved, should result in a positive contribution to the fundamental purpose and mission of the corporation.

Objectives should be guides to and initiators of action. They should aid the decision-making process by setting criteria for the selection of alternatives among possible courses of action.

Objectives should be stable over time, to whatever extent possible. They represent the general directions of a corporation's growth, and these ordinarily do not change very frequently. The longer the development time of a company's products, the more stable should the objectives be. Research and development often last years for certain products, and stability of corporate objectives is important in such cases. If they are not stable, R & D objectives move out of synchronism with corporate objectives.

Objectives should be general and flexible enough to accommodate all anticipated changes over the plan period, as well as some that are not anticipated. If objectives are too specific, they will likely require frequent modification. If, for example, an objective defines a product line with rather precise specifications, it is almost certainly to become obsolete as markets evolve, necessitating a shift from this objective. It is better to define the product line loosely, referring to the type of business. Furthermore, because of the uncertainty associated with research and development, flexibility is essential. Products planned for the future should be specified in somewhat general terms, pending technological results. As these results evolve, objectives can be sharpened as needed.

Objectives should be achievable yet offer challenges. It is important for a company to be able, with good likelihood, to achieve its objectives. It is equally important that the company has to reach to do so. If objectives are beyond any reasonable stretch, however, they may serve little purpose. It is not always easy to define objectives that are achievable and require reaching. One approach is to require that each objective has at least 50%, or perhaps 75%, probability of being achieved. A company's management should not consider itself a failure if all stated objectives are not achieved in the plan period. In fact, if all are achieved, management may not have aimed high enough.

Finally, objectives must be understood by and acceptable to those who must work towards achieving them. Sometimes objectives are not comprehensible to the managers who must apply them to the operations of a firm. In such a case, they serve little purpose. If those who work towards achieving objectives have been involved in defining them, the likelihood of their success is increased.

In the face of all these guides to objectives-setting, management must not lose sight of what the corporation's mission and objectives must really aim to do: to address the end result, which in all cases must be what the customer wants. A machine tool manufacturer must remember that a customer doesn't want drill bits; he or she wants holes. An office products concern must remember that customers do not want word processors — they want documents.

Where to Begin Planning

As we saw in Chapter 1, in order for management to plan for its company's future, it must begin by determining where it is heading and deciding where it wants to go. The order in which these two tasks are answered is not usually critical, but in certain cases management should start with one or the other.

If a company intends to expand its product line where it already holds a large, established share of a market, it is best to begin planning by analyzing the company's present situation and studying its environment. With a large market share, the company has a good deal of momentum, and it is valuable to determine where this is leading the company. On the other hand, if the company intends to develop a new product line in a market where it holds no share at all, it should set its objectives first, since it is planning totally new products and must have a clear idea of product goals.

In practice, the situation is not as clear cut and thus the choice is not, either. A large corporation is likely to have plans in both situations. In that case, management is likely to use a combination of the two approaches. For parts of the company, analysis will come first; for others, setting objectives will. Writers

in the field vary in their views on the sequence of events; most prefer beginning
with the analysis. The best approach is to start with whatever management feels
is appropriate. The two tasks usually proceed essentially simultaneously and
iteratively, so that the final result strongly reflects the influence of each.

The author conducted a survey of strategic planning methodologies, as
practiced by technology-based companies. It revealed that almost half the
companies responding began with objectives-setting and about as many with
information gathering and analysis. A small fraction claimed they did these tasks
simultaneously.

When management chooses to start the planning process by setting
objectives, for whatever reasons, it can do so only tentatively. After the
information gathering and analysis phase is accomplished, those objectives may
need revision. If management works with objectives without a consideration of
the company's present state and that of its environment, unrealistic goals may
result. Objectives must be reviewed after the analysis is finished to avoid this
situation.

5.4 SETTING OBJECTIVES

The Responsibility

Top management and the board of directors share the responsibility for setting
corporate objectives, and the CEO has the responsibility, with top management's
help, for carrying them out. The situation obviously varies among corporations,
but a point to note is that the objectives should represent the views of top
managers, in addition to the CEO. Ideally, all managers should participate in the
process, but practicality rules this out. H. Igor Ansoff stated it this way: "The
objectives of a firm are in reality a negotiated consensus of objectives of the
influential participants [8]."

Factors to Consider

The procedures whereby objectives are set within a corporation will by necessity
vary from company to company, because of different management styles,
different kinds of products, and other different circumstances. There are,
however, some general guidelines that apply to most situations; these follow
below.

1. Current objectives. The logical starting point in developing objectives is the
   current list of corporate objectives, originally set at the time of the last
   strategic planning cycle. Each objective on that list should be reviewed for
   currency and continued relevance, in the light of the events of the past 12
   months.

2. <u>Technology alternatives</u>. Top management, together with technical management and the planning staff, should carefully examine both the potential for significant improvements in products and the inherent limitations imposed and opportunities provided by technologies available within the company and outside. The state of the art of all relevant technologies defines the base upon which new products can be built; the expected future of these technologies represents new products that will be available later. These technology alternatives provide a portfolio from which management can develop concepts for objectives.

3. <u>Corporate strengths and weaknesses</u>. The self-analysis previously performed identifies the company's strengths and weaknesses. These were identified in the preplanning analysis report (PAR). It is likely that a technology-based company's greatest strength is its technology, and if so the company must capitalize on this. Its strength in a particular technology is a function of its proprietary position and experience in that technology, as well as the strength of its R & D activities. Additional company strengths may lie in marketing, service, product reliability, finances, or other areas. Similarly, its weaknesses may lie in any of these areas.

4. <u>Opportunities and threats</u>. The environmental analysis identifies opportunities and threats, which also appear in the PAR. Objectives based on opportunities are "offensive" in nature and generally relate to new ventures. These may be to improve products, develop new products in present product lines, or provide totally new offerings. Objectives based on threats are "defensive" and generally relate to competitive pressures, often due to technological competition. Responses are commonly to cut prices, improve reliability of products, and to redefine product lines.

5. <u>Internal constraints</u>. The company's philosophy of operation and its code of conduct will impose constraints on all aspects of company operations, including the setting of objectives. The "image" that a corporation projects to the public is also a factor in determining corporate objectives.   A technology-based company is often anxious to project its role in research activities, and the nature and extent of those activities is a factor in its image.

6. <u>External constraints</u>. The analysis of the environment will reveal constraints that exist quite apart from the company's own limitations and the pressures of competition. These are due to such factors as government regulations on prices, import limitations, duties, and pollution control, labor unions' agreements with management, and stockholder expectations on the rate of return on their investment.

The many forces that shape corporate objectives are illustrated in Fig. 5-1. The diagram summarizes the guidelines just described, as well as other factors that influence the objectives. The figure can be related to the flowchart outline of strategic planning given in Chapter 1.

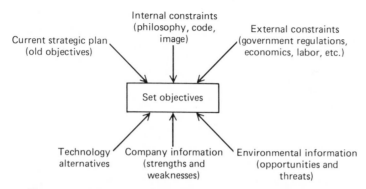

Fig. 5-1. Forces influencing corporate objectives.

Approaches

The process of setting objectives can proceed from the top down, from the bottom up, or as a combination of the two approaches. The last of these is usually the best approach. Corporate objectives must reflect the directions that the company as a whole plans to take, but they must be based on the capabilities, strengths, and needs of all divisions of the company. This bilateral interaction can take place as follows. Top management and the division managers simultaneously develop their own views on both corporate and divisional objectives. The objectives from the lower managers are passed to top management, who uses them as added information for setting down their views on corporate objectives. Corporate objectives then represent both a consensus of the views of managers at the several levels and a coalescence of divisional objectives. Ideally corporate objectives are a "summation" of the objectives of each of the corporation's component parts.

An important reason for top management to consider the views of division managers on corporate objectives is that the latter are closer to daily operations and are likely to be more aware of how realistic a proposed objective may be. Technology limitations are especially important and technical management must make top management aware of these.

Regardless of how the process is carried out, it should be clear that a "dialogue" between top management and divisional management is valuable. The dialogue exists in the sense that a consensus should be reached by taking the viewpoints of both groups into account, with top management, along with the company's board of directors, having ultimate responsibility. The precise manner in which it is carried out in a given corporation will depend upon the style of management in that firm.

Among the companies responding to the author's planning survey, the process is predominantly top-down. The board of directors, the CEO, and other top managers develop objectives and send them down to divisions to set targets for strategy development.

It is clear, from this discussion on the nature of corporate objectives and the process of setting them, that many factors come into play. Management will find itself considering conflicting forces and information and so must make trade-offs among them. The weights of the several factors mentioned above must be set by management. It is not feasible to set down general rules here; there are too many individual situations.

Trade-offs Among Objectives

It is important for top management to establish a structure of priorities among objectives. When a strategic plan is completed, the set of objectives derived in the process is presumably optimized, at least for the time being. We have seen that there are many forces that shape the objectives-setting activity. As the events in the plan unfold, i.e., as time passes and progress against the plan is noted, it is likely that management will observe that not all objectives are going to be met as planned. To prepare for that contingency, or to prepare for the following plan period a year hence, management should answer the question, "To what extent will we trade off among the several corporate chosen, if we must?" In other words, relative weights should be assigned to corporate objectives, in the event it is necessary to pull back from the attempt to achieve all of them simultaneously.

Communication

Since corporate objectives form the basis not only for the development of a strategic plan but also serve as guidelines for management decision making, they must be widely communicated. They should be transmitted to all managers, who must be aware of them for both strategic planning and decision making.

ConTronics' management defined the following corporate objectives and subobjectives:

Business objectives

* To be in the business of manufacturing and marketing (a) control devices for use in information processing and information management systems for industrial and consumer markets and (b) small, self-contained electronics devices for these markets.

* To establish the reputation of the Company as a significant producer of high-quality small electronics systems in industrial and consumer markets.

* To maintain currency with the latest advances in electronics markets, offering products that are competitive in those markets.

Financial objectives

* To grow revenues from 1981 to 1986 at an average annually compounded rate of 30%.

* To grow profits from 1981 to 1986 at an average annually compounded rate of 40%.

  (The growth rates shall be less than these targets in 1982 and 1983 in order to fund heavy R & D investments and be greater thereafter.)

Subobjectives

* To improve all products in incremental fashion over their commercial lifetimes, in such areas as new features, price, reliability, size, speed of operation, and cost of operation.
* To extend product lines, downward, into "niches", and upward, as appropriate, thereby extending present markets.
* To design and build replacement products for the current line that are less expensive, are smaller, and offer more features than present products, thereby enlarging present markets.
* To develop new controller products and self-contained systems and devices for the "office of the future" market.
* To develop new controller products and self-contained systems and devices for the home electronics markets.
* To rely to an ever-increasing extend on proprietary technologies.
* To reduce the Company's dependence on the sale of OEM products and components, thereby broadening the customer base.
* To introduce innovative new technologies in materials, special-purpose software (for information processing and control applications), and circuit design.
* To strengthen technical skills where the Company is vulnerable, to the point where it has a capability equal to its competitors.
* To acquire automatic systems where studies show them to be cost-effective for internal operations.

5.5 DIVISIONAL OBJECTIVES

Corporate objectives are, by their nature, too remote from and too unrelated to divisions' and departments' specific responsibilities to be useful for formulating programs. They must be translated into lower-level objectives that can be stated in terms more specific to those organizations. Thus, each division must set its own objectives, created from the previously set corporate objectives. The dialogue that took place between top management and divisional management on setting objectives would have suggested divisional objectives. The goal is for each division to develop its own strategic plan, once the corporation as a whole has done so. Theoretically, the divisions' plans follow from the corporate plan, but in actuality these plans are done simultaneously in an integrated manner. This process is discussed in Chapter 7, *Setting Strategy*.

Though divisional objectives follow from corporate objectives, they differ from them in two important ways. First, they are more specific; they relate to the divisions' roles within the corporation. Second, they are narrower in scope, since they apply to specific divisions. The set of all divisional objectives, taken together, must not conflict with the set of corporate objectives in overall scope, achievability, and feasibility; rather, they represent a more detailed exposition of the latter.

The set of objectives of any one division cannot be in conflict with the objectives of any other, if the corporation itself is to have a consistent and realistic set of objectives. The sets of divisional objectives may be different in scope and type from each other.

Corporations are usually organized either by product line or by corporate function. Some use combinations of these structures. In a company organized along product lines, divisional objectives need relate to each other only relatively loosely. If divisions are very different from one another in the products they offer, their strategic planning may also be different.

In a company organized by function, the divisional objectives will tend to be more closely integrated, and coordination among all objectives is necessary. A manufacturing division must plan its future around those of the research and development divisions, while product-oriented divisions can plan more independently.

Divisional objectives are developed in a manner similar to corporate objectives, but fewer factors come into play because of their more limited scope. The basic questions asked about the corporation as a whole are generally not asked of divisions. A possible exception is that the "businesses" (or "missions" or "charters") of product divisions must be defined. Divisional objectives have the same traits as corporate objectives, however; they should be general, flexible, quantitative, achievable, consistent with missions, and understood by and acceptable to all who must work with them. Technology alternatives will guide divisional management in setting objectives, particularly in Research, Development, and Manufacturing. Divisional strengths and weaknesses should also be considered.

Divisional plans often depend on *issues*, which are matters beyond the direct control of the divisions themselves. The inclusion of issues in divisional plans is important because of the interdependence of divisional objectives, especially in the case of functionally organized companies. Issues are similar to corporate assumptions, since they refer to conditions outside direct divisional control. They represent conditions, however, that top management, having control over all divisions, can in many instances resolve.

As an example, one issue raised by Engineering might be that a particular technology, about to be transferred to it from Research, is not ready for conversion into product prototypes. Research, in turn, may not be able to develop the precursory "research prototypes" because of budgetary constraints. If top management sees this gap as a serious enough problem, it can provide additional resources to bridge the gap, perhaps by supplementing the research budget. If this is done, the issue disappears; if not, it must remain as an issue in the strategic plan, for its existence will have some impact on the plan and its execution. When conditions change subsequently, issues demand the attention of management.

The process of developing objectives for divisions should extend to lower organizational levels, to divisions, departments, etc. The objectives of a department bear more or less the same relation to divisional objectives as the latter do to corporate objectives, particularly if a company is organized by product line. The number of levels of objectives that management should develop depends upon the nature and size of the firm; in large corporations, three or four levels usually suffice.

ConTronics' management developed these divisional objectives:

Research

* Develop technologies which utilize new proprietary materials that provide a variety of properties useful in sensors.
* Develop new software for use in controllers
* Develop advanced automated circuit design systems easily adaptable to evolving electronics technologies.

Development

* Achieve engineering improvements in product cost, reliability, size, and features.
* Develop a new miniaturized product line.
* Develop new products for the low end of ConTronics' current markets.

Manufacturing

* Establish equipment and resources for planned products.
* Decrease manufacturing costs by an average of 8% per year.

Planning and Marketing

* Identify product feature tradeoffs for improved and new products in present OEM and retail markets.
* Characterize clearly the planned new markets in office automation and home electronics; identify customers, their number, and their needs.
* Define new small, self-contained electronics devices for new markets, basing product specifications on Company technologies.

Sales

* Plan an approach to marketing the new planned products.

5.6 SUBOBJECTIVES

Corporate objectives not only lead to divisional and lower-level objectives; they also lead to *subobjectives*. The subobjectives that follow from a corporate objective represent more specific achievements to be attained to meet that objective. Similarly, sub-subobjectives follow from subobjectives. Consider this example. If a corporate objective is to attain a certain profit margin over a period of five years, subobjectives that follow from that might be (a) to increase sales over that period by a stated amount, (b) to increase its work force's productivity by 20% over that period, and (c) to build a major new plant. In turn, the sub-subobjectives that follow the first of these (to increase sales) might be (a1) to increase market share by 20 percentage points, (a2) to invest 50% more in R & D for each of the next three years, and (a3) to double the advertising budget within the last two of the next five years.

Sometimes, what may be stated as a subobjective by one firm may be a corporate objective to another. A corporate objective may be to increase market share, and one of its subobjectives may be to increase sales. Though the process may thus seem arbitrary, the point is that management must select its primary objectives, the ones deemed most important in the long run to its company's survival and growth. Subobjectives then follow from these. Clearly, subobjectives sometimes are the same as or are related to divisional objectives, but in general this is not the case.

5.7 GOALS

In addition to having objectives for strategic planning, a corporation and its divisions should also establish goals. The terms *objective* and *goal* are often used interchangeably, but here we make a distinction between them. Goals are the means by which objectives are attained. As Richard Vancil pointed out [9]:

> One of John F. Kennedy's *objectives* in 1960 was to reestablish this country's position as a leader in the fields of science and technology, while one of his *goals* was to land a man on the moon and return him safely by 1970.

Objectives usually relate to the desired nature of the business to be in and to broad issues such as growth, profitability, stability, or image. They tend to be enduring, at least for years at a time. Goals are more specific and relate to the means by which objectives will be attained. They are shorter term than objectives. They can provide scales of value against which progress toward objectives can be measured; such scales include growth rate in sales and earnings, profit margins, earnings per share, and the like. They provide the means whereby management can determine whether objectives have been achieved on time and to the extent desired. Goals are related to a specific time frame, while objectives are not necessarily so related.

Goals generally have these traits as well: (a) they are specific, stated in terms of particular results and a time schedule; (b) they are measurable rather precisely; (c) they are focused internally, carrying implications on how company resources shall be utilized.

As an example, it is almost useless to state that a goal is "to improve productivity". It is far more valuable to state (if it is feasible) that the goal is "to improve productivity by 10% each year for the next five years". Another goal may be to capture 25% of the electronic printing market by 1985. Still another may be to achieve 30% of all corporate revenues from office automation products.

ConTronics' defined the following goals for the Company:

* To capture 40% of the home controls market by 1986, 30% of the office automation controls market by 1988, and 20% of the office systems small device market by 1988.

* To increase market shares in all product lines by amounts varying from 5 to 20 percentage points.

* To increase the business division revenues most rapidly in the 1982–1984 period and the office and home divisions revenues most rapidly in the 1984–1986 period.

* To reduce the OEM share of revenues from its present 65% to approximately 30 to 35% in five years.

* To increase the customer's perceived "value" of each product, using some measure, by 5% each year per unit constant-dollar price.

* To improve product reliability by 10% each year, on the average across all products.

* To start R & D funding in all the new areas of the Company's businesses by 1985, phasing this funding in gradually from 1983 to 1985.

* To reduce manufacturing costs, on average, by 8% each year, for all product lines.

* To increase company productivity by 12% and manufacturing costs by close to 10% each year, on average.

5.8   THE SCHEDULE

The development of objectives and goals is a task that can occur at any time in the planning cycle, i.e., at any time during the year. It should occur at least once a year for the strategic planning task under way that year, optimally close to the start of the planning process. Generally, objectives setting should occur at about the middle of the second quarter of the year. In companies where the strategic planning starts with objectives setting and information analysis follows, objectives setting should occur at the start of the year, in a tentative fashion. Then, about three or four months later, the objectives can be made definite, with the information analysis done. Fig. 5-2 shows a schedule for setting objectives and goals.

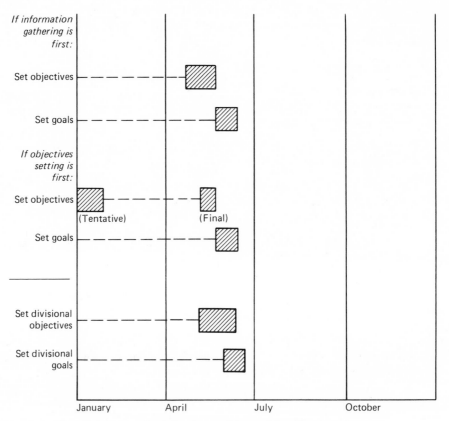

Fig. 5-2. A schedule for setting objectives and goals.

5.9   PROBLEMS IN SETTING OBJECTIVES

There are several problems in the setting of objectives within a corporation. One problem results from the tendency of line managers to give priority to objectives which tend to make them "look good" in the short run, because corporate reward systems usually stress performance in this area. It may be very hard to convince them to give their full support to an objective which may only be reached in a relatively distant future.

Another problem results when objectives are highly business oriented and fail to take technology needs fully into account. As an example, top management's primary objective may be to maintain a certain profit level, despite the need for uneven R & D expenditures. The tendency may be to trim the R & D budget one year when, for the long term, it might be better to increase it. Budget allocations tend to be a function of current expenditures in the company, while R & D programs address technologies for products several years into the future.

A potential source of conflict in the setting of objectives relates to the forces that drive research and development objectives and corporate objectives. The researcher may be interested in science for its own sake and for the prestige it offers. The engineer may be interested in building something that works. R & D management cannot but help reflect these views in part. Top management, on the other hand, is more concerned with results than with the science or technology. R & D contributes to these results, but there is a long time delay from early technology development to product introduction, and goals at the two ends can easily fall out of step. For this reason, top management must be certain that R & D objectives bear the proper relationship to corporate objectives.

The transmittal of needs upward to aid in the definition of corporate objectives and the subsequent transmittal of objectives downward in order to guide setting lower-level objectives can lead to distortions. These result from the interpretations put on them by managers at the several levels of organization. This is the problem of the "noisy channel" of communication.

The role of corporate culture in the top-management attempts to implement change is often overlooked. Sometimes management will attempt to set objectives that are new for the company and run contrary to its traditions and values. If so, employees may very well resist the change and sabotage the efforts.

SUMMARY

The one "true objective" for a corporation is to make a satisfactory profit, so that it can continue to exist. Since this objective offers no guidance to management in running its company, more specific objectives are necessary. Management starts the process of deriving objectives by asking key questions on the business the company should be in, on its acceptable rate of growth, and on how it should grow.

It is desirable for a corporation to articulate its mission, which provides a rationale for existence, and its philosophy of operation, which provides guidance on how the company is to be operated.

Corporate objectives should be (a) consistent with the company's mission, (b) be guides to action, (c) be stable over time, (d) be general and flexible to accommodate to change, and (e) be achievable while offering challenge.

Objectives must be understood by and be acceptable to those who use them.

Top management and the board of directors have responsibility for developing objectives. Among the factors that should be considered in developing objectives are (a) current objectives, (b) technology alternatives, (c) corporate strengths and weaknesses, (d) opportunities and threats, (e) constraints, and (f) corporate image. A dialogue among managers at different levels should be used to help develop objectives.

Prior to setting objectives, management should develop positions on corporate missions and a philosophy of operation. In addition, it should define the mission of each of its divisions.

Divisional objectives must also be established. These evolve from corporate objectives and, as a group, must be self-consistent. Divisional objectives are more specific and narrower in scope than corporate objectives. Divisions should also raise issues, which are matters beyond their direct control, for top management's attention.

Subobjectives are the component parts of objectives and represent a different means of breaking down objectives. They are based on specific goals rather than on organizations.

Goals, which are more specific and more inner-directed than objectives, should also be defined. They provide measures for objectives.

REFERENCES

1. Argenti, John, *Corporate Planning: A Practical Guide*, Dow Jones — Irwin, Inc., 1969, Chapter 1.

2. Drucker, Peter F., *The Practice of Management*, Harper & Brothers, New York, 1954.

3. Drucker, Peter F., *Management: Tasks, Responsibilities, Practices*, Harper & Row, New York, 1974, p. 75.

4. Shepherd, Mark, Jr., and J. Fred Bucy, "Innovation at Texas Instruments", *Computer*, IEEE Computer Society, September 1979, vol. 12, no. 9, p. 82.

5. Neubert, Ralph L., "Strategic Management the Monsanto Way", *Planning Review*, January 1980, vol. 8, no. 1, p. 46.

6. Steiner, George A., *Strategic Planning: What Every Manager Must Know*, The Free Press, New York, 1979, pp. 149–150.

7. Quinn, James Brian, "Long Range Planning of Industrial Research", *Harvard Business Review*, July/August 1961, vol. 39, no. 4, p. 96.

8. Ansoff, H. Igor, *Corporate Strategy*, McGraw-Hill Book Company, New York, 1965.

9. Vancil, Richard F., "Strategy Formulation in Complex Organizations", *Sloan Management Review*, Winter 1976, vol. 17, no. 2, pp. 1–3. (Also in *Strategic Planning Systems*, Prentice-Hall, Inc., Englewood Cliffs, N. J., 1977, pp. 5–6.)

Additional References

"Corporate Culture," *Business Week*, October 27, 1980, pp. 148–160. (This article discusses corporate traditions and values, which must be considered when new objectives and strategy are set.)

Pearson, G. J., "Setting Corporate Objectives as a Basis for Action", *Long Range Planning*, vol. 12, no. 8, August 1979, pp. 13–19. (This paper describes a number of objectives-setting systems and relates the process to Maslow's hierarchy of human needs.)

Vancil, Richard F., "Strategy Formulation in Complex Organizations", <u>Sloan</u> <u>Management Review</u>, Winter 1976, vol. 17, no. 2, pp. 1–18. (This is a chapter in *Strategic Planning Systems*, by Peter Lorange and Richard F. Vancil, listed above.)

Levitt, Theodore, "Marketing Myopia", <u>Harvard Business Review</u>, Sept.–Oct. 1975, Vol. 53, No. 5, pp. 26–48. (This is an updating of a classic paper that discusses the fact that companies sometimes fail to identify their true objectives and so fail to aim their strategies properly.)

Knoepfel R. W., "Establishing Corporate Objectives at Solvay," from *Long Range Planning for Management*, 3rd edition, edited by David W. Ewing, Harper & Row, New York, 1972, pp. 392–420.

Granger, Charles H., "The Hierarchy of Objectives", <u>Harvard Business Review</u>, May-June 1964, Vol. 42, No. 3, pp. 63–74. (Many levels of "objectives" are considered, from missions and visions down to strategies and budgets.)

6

ISSUES ON TECHNOLOGY

INTRODUCTION

There are several issues on technology that are of concern to those who do strategic planning in technology-based companies. These issues, to a large extent, define the task of technology or R & D management. They can be expressed as a series of questions. First, how does a company gain a lead in its technological domain and maintain that lead, as technology advances, often very rapidly? Second, how does a company deal with the risks associated with technology development? Third, what is the better way, under appropriate circumstances, of handling technology acquisition, by internal means or by acquisition from various external sources? Fourth, what is the impact of the development of technology alternatives on corporate objectives and on planning? Fifth, how does a company undertake the assessment of technology, to evaluate its technological position relative to the outside world and to its corporate business objectives and goals? Sixth, what are the forces that drive innovation? Seventh, what are the special problems in the development of new technology? Eighth, what is the effect of technology maturity on planning? Ninth, how should management address the issue of technology transfer, moving technology advances from Research to Development?

This chapter interrupts the description of the strategic planning process provided thus far in Chapters 2 through 5. That description resumes in Chapter 7. Such a review of technology issues is important at this point because strategy formulation for a technology-based company cannot be done properly without taking these issues into consideration.

6.1 OBJECTIVES FOR TECHNOLOGY

Developing Technology Objectives

Just as a company's technology alternatives are factors in the selection of corporate objectives, so are those objectives factors in guiding technology development within a firm.   The process is bilateral.   In technology-based companies, research and development objectives influence corporate objectives, and vice versa.   Corporate objectives help determine the size, nature, and timing of the company's technology programs.   They do so by defining businesses and products of concern to the company and by stressing the kinds of product functions the company should provide.   These functions relate to technological embodiments, and in this manner technology programs are guided by corporate objectives.   Objectives for research and development are determined in this manner.   Without this linkage between objectives and technologies, research programs might not be consistent with those objectives.   The technology requirements of planned products in turn guide the development of strategy, whereby particular technology development programs are funded and given priority over other programs.

Some general comments about R & D objectives can be made.   The objectives of a corporate research program generally are (a) to achieve sufficient understanding of materials and processes of concern to the corporation so as to control and utilize them, (b) to develop and maintain competence in scientific disciplines which hold promise for present and future company products, and (c) to provide research support to operating organizations by demonstration of feasibility to the point where results can be exploited by such organizations.   The objectives of a corporate development program generally are (a) to demonstrate economic feasibility of technological embodiments in products, (b) to develop new products for the company, and (c) to improve existing products.

The objectives developed for a company's R & D organizations are, of course, divisional objectives.   In technology-based companies, R & D objectives drive all other divisional objectives, since technology drives such companies' other operations.   Consequently, R & D objectives must be defined before other divisions' objectives.   For R & D programs to be successful, they must be keyed to corporate objectives, and this is accomplished through R & D objectives.   The greatest influences on these objectives are corporate objectives and technology alternatives.   The need for divisional management to be involved in setting corporate objectives, to understand those objectives, and to have a commitment to them is nowhere as important in a technology-based company as in the R & D organizations.

In order for technical management to develop specific objectives for its R & D organizations, corporate objectives must be established.   Then, management should receive information from those parts of the company that have interests in technology developments.   These include the top management, technical staff,

Planning, and Marketing.   To facilitate this information-gathering process, a planning structure that delineates products, product lines, and markets is important.   The structure should comprise a common language for all to use, a description of current and planned products, and a description of the company's markets.   Such a structure permits communication across diverse organizations in a manner understood by all.

The information gathered must be translated into a form that allows R & D management to formulate technology objectives.   It must be in the form of product specifications which identify particular technology needs.   This information will also be needed to formulate strategy, as discussed in Chapter 7, *Setting Strategy.*

Linkage of Objectives

It is sometimes difficult to link technology objectives and planning with corporate objectives, because the former are technology-oriented and the latter are product- or business-oriented.   This is especially true for research activities, where time scales and attitudes toward risks often differ greatly from those in Manufacturing, Sales, and Service.   One approach used to link R & D objectives with corporate objectives is given by J. M. Hubert [1].   He uses relevance trees to break down both sets of objectives into subobjectives and sub-subobjectives.   Three levels are used for R & D objectives, and four levels are used for corporate objectives, as shown in Figs. 6-1(a) and (b).   The two relevance trees can be linked to form one structure, as in Fig. 6-1(c), where the lowest-level objectives of each, termed "approaches", are matched.   The extent to which these levels can be matched for a particular company reflects the inherent relationship between its R & D and corporate objectives.   This method aids the goals of linking R & D programs to corporate products or businesses and of increasing the likelihood of the results of research being utilized.   It also provides a relevance analysis of R & D operations.

A Conflict

A conflict arises between the ways that Research and top management view the passage of time and events.   Researchers view time as the dependent variable, while businessmen view time as the independent variable.   Researchers believe that one cannot dictate schedules for research; rather, one sets goals based on achievements to be sought and accomplished, with the timing of those achievements to be indeterminate in most cases.   Businessmen, by contrast, look at schedules because their point of view dictates that products must be commercially available on certain dates.   This same type of conflict exists between Research and Development, though less sharply, since the latter is more schedule-oriented.   This is understandable, for tasks in Development are more readily predictable as to timing than those in Research.

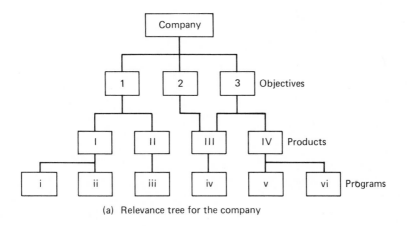

(a) Relevance tree for the company

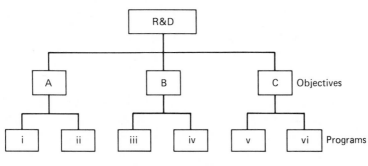

(b) Relevance tree for R&D

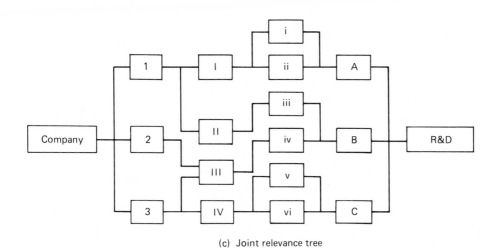

(c) Joint relevance tree

Fig. 6-1. Linking R & D and corporate objectives.

6.2   THE RAPID CHANGE OF TECHNOLOGY

A potentially serious problem facing the management of technology-based companies is the rapid pace of technology advancement in the outside world. This is a problem because new technologies and new advances in older technologies threaten those that a company builds into its products. A new product's very existence may be threatened by yet another new or improved one after only a short while in the marketplace.

Management in such firms can take several steps to decrease the probability of having this problem become serious. A company can try to develop products that provide significant "value added" to the raw technology. This means that it would make unique, proprietary advances in technology development that yield results of significantly greater value than it started with. This approach is successful if the results are unique (for then patent protection may be available) and provides product advantages in cost, reliability, quality, etc. Even if the results are not unique, early product introduction or marketing strength can bring success. Further, the company can attempt to design products in a modular fashion, with identifiable, separable subsystems. In this way, the modules whose technological bases are threatened with obsolescence can more readily be replaced by their successors.

Serious and intense investment in technology development and product design are also important in rapidly changing technical environments. The R & D budgets have to be large enough to allow the company to keep pace with or outdistance its competitors. Small investments in such situations probably represent wasted expenditures. It is also important to move advanced technology products to the marketplace as quickly as is feasible, since the time element may be critical. Obviously, rushing a product in this way before its design is thoroughly tested and before appropriate market studies are made is a mistake, but speed is often nonetheless important. Also, it is true that merely displacing one's own products may have little advantage.

Finally, it is particularly important for a company to maintain an in-depth awareness of the state of technology development in the outside world in its fields of interest. (This process is, of course, important for other reasons as well, as we have seen.) This is necessary if the company is to anticipate technology advances early and accurately. The task is accomplished by having its technical management scrupulously follow the technical literature, as discussed in Chapter 3. The acquisition of external technology, discussed above, is yet another way to keep pace with rapid technology advances.

The task of doing strategic planning is, by its very nature, not fully reconcilable with the need to act rapidly in the face of sudden changes in technological development. What this conflict implies is that, while doing the planning, management must nevertheless be ready to act quickly when threats arise quickly. It must be flexible in its thinking and planning, to maximize its ability to respond to surprises. However, it is not possible to be prepared to respond to all the threats that may arise.

6.3 RISKS IN TECHNOLOGY DEVELOPMENT

Risk

Each research project and each development program carries a risk with it. *Risk* measures the uncertainty in successfully completing activities and the accuracy of estimating the cost of and time to completion. Theoretically, it can be measured quantitatively as a probability, i.e., on a scale of 0 to 1. In practice, one cannot be this precise, and such terms as "high risk", "moderate risk", and "low risk" are more appropriate and generally just as useful.

There is uncertainty associated with pushing the state of the art in science or technology and with the costs of product development. The greater uncertainty lies with the former, which involve technical breakthroughs. Allan Baillie suggests that there is a need to separate technological uncertainties from product development uncertainties [2]. He points out that probably all R & D projects encounter substantial cost overruns and schedule slips due to technical problems that were not anticipated. Such problems plague most projects, even when technology is not an issue, as in building construction projects. When the uncertainties of pushing the state of the art in technology are present as well, the problems are compounded. Baillie also reports, not surprisingly, that R & D managers tend to be risk-averse (as do individuals in general). This conclusion is based on a broad study of firms carrying on military and space R & D activities.

As each activity is considered for inclusion in the strategic plan, its risk should be assessed. There are several factors that tend to determine the level of risk associated with a project or program.

First, it is generally true that as a program moves through the path from basic research, through applied research and engineering, to manufacturing, and finally to sales, its risk diminishes. Programs that fail are eliminated along the way, and the survivors are the most likely to become commercialized.

Second, technology programs that deal with mature technologies, which are discussed in Section 6.9, usually involve much less risk because past history has shown the viability of the technology commercially, and management can be more certain of the outcome of investments in technology improvements.

Third, the further away the projected completion date of the project or program, the more risk is involved, provided there is a competitive threat. The existence of competition simply means that the uniqueness of the technology is less likely and so are the chances of the company's commercial success.

Pay-off is another factor that should be considered. If two programs are equally likely to be successful and one has twice the expected pay-off (e.g., expected profits over the product lifetime), that one is most probably preferable.

Both risk and payoff are considered in Chapter 7, where methods of evaluating activities are discussed.

Levels of Risk

Top management is not particularly concerned with the several types and phases of R & D activity. Rather, it is interested in results, i.e., products and their capabilities. From its point of view, characterization of R & D projects and programs by their degree of risk is far more meaningful than by the technical phases they are in.

Some technology programs involve applying the state of the art to existing products or to new products. Attention is focused here on such matters as reducing cost, increasing reliability, and adding new features. There is little concern on technology advances. The risk in this case is quite low, since the cost and timing of completion can be fairly accurately predicted.

Other technology programs attempt to extend the state of the art, perhaps by using improved materials, better designs, or cheaper manufacturing costs. Risk is greater than for the case just above, since there is less certainty of success.

Finally, some technology programs involve the development of new technology. The aim is either to replace an existing technology with a better one, in a capability now existing, or to offer a totally new capability. Clearly, the risk in these cases is the greatest of all.

Management and Risk

A conflict between Research and top management also manifests itself with respect to the matter of risk. All R & D activity involves some degree of risk. The pressures on top management for ever-better profitability come into conflict with the acceptance of uncertainty and risk. Technical management and top management must resolve this inherent difference of views. An ongoing dialogue between technical management and top management is valuable. Each must understand the pressures under which the other operates. Each must convey information on its own responsibilities to the other. Top management cannot make decisions on technology, but it can provide guidance for technical management to do so.

Risks always present problems. A consequence of this is that managers who are risk-averse hesitate to undertake any project or program that can be classified as "high risk". The result of this inaction may be that breakthroughs do not occur. Advances in technology-based products are then limited to incremental or evolutionary changes in products.

The best way for management to deal with risks is to try to have a broad spectrum of risk levels among R & D programs and to include high-risk ventures that have high pay-offs. This balanced approach tends to minimize losses over the long run. The uncertainty of some programs counters the greater certainty of others. Management should evaluate expected benefits and costs as carefully as possible and maintain a comprehensive surveillance program to remain aware of competitive advances in technology.

6.4   TECHNOLOGY ACQUISITION

The Alternatives

A corporation's early consideration in planning its technologies is the manner of their acquisition. It has basically two choices, internal development and external acquisition, and most likely it will exercise both options in some combination. Once a company has determined its technology needs, it then must decide which approach to take regarding particular needs. The following questions should be addressed in an attempt to make such decisions. Implicit is the assumption that the technology is in fact available outside.

What is the nature of the company's experience in the technology?

How much time does the company have before the technology will be required?

How much time and money will be required to develop the technology internally, considering the skills and facilities available and those that can be acquired?

What is the cost of external acquisition?

What is the timing of such acquisition?

How exclusive are the rights to the technology that can be obtained?

In brief, the main considerations are the company's expertise in the technology, the cost and time needed to develop it to the point of feasibility, and the cost of external acquisition. There are other factors also; these are reviewed below.

Internal Technology Development

The development of a technology internally provides a company with its best chance for the security and exclusivity of a technology. Internal development allows a company to conduct development in a way most suitable to its needs. On the other hand, internal development requires the most involvement and longest time commitment among the several approaches to technology access. It also involves the most risk, since expenditures of funds may be made for naught, if development results prove inadequate or show infeasibility, either technically or financially. Another risk is associated with the long development time generally involved. During that time, competitors have the opportunity to catch up or even pull ahead in the technology race. The decision to move ahead with the development of a technology must be based on these factors. It must be preceded by an analysis of the resources required to effect internal development, which include technical and managerial skills, money, equipment, and related experience. Further, a program of competitive surveillance, described in Chapter 4, will be of continuing utility as plans move ahead in technology development.

Outside technology developments can be threats to a company, so there is sometimes a reason for *defensive* research and development, i.e., research and development undertaken to maintain parity or leadership in a technical field. If an outside firm develops and thus owns a new technology or an improved one, the company may be at a disadvantage. By doing defensive R & D, the company may be better able to defend its position.

Among the largest companies, internal development is most common. We have noted that the expenditures for such development typically run from 3% to 6% of a company's revenues. Strategic planning is especially important in this approach to acquisition, since internal technology development is inherently a lengthy process, taking perhaps up to five years or more. Furthermore, since most research projects and many development programs do not achieve commercial success, careful planning of technology is vitally important.

External Technology Acquisition

External technology acquisition must be treated rather differently from internal development. The main differences lie in the plan period involved and the matter of exclusivity. Decisions on whether to acquire a technology externally can be made in a relatively short time. The time to acquisition can also be relatively short. If a company plans to watch a technology evolve outside before making a decision to acquire it, then acquisition may take a long time. Technology purchase can be accomplished by outright acquisition of an entire company, of the division of a company, or of the rights to the technology alone. The decision to go outside, however, may follow an internal development activity that has had poor results, in which case the overall acquisition time may be lengthy. Ideally, a decision to go outside for a technology would be made without such internal work, but that cannot always be the case.

The successful identification, evaluation, acquisition, and use of external technologies requires a certain internal capability. The company's staff must be knowledgeable of the state of the art in the field in question, so as to aid the decision on acquisition, and it must be able to integrate the technology, once acquired, with the company's development programs, a progress sometimes called *internalization*.

If a company acquires an externally developed technology, it may not be able to obtain exclusive rights to its use. Alternately, it may only be able to use it under a licensing arrangement, which may also be available to others. Exclusive rights are likely to be rather expensive. Another aspect of external technology acquisition is the lack of privacy involved; clearly a licenser is aware of certain of its licensees' interests. It is possible, though, for this knowledge to be constrained. Finally, access by license involves paying royalties to the owner of a technology for its use, and this may be costly, though it is generally less so than the cost of internal development.

Among the future decisions that a company may address in its strategic plan are those concerning future acquisition of external technology. Such decisions would depend upon the nature and timing of outside developments in technologies of interest, as well as internal developments. The strategic plan should include points of decisions over time that relate to external technology development.

The results of the planning survey taken by the author indicate that companies use at least the following criteria for deciding on outside acquisitions, with the most frequent responses listed first: lower cost relative to inside development, shorter acquisition time, lack of the ability to develop the technology inside, and the uniqueness of the technology outside.

We have seen the need to monitor outside developments in technologies relevant to the company among competitive firms and elsewhere. While this task serves primarily to monitor competition, it may also serve to identify technology candidates for acquisition.

The uncertainty about technological feasibility associated with internal development is largely absent in technology acquisition from outside sources, since feasibility will often have been established. The probability of failure in the latter case is greatly diminished, though commercial success is certainly not guaranteed.

A corporation that is interested in acquiring external technologies can go to a commercial "broker" for this purpose. Potential acquirers and sellers of technology can be put in contact with one another much in the way that buyers and sellers interact through advertisements [3,4].

Corporations sometimes develop technologies jointly with other corporations or with universities. The criteria for deciding on such ventures include the extent of mutual interests, the nature of what all parties have to offer one another, and whether a joint venture provides advantages over the alternative approaches to technology acquisition, namely internal development and outside purchase or lease.

Selling Technology

A company may be in a position to sell technology and thereby gain by its distribution to other firms. There are several questions to ask in this regard. The assumption made here is that a decision has been made not to develop the technology for internal use. Commercial brokers may be of help here too.

Should the technology be sold outright or be licensed?

To whom should it be distributed?

Should it be distributed exclusively to one acquirer or to many?

What is an appropriate price to charge?

What are the risks in distributing it?

It may be best not to distribute a technology because of the potential harm resulting from a competitor's successful exploitation of it. It is also possible to retain a technology that will not be used, simply to prevent its use by others.

6.5 TECHNOLOGY ALTERNATIVES

Alternatives

The development of technology advances within the company, coupled with other advances outside, presents the company's management with a variety of alternatives for technologies. Most of the technical activity in a company is strongly directed toward product programs, but the research and exploratory or advanced development work generally is not. The latter are primarily motivated by long-term objectives and goals, by the drive to discover new scientific phenomena, and by a desire to understand and control new processes. Management should view such work as eventually yielding commercial successes but should also understand that no particular successes are guaranteed. The results of this work will be mixed; there will be total successes, partial successes, and failures. Among the successes will be new technology alternatives. Besides, as discussed earlier, other alternatives exist outside the firm.

As internal technology develops, it is the responsibility of technical management to keep top management informed of advances. The most uncertain and most changeable functional areas of a company are its research and exploratory development activities. For that reason, technology advances should be brought to the attention of top management frequently and regularly. There may be some difficulty, however, in doing so. Top managers often cannot appreciate the significance of technology advances; they generally do not have technical backgrounds. The two groups must maintain close communication with each other in order for the advances to have appropriate impact.

Management Responses

As technology alternatives confront management, it may react in at least two ways. It must consider whether or not corporate objectives require modification and whether the strategic plan strategy must be changed. Since it is not wise for objectives to be changed too frequently, management should note a possible change in objectives, if indeed one is needed, for use at the time that the planning process calls for objectives setting. If a technology alternative is presented that calls for a major revision to corporate objectives, then that change should be effected right away. Corporate objectives might have to be modified if significant advances were made that promised new or improved products that previously seemed impossible or unlikely. They might also have to be modified if technology developments proved that plans for products were unduly optimistic.

Just as technology advances can change corporate objectives, the reverse is also true. Changes in corporate objectives might call for a change in the direction of technology development. If, for example, a company decided to concentrate henceforth on major cost reductions in the manufacture of one of its products through the use of new materials, its research division might have to triple its efforts in materials exploration.

Technology alternatives and objectives each can have impact on the other. The result is an iteration in the strategic planning process that goes on throughout the year. Management should examine the interaction of these two sets of information on a regular basis, the frequency depending on the nature of a company's business. In a large technology-based company, this examination need not be done more than monthly, and perhaps even a quarterly survey will suffice.

The second appropriate management response is to consider a strategy change, which is easier to effect because its impact on the corporation as a whole is less. Initially, a change in strategy may only affect one division or part of one, though eventually it may affect the entire firm. A strategy should change (a) if the assumptions made for its development no longer are valid because of technology alternatives sent up to management, or (b) if events take place that were unexpected and a significant change in activities is required as a result. It is important, however, that management not overreact to technology developments. Before any changes in strategy are planned, all ramifications of such developments should be explored.

There may be outside technology developments that demand some internal action. There may be a new, unexpected product announcement by a competitor who uses a technology not previously known or a technology that the company's technical management had not expected to see implemented in a product by that time. Management may have thought the use of the technology was months or even years into the future. If the technology is one the company was developing for its own use, a change in strategy may be essential, either one whereby further development on the technology is abandoned or one whereby more resources are applied to its development. Another possibility is that the company may be interested in acquiring the technology or even its product embodiment.

Movement Upward of Alternatives

Technology alternatives should be initially developed at the lowest feasible levels in the company and move upward for management action in response. As they move up, they should be combined and filtered, so that when they reach top management, they are fewer in number and broader in scope, comprising only major items. The combination and filtering must be carefully done so as not to obliterate critical choices at too low a level. Some alternatives filtered out at one time may emerge subsequently when they prove to be more significant than before.

The process of sending technology alternatives *up* to top management and the process of sending objectives *down* to technical management occur during the same time period. This was shown in Fig. 1-4. Over the course of a year, both processes occur, and while changes in both objectives and in technology development are relatively infrequent, management at all times must be responsive to them. Both processes actually have potential impact on each other, so they must be managed coherently in an iterative manner. Technical management also has an obligation to send up to top management technology advances that occur outside the company, for their existence may also influence objectives setting.

As top management receives information on technology advances within the company, it not only should consider the modification of objectives and strategy at some time in the future, but it also should help technical management make decisions on which technology projects to continue. Projects will continue to be funded as long as their probability of success seems high enough, but they will require increasing resources and commitment by management. Some projects must be diminished in size or eliminated, and the decision to do so must be made by technical management, aided by top management. The latter become involved to the extent that technology advances are related to objectives setting and strategy.

6.6 TECHNOLOGY ASSESSMENT

As management weighs various alternatives regarding technologies — internal or external acquisition of a technology, more or less support for technology programs, whether to transfer the technology to Development, etc. — it is usually appropriate to undertake a *technology assessment*. A technology assessment is a detailed examination of the state of the art in a technology, with particular emphasis on (a) the possible utility of the technology to the company and (b) the impacts of the technology on the company or on the outside world. The terms *technology utility assessment* and *technology impact assessment* can be used, respectively, to describe these two tasks. (Some writers strongly emphasize one of these to the exclusion of the other.) The impacts considered include those that are socioeconomic as well as technological. Since this book is concerned with planning, greater emphasis is on the utility of the technology, though management should give consideration as well to the impacts of external technologies on the company.

The specific questions that management should address in an assessment that stresses technology utility are the following.

What has been the historical development of the technology, both inside the company and outside?

What are potential applications of the technology and when can these be achieved?

What areas of opportunity exist for further research in this technology?

What is the state of the technology in the company?

What are current plans for continued work on the technology?

How much more time and money are required to show technical feasibility?

What is the probability of proving technical feasibility?

Where can we proceed with the technology and how much would it cost?

Where do we stand relative to the outside world in this technology?

What is the state of the technology in other companies and at universities?

What do other companies appear to be doing with the technology?

The answers to these questions provide information for use in developing a strategy. They permit decisions to be made on new and existing research and technology projects.

Many of these questions were addressed by the technology questions of Chapters 2 to 4. They are brought together here to focus attention on technology strategy issues to accomplish the following:

a) To decide whether to develop technology internally or to acquire it externally;

b) To determine which technology projects to fund internally and to what extent;

c) To decide when internal technologies will be available for product development and commercialization.

There are problems in undertaking technology assessments. One is the same as any projective analysis encounters. Since the future cannot be known, only projections can be developed, which are based on the best information available and the best judgment of experts. A second problem is that it is hard to obtain some of the information required to do an assessment of the states of the technologies and their uses in other firms.

6.7 FORCES ON INNOVATION

Much has been written about the management of technological innovation — how to motivate it, how to guide it, and how to reap benefits from it. We shall not discuss it in any detail, except to comment on its relationship to planning. We have already mentioned *supply-pushed* and *demand-induced* innovation.

These can be thought of as two forces that motivate innovation, wherein a "creative tension" exists that together lead to innovation. This concept has been elucidated by Lowell W. Steele [5].

Supply-pushed innovation results from inventions and developments within the R & D organization and does not depend on the existence of any needs for the new capabilities. Subsequently, R & D management may, if the work is successful, attempt to adapt such advances to planned products or to convince top management of the utility of the technologies in new products. This type of innovation is a consequence of the nature of technical staff and the work they do. R & D organizations, having worked in technology invention and development, build expertise and have ongoing projects and programs. The technology alternatives they generate are a natural consequence of this activity. There is much more risk in this approach to technology development, since an identified need was not there at the start and may indeed never be there. The probability of success is small, though when it occurs it is more likely to yield a true breakthrough than the other approach.

Demand-induced innovation is driven by forces outside the R & D organizations. A need is perceived by someone in the firm and a demand is placed on R & D to develop a technological solution. The needs might be, e.g., for a new specific product, for improvement of an existing product, as a response to an opportunity, or for meeting the request of an important customer. Innovation and technology development that proceed in this manner generally involve relatively little risk; success is more or less predictable. It has been estimated that about two-thirds of all innovation is of the demand-induced type, and that fraction has been steadily increasing in recent years.

Sometimes, the customer is indeed a valuable source of innovative product ideas. Eric von Hippel has studied the role that customers play in innovation; he has found that very often they are a valuable source of ideas. He writes, "In some industries, most commercially successful products are developed by product users, not product manufacturers [6]." It is important, where this is true, that companies monitor their customers closely, seeking from them not only information on their needs but also proposed solutions to those needs. Sometimes much of the early engineering is done by those companies.

Management must retain a balance — the creative tension mentioned above — of the two opposite forces for innovation. A technology-based company usually needs both forces. The demand-induced approach allows perceived needs to be met, while the supply-pushed approach yields an occasional large success and, equally important, permits the creativity of R & D staffs to be fostered and utilized.

Management should recognize the characteristics and roles of these two forces in developing strategy in planning. An appropriate strategy encompasses both methodologies in a balance appropriate to the needs of the company and to its perceived opportunities and threats.

6.8   NEW TECHNOLOGY DEVELOPMENT

Among the most important decisions regarding technology that management makes are those having to do with undertaking the development of new technologies. These are strategic decisions and so are addressed in Chapter 7, *Setting Strategy*. The decisions are important enough, however, to warrant some attention at this point.

The decision to fund the development of a new technology project is usually made when (a) a research advance proves very promising for possible technology development for a product, (b) a need has been identified by product planners, the marketing staff, or others within the corporation, or (c) a competitor has made significant advances in a technology that management wants to match.

The steps that technical management takes, in order to make a decision on a new technology project, are these:

a) A technology assessment of the state of inside knowledge and experience in related areas and of the state of the technology outside;

b) Identification of new products by using the technology and new or expanded markets for those products;

c) Identification of the required time and resources.

The result of taking these steps leads to planning in the usual manner. The proposed new program becomes a candidate for inclusion in the strategy. The issue of technology development is related to some of the other technology issues reviewed in this chapter. The pace of technology advances outside, the risks inherent in R & D work, and the possibility of acquiring external technologies may all be factors in a decision by management to proceed with its own internal technology development.

6.9   TECHNOLOGY MATURITY

A technology is, at any time in its development, in a particular state of maturity. One can say that a technology is born when a new process or material is embodied in a device or a component so as to yield something of value. Xerography, e.g., was born in 1938 when Chester Carlson demonstrated that the technology could produce a copy of something handwritten or printed on another piece of plain paper. Over 20 years passed before that technology was embodied in a machine that could be sold or rented. Today, about 20 years after that, the technology is still being improved, by many corporations, in generally incremental ways. Xerography can be classified as a mature technology.

it is difficult to define *mature* with respect to technologies in a precise manner, but it should be clear that xerography, for example, is mature. One might arbitrarily state that a technology is mature once it has been utilized in a commercial product for several years, perhaps three or five. The precise definition is not important. What is important is the realization that technologies pass through stages of maturity, from initial birth, through research and engineering development, and continuing on through successive embodiments in a series of products.

In mature technologies, a company is likely only to make incremental evolutionary changes, which lead to such product advances as improved reliability, lower operating costs, reduced size, and reduced cost of operation. In the case of an immature technology, the changes can be revolutionary, as, e.g., were xerography, the transistor, and the jet engine when they were first introduced commercially. In fact, almost by definition, if a technology experiences evolutionary changes, it is not mature. Mature technologies are generally driven by demand-induced innovation.

The other issues on technology discussed in this chapter relate to this one of maturity. Technology acquisition decisions will depend, in part, on the state of the technologies' maturity. The maintenance of technological lead in the face of rapid advances also depends on the maturity of the technologies, since one has a likelier chance of making a breakthrough to challenge the leader in the case of a less mature technology. Risks are lower in mature technology development. Technology assessment deals directly with maturity. On the other hand, it is hard to say, however, just how technology transfer relates to technology maturity. Other factors seem to play larger roles in transfer, as discussed below.

6.10   TECHNOLOGY TRANSFER

When It Occurs

Technology transfer is defined here as the transfer of developed technologies from Research to Development. (The term is also used in other senses, referring to the transition of technology from Development to Manufacturing, from one application to another, from one company to another, from government to industry, and from more developed to less developed countries.)

Although technology transfer is a critical step, it frequently fails to occur satisfactorily. Strategic planning must take the process into account, since proper technology transfer is essential for commercial success and must be planned in advance. When management decides that the results of a research project are promising enough for it to plan a new product or product line around the technology involved, it effects a technology transfer. It may also effect the transfer when the technology promises to provide major changes in existing product lines. In short, the transfer occurs when the company has made a decision to develop a new or modified product based on the new technology. The responsibility for the work passes from Research to Development and the *research project* becomes a *development* or *product program.*

The optimal time for transfer to occur is not easily identifiable, for it will not always be the same point in technological development from one project to another, or indeed from one company to another. Generally, the decision to effect a transfer will occur when a technology, embodied in an early prototype, appears to be feasible enough to warrant consideration in a product. The transfer is actually effected when technical feasibility in the prototype is proven, and the next task is engineering the product. The actual timing of the transfer is not nearly as critical as the manner in which it is accomplished.

Effective Transfer

It is necessary that there be incentives to promote transfer. If top management strongly pushes the development of a product which required research activity, there will be a strong incentive to transfer the resultant technology. This push may be in response to the existence of some form of the technology in a competitor's laboratory or a product announcement by a competitor. The effect of the push is to provide unified goals and guidelines for both Research and Development, which is essential for transfer.

A well-defined set of corporate objectives and a strategy for attaining them will go a long way towards motivating technology transfer, for this also provides consistent goals to Research and Development. Both organizations will have a clear idea of what they are striving for, and those ideas will be consistent. In other words, if a corporation has a well-defined strategic plan, that plan will doubtlessly provide the motivation for transfer. By the same token, the need for such transfer will in part define the plan.

A key to effective technology transfer is constructive communication among the various functional groups involved. Such communication should be established at the time of initiation of the technology development activity. It should be continued in such a manner that the technical staff, scientists and engineers in Research and Development, know at all times the state of the developing technology and the technological needs of the products.

Because Manufacturing and Marketing will eventually be involved in technologies as they become embodied in products, the early interaction of these organizations with Research and Development is also important. It is best if they become aware of technology developments shortly prior to the time of transfer to Development, so they can plan appropriately for their future roles. Such an approach increases the likelihood of eventual product success. This implies that there be a transfer of information quantifying the needs of customers to the technical community.

An important force in effecting transfer is the presence of a "champion" for the technology and its application in a particular product. Someone in Research, perhaps aided by someone in Engineering, must take the responsibility of seeing that the work be transferred, sometimes driving it against odds. This person must be an active, persuasive seller of the technology.

Finally, the presence of an "advanced technology" group in Engineering increases the likelihood of successful transfer. Such a group's responsibilities are to develop a technology from a state of indicated technical feasibility to proven technical and economic feasibility as embodied in a product, before a full product commitment is made. The task precedes actual product development. Rather, it stresses the technology and its possible use in a variety of products.

Research and Development Interactions

Communication between Research and Development is especially important in effective transfer. A useful way to aid the transfer process is to have staff from each organization move to the other. Fig. 6-2 shows how this can be accomplished. Basically, what it shows is that the extent of both Research's and Development's involvement in a technology resemble bell-shaped curves over time, and that there is overlap in the curves. Specifically, this means that Development personnel are transferred temporarily to Research somewhat before transfer, and that Research personnel are similarly transferred to Development for a time somewhat after transfer. Transfer occurs during the overlap period. At the very least, the principal investigator or project leader should transfer. There should be a means whereby some Research personnel transfer back to Research and some stay on in Development with the program. This approach assures close communication between the organizations and is probably the best way to promote smooth and effective transfers of technology. If more advanced

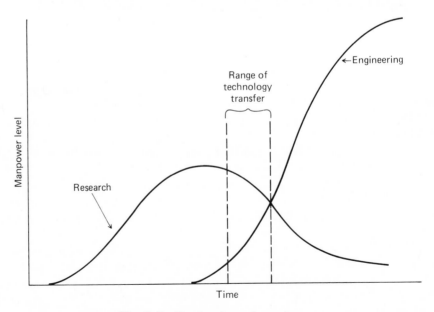

Fig. 6-2. Technology transfer.

work in a technology is needed, the transfer back to research of some staff is particularly appropriate.

Communication between Research and Development can also be improved by the free exchange of technical documents issued by the organizations, as appropriate to the transfer process.

Research and Development must agree on what constitutes technological feasibility. Feasibility usually refers to the existence of a working device, performing a function, with a demonstrated fabrication methodology. Feasibility should be demonstrated prior to transfer. Further, the organizations must agree on the timing of the transfer.

It is important to have Research plans for technology development match Development's needs for the future. Development should make its needs known to research in advance of strategic planning time, so that those needs can be considered. It is best if Development is involved in the development of those plans.

It is important that both Research and Development understand where a project to be transferred will fit in the product line of the company and what requirements must be met by it for that purpose.

Problems

Although technology transfer and the conditions for its satisfactory occurrence can be well defined, it often fails to be effected properly. Some of the problems companies have with the process are described here.

If a company's research program is not integrated into corporate-wide plans, transfer may not occur properly, because the research may not be guided by corporate objectives. The development organization may or may not be striving for the same corporate objectives.

There are biases that restrict the flow of technology developments from Research. There is a tendency, in research organizations, for managers (a) not to recognize the commercial implications in their work, (b) not to release work until all of its possible technical ramifications have been covered, and (c) to emphasize technical accomplishments over business requirements.

At the same time, there are biases that restrict the flow into Development. There is a tendency, in engineering organizations, for managers (a) to view research results as impractical because they were developed by persons who don't understand engineering problems, (b) to resist taking on research ideas which will add engineering development costs to their operations, and (c) to be averse to risk taking and to committing significant funds before technology is fully proven.

There are other barriers to technology transfer. If there is a lack of formal transfer procedures, transfer is less likely to occur since planning for it probably won't be done. If Research results are ready for transfer at a time when Development cannot address them and carry them on to development, the transfer will not occur optimally. If Development has not properly planned for the transfer, the transition process is hindered.   Finally, a company's reward system often acts as a barrier to transfer.   If it promotes a risk-averse attitude, e.g., by rewarding only success, transfer will be hindered.   There are risks in undertaking the transfer, as there are in other aspects of technology management.

6.11   AN APPROACH TO TECHNOLOGY ISSUES

We briefly describe the approach taken by a technology-based corporation to deal with the issues of technology and R & D planning.

Whirlpool Corporation

Whirlpool Corporation uses several bodies of information for the research planning process [7].   These include detailed corporate objectives from top management, detailed needs from the manufacturing engineering departments, and marketing needs expressed by the marketing department and customers.   The customers for R & D results are the manufacturing divisions.

The major factors that influence the business of the corporation are these: energy (energy-saving products), critical resources (materials, water, people), sociopolitical pressures (expectations of consumers), competition, ecology, and new science and technology.

The company has a Technology Forecasting Department which annually issues a forecast of events in technology of interest to the firm.   The report offers guidelines on the extent to which each major external factor should be addressed.

The company also has a Technical Advisory Group made up of individuals with backgrounds in engineering, science, and business.   The group's responsibilities are (a) to assess current and future science and technology, (b) to advise the company on trends, attitudes, and emphases, (c) to act as a catalyst to keep research looking ahead, and (d) to identify technical manpower skills needed for the future.

Five missions have been identified for research: current-product R & D, manufacturing-systems R & D, new opportunities, technological research, and continuing support.

The process of planning R & D comprises these steps:

1. Research department heads make proposals for research projects, indicating goals, mission addressed, and impact on external factors.

2. The urgency and expected benefits of all proposals are reviewed at an annual "client conference", attended by representatives of engineering, manufacturing, sales, customer service, international operations, and quality control.

3. Proposals are prioritized; the top ones are selected as limited by the budget. As more funds become available subsequently, other activities are selected.

SUMMARY

There are several issues of concern in technology that management must address during the planning process: the rapid change of technology, risks in technology development, technology acquisition, technology alternatives, technology assessment, forces in innovation, new technology development, technology maturity, and technology transfer.

Dealing with the rapid pace in some technology fields is a difficult problem for companies. Management must do what it can to avoid being seriously threatened by such change. It should attempt to maximize the "value added" to raw technology, put substantial R & D resources into its key technologies, and maintain an awareness of technology developments in its fields of concern.

Every R & D program carries a risk. The further along an activity moves from basic research to manufacturing, the less is its risk. The longer the time to completion of a program, the greater is its risk. Those projects that apply current technology have little risk; those that attempt to extend current technology have more risk; and those that involve developing new technology have the most risk of all.

The specific issue on technology acquisition is the matter of whether a company should develop its own technology, internally, or whether it should acquire it from the outside. The extent of the company's own experience with a technology, the estimated cost of continuing that development, and the greater privacy and exclusivity of the results must be weighed against the generally shorter time and lower cost of acquiring it outside. If the approach taken is that of internal development, top management must be kept informed about its progress, since it affects corporate objectives.

Technology alternatives represent a set of choices to management. As these alternatives evolve, top management may choose to modify corporate objectives or strategy. In any event, when objectives are being developed, the alternatives must be considered. Technology alternatives are generated in small technical groups and move upward, providing top management with technical guidance. These alternatives interact bilaterally with corporate objectives.

Technology assessments are important to companies from both the standpoint of learning how technologies may be used and the impact of outside technology development on the company. The status of technologies both inside and outside should be assessed, and the potential areas of opportunity for them should be identified. The purposes of the assessments are to decide how to acquire a technology, inside or outside, to determine which technologies to fund internally, and to decide when technologies are ready for commercialization.

Technological innovation can be considered to be driven by two opposing forces that provide a creative tension. One force is supply-induced innovation, where the R & D organizations generate inventions and developments without any particular need having been identified. The other force is demand-induced innovation, which results from factors outside R & D; a need perceived somewhere else in the company creates a demand on the technical organization.

Management may decide to undertake a new technology project when a research advance is very promising, when a need has been identified for it within the company, or when competition has made technology advances that management wishes to match.

Technology maturity underlies each of the other issues, since the state of the maturity of a particular technology will play a role in decision making on those issues. Mature technologies are those that have been utilized in products for a number of years; generally, only evolutionary changes are likely.

The issue of technology transfer, from Research to Development, is a vital step in the commercialization of technologies. It should generally take place when a technology has been shown to be technically feasible, but more important than *when* the transfer is effected is *how* it is effected. There must be certain incentives to transfer, including support of top management, well-defined objectives, an associated strategy, and proper communication between Research and Development.

REFERENCES

1. Hubert, J. M., "R & D and the Company's Requirements", *R & D Management*, October 1970, vol. 1, no. 1; also in a paper by Alan Pearson, "Planning of Research and Development", *Long Range Planning*, March 1972, vol. 5, no. 1, pp. 56–61.

2. Baillie, Alan S., "Management of Risk and Uncertainty", *Research Management*, March 1980, vol. 23, no. 2, p. 20.

3. TECHNOTEC Technology Exchange Service, Control Data Corporation, P. O. Box 0, Minneapolis, Minnesota 55440. (Technology listings reside in a computer data base and matches between buyers and sellers are performed by computer programs.)

4. TechEx – The World Fair for Technology Exchange, Dr. Dvorkovitz & Associates, P. O. Box 1748, Ormond Beach, Florida 32074. (This is an annual fair at which new technologies are displayed in an exhibition area. A technology data base is available for licensing, called *Licensable Technology*.)

5. Steele, Lowell W., *Innovation in Big Business*, American Elsevier Publishing Company, New York, 1975, Chapter 2.

6. von Hippel, Eric A., "Users as Innovators," *Innovation*, by the editors of *Technology Review*, M.I.T., Cambridge, Massachusetts, 1978.

7. Cutler, W. Gale, "Formulating the Annual Research Program at Whirlpool", *Research Management*, January 1979, vol. 22, no. 1, pp. 23–26.

Additional References

Bisio, Attilio, and Lawrence Gastwirt, *Turning Research and Development into Profits: A*

Systematic Approach, Amacom, New York, 1979. (This book discusses many aspects of R & D management. Of particular relevance here are chapters on risks and benefits of R&D and on the relationship of strategic planning to R & D; of value for Chapter 7 also.)

McPherson, Joseph H. and Dominic A. Guidici, "Advances in Innovation Management," *Business Intelligence Program*, SRI International, 1978. (This report discusses the role of innovations as the source of creative solutions to the concerns of a corporation.)

O'Dochartaigh, Aodh, "Total Technology Transfer in Transnational Corporations", No. 14 of series, Cranfield Research Papers in Marketing and Logistics, Cranfield Institute Press, 1976. (This paper deals with several types of technology transfer, including the transition from Research to Development and then to Manufacturing.)

Innovation, by the editors of *Technology Review*, M.I.T., Cambridge, Massachusetts, 1978. (This is an anthology of papers presented at a symposium on the management of innovation in December 1976. It addresses many issues in innovation and technology.)

Maidique, Modesto A., "Entrepreneurs, Champions, and Technological Inno-vation", *Sloan Management Review*, Winter 1980, vol. 21, no. 2, pp. 59–76. (This paper discusses successful innovation and the forces needed to motivate it. Entrepreneurial, managerial, and technological roles are reviewed.)

Baillie, Alan S., "Management of Risk and Uncertainty", *Research Management*, March 1980, vol. 23, no. 2, pp. 20–24. (Cited in this chapter.)

Cohen, Hirsch, Seymour Keller, and Donald Streeter, "The Transfer of Technology from Research to Development," *Research Management*, May 1979, vol. 22, no. 3, pp. 11–17. (This paper describes the problems encountered in technology transfer and proposes solutions.)

Donaldson, James R., *Trends and Applications 1976: Computer Networks*, IEEE Computer Society publication, November 17, 1976. (This paper includes a discussion of TECHNOTEC Technology Exchange Service.)

Rothwell, R., C. Freeman, V. T. P. Jervis, A. B. Roberson, and J. Townsend, "Sappho Updated – Project Sappho Phase II", *Research Policy*, 1974. (Sappho was a study designed to discover the factors leading to both successful and unsuccessful innovation.)

The May 1979 issue (vol. 23, no. 3) of *Research Management* has several articles devoted to acquiring and selling technology.

The November 1979 issue (vol. 23, no. 6) of *Research Management* is devoted to stimulating technological innovation.

7

SETTING STRATEGY

How do we get where we want to go?

INTRODUCTION

A corporation can attempt to achieve its objectives in many different ways. In selecting an optimal approach to doing so, it is subject to constraints in money, manpower, equipment, and time. Consequently, its management must make decisions on what to do and where to put its available resources. The particular approach chosen constitutes its strategy, which is formulated with those constraints as a backdrop. The strategy formulation process has two basic steps: (a) identifying feasible activities to undertake and (b) selecting those the company is able to undertake with its resources. There are numerous ways to identify the activities. These include a study of the current strategy and its provisions and a review of all the information that has been collected on the company and its environment. Particular emphasis should be placed on a company's own product line, the product lines of the competition, and the areas where there are product "vacancies", i.e., where no products exist. The "futures gap" also provides direction to strategy formulation.

There are several approaches to making a selection, including setting priorities, matching activities to corporate objectives and goals, and scoring and evaluating identified activities. Management will generally use several of these approaches for both identification and selection and include its own particular methodologies as well.

7.1 STRATEGY

What a Strategy Is

With analyses on the company and its environment completed, with objectives and goals set, and with forecasting the future and making assumptions accomplished, it then becomes necessary for management to set the strategy for the corporation. This is the heart of the planning process, since the strategy represents the plan of action for the strategic plan period. A company's strategy comprises a time schedule of activities to be carried out to achieve corporate objectives and goals, an explanation of how the activities relate to these objectives and goals, as well as strengths, weaknesses, opportunities, and threats (called the *rationale*), an allocation of resources to those activities, information on how those resources are to be used, and a way of measuring progress against the schedule. In brief, *a strategy is the method whereby corporate objectives and goals are to be attained by the allocation of resources to activities.*

In the development of a strategy, management should address such matters as the planned scope of products (which may include diversification), the markets its company is in and hopes to become active in, the nature and extent of research and development expenditures, the purchase of laboratory and manufacturing equipment, the hiring and training of new employees, manufacturing activities, sales and service, possible acquisitions, financial needs, organizational structure, and social responsibilities. In short, strategy issues encompass all the areas addressed by the self-analysis performed and possibly other areas as well.

It is useful to differentiate between two diverse but related areas of activity for which strategy must be developed. The more important area by far involves the relationship of a corporation to its environment. This area receives virtually all the attention in this book. The other area involves the internal operation of the firm and the manner of that operation. One can refer to these areas as *effectiveness* and *efficiency*, respectively.

Less-structured Strategy Setting

Strategy setting in practice is often performed in an informal, evolutionary, and largely intuitive manner. Strategy may evolve as external events, internal decisions, and managers' desires come together and yield a consensus among top management. Charles Lindblom suggests that the concept of *logical incrementalism* describes this process [1]. This concept suggests that strategy decisions do not lend themselves to use of one large decision matrix. There are simply too many internal and external variables and combinations of local decisions to address exhaustively. James Quinn has found, from his study of corporate strategy formulation, that *strategic subsystems* are used, each addressing a specific, relatively small class of issues in a structured way. These subsystems are combined into a cohesive whole that becomes the company's strategy [2].

The material in this chapter is presented with acknowledgment of the fact that strategy is most realistically developed in this manner. A series of approaches is suggested whereby strategic issues can be identified. Several methods for choosing among the activities to be selected for inclusion in a strategy are given. Managers should realize, while attempting to develop a unified strategy, that the logical-incrementalism approach described may be easier and more viable for their company than a formal and unified one. In any event, overall cohesion must eventually be sought in the process.

Steps in Strategy Setting

A strategy is developed generally by proceeding through these steps:

1. Identification of all feasible activities intended to move the company towards its objectives.
2. Selection of activities to be undertaken from among all feasible ones.
3. Allocation of resources to the selected activities.
4. Determination of how resources are to be used and over what time periods.
5. Identification of measures of progress towards objectives.

In technology-based companies, the major strategic issues relate to R & D, since all other company operations follow from them. Quinn describes the situation as follows [3]:

> No company can be pre-eminent in all technological fields. Because of limited resources, a company must expose itself to some risks and pass up some opportunities. The research strategy is to establish — in light of expected competitive action — where the company should (a) concentrate its research efforts, (b) remain "on the grapevine" (in touch) with the scientific community, or (c) virtually ignore developing technology.

In other words, of all the possible areas of research and technology development that a company could reasonably undertake, it must be selective among them and concentrate most heavily on a few and pay varying, lesser degrees of attention to the others. Making this selection is central to the strategy development process.

Approaches

Business strategies are often based on combinations of four fundamental options, as Lowell Steele points out [4]:

1. Harvesting the present businesses. Sometimes there is little or no opportunity for growth in a product's business. The strategy then can be to

generate as much profit from this nongrowth situation. The only added investments will be those to maximize future return from a business that exists by virtue of past efforts.

2. Growing the present businesses. Some products have the potential for growth by offering improvements in quality, price, and features. The strategy then can be to provide these improvements and so grow the product's business in the same market. Attempts are made to broaden that market. The business grows but its nature does not change.

3. Extending the present businesses. Sometimes existing products can be extended to associated markets and opportunities, by adding new or improved products, or by integrating vertically.

4. Creating new businesses. The strategy can be to open up new markets and businesses for the company. This is accomplished through the use of new, internal technologies or by acquisition of outside technologies or companies. New products are developed in this approach.

The growth cases, the last three options, can be illustrated by an approach described by Robert Allio and Malcolm Pennington [5]. The cases they describe are approximately the same, though there are some differences. Consider a company that has a relatively simple product—market relationship. Fig. 7-1(a) represents its product—market matrix. This is a commonly used matrix that relates the extent of product lines and markets for those products. The figure shows its base business. Three different growth strategies are shown; they modify this base case and are applied successively. *Expansion* is illustrated by Fig. 7-1(b), which shows both an extension of the product line (i.e., selling new products in existing product families) and an expansion of market share. *Augmentation* is illustrated by Fig. 7-1(c), which shows the sale of new products to existing markets and existing products to new markets. *Diversification* is illustrated by Fig. 7-1(d), which shows the selling of new products to new markets.

ConTronics Corporation's position on the four options is as follows:

1. Harvesting. The Company's present OEM product line will continue to be marketed, with improvements made in cost. These products will be phased out by 1984 or so.

2. Growing. The Company's retail product line will be significantly improved in price and will have new features added, in order to increase its business.

3. Extending to associated areas. Planned are (a) low-cost versions of the product lines, (b) miniaturized products, to expand into new, associated markets, and (c) controllers for office automation products.

4. New businesses. Plans are for new businesses, in the home electronics devices and stand-alone office electronics systems markets.

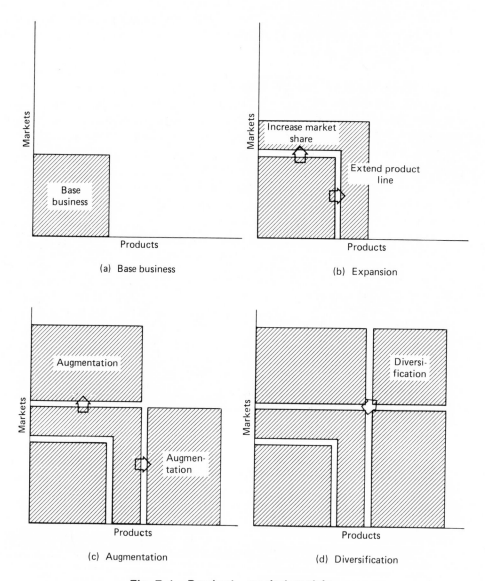

Fig. 7-1. Product – market matrix.

There is another useful classification of approaches to strategy development. It characterizes the forces that drive strategy development, as follows:

1. <u>"First to market"</u>. Here, a company decides it wants to be a technical leader in a particular market; research plays a major role in this philosophy, which involves the most risk.

2. "Catch up" or "me too". Here a company moves into a new product area because its competitors have done so and it feels it must copy the move for defensive purposes. The company generally utilizes little or no R & D activity in this approach.

3. "Have technology; must find use". Here the company has a technology for which it seeks a use. This is the supply-pushed situation.

4. "Have need; must find technology". Here a need has been identified, and the company now seeks a technology to meet it. This is the demand-induced situation.

5. "Customer defines the product". Here customers identify their own needs and actually design a "product" that a company subsequently develops and markets.

ConTronics position on these five approaches is as follows:

1. First to market. The plan is to be first in controllers and sensors.

2. Catch up. Nothing is planned here.

3. New technology. The work in new materials with interesting properties applies here.

4. Have need, find technology. This is a major driver of technology development; specifically, a need for smaller units and for new products in offices and homes has been identified.

5. Customer defines product. Nothing applies here, but this will be explored.

These sets of options and approaches are simplifications of strategy development. Nonetheless, they provide useful means for starting the formulation of a strategy by segmenting the company's businesses. They may also be useful in analyzing an already developed strategy for completeness.

Texas Instruments

It is instructive to learn how one large electronics firm undertakes its planning and manages innovation. Texas Instruments uses its Objectives, Strategies, and Tactics (OST) System, which is described by Mark Shepherd and Fred Bucy [6]. Its roles are to focus management's attention ten years out, to reserve major resources for strategic programs, to provide continuity of funding, to provide a system that utilizes all company resources, to ensure visibility and recognition of innovators, and to monitor progress towards goals. It calls for three stages in planning:

1. Objectives. Establish long-range, ten-year goals, with several intermediate points, for each major business.

2. Strategies. Focus on an intermediate set of goals relating to product lines and define directions.

3. Tactics. Identify funded action programs oriented to the realization of goals.

There are nine business objectives, over 60 strategies, and over 250 tactical action programs.

The principal characteristics of the OST System are these: (a) it is a hierarchy of goals that links current projects, product strategies, and corporate objectives and goals; (b) it is implemented by the line organizations; (c) it provides a means to gain synergy among diverse businesses.

The capstone of the OST System is the Corporate Objective, quoted in Chapter 5. Supporting it are nine business objectives, which establish the long-range scope and strategic goals for each major business of the company. Each objective includes a business charter, appraisal of market potential, projections of technical and market trends, potential barriers to success, and performance measures. (These are more than objectives, in the sense of the term used in this book. They include future projections and potential problems.)

These objectives often suggest strategies required. Strategies define the innovations in design, manufacturing, or marketing that are necessary to support the objectives. The analysis required to develop strategies suggests the tactics needed to support it. Tactical action programs establish the programs necessary to the success of the strategies. These programs cover all business activities. They set down quantitative goals in detail.

Many of the company's strategies center on a continuous improvement of their productivity, which comes primarily from innovation. They stress innovation in all aspects of company operations.

The following four-loop planning system is used by the company:

1. Long-range planning. The focus is on where the company is going over the next ten years. Quantitative goals are set, markets and products are projected, and needed technology advances are identified.

2. Intermediate-range planning. Planning is done for the next three years. Authorizations for new products, personnel additions, and capital expenditures are based on this planning.

3. "Rolling planning". This is a quarterly updating of the current and following years. This involves operating in near real time, with quick responses to changing conditions.

4. Four-month forecasting. This is a monthly activity; it constitutes the company's real-time problem detection and control mechanism.

7.2 QUESTIONS FOR STRATEGY SETTING

The strategy setting process answers three questions:

1. *What can we do and where can we go during the plan period?*

2. *What should we do and where should we go during the plan period?*

3. *What will we do and where will we go during the plan period?*

The answers to question 1 comprise the set of possible activities that can be selected as part of the company's strategy. The answers to question 2 comprise the activities that should be considered for the strategy. The answers to question 3 comprise the strategy itself. Section 7.3, *Identifying Activities*, and Section 7.4, *Selecting Activities*, deal with these questions.

The specific questions that management must ask under the broad question 1 follow directly from those given in Chapter 2. A tabulation of such questions appears in Appendix for Chapter 7.

An appropriate starting point of the question-answering process is to address the question posed early in Chapter 2, which could then be only partially addressed:

> *What are the major decisions that management must make during the plan period?*

This question sets the stage for all the subsequent questions- and issues-addressing activity that takes place.

7.3   IDENTIFYING ACTIVITIES

Activities

The first step in setting strategy is the identification of feasible activities that the company should consider undertaking. A partial tabulation of activities is given in Table 7-1. The listed activities represent new activities or changes in direction. A strategy clearly does not comprise only activities that are new or different. The list must be supplemented by a tabulation of the activities now under way in the company. Besides, any others that can be identified as potentially important should also be considered. There are several approaches that can be used to identify such activities.

Analysis of Current Strategy

Many of the questions asked in Chapter 2 can be collected and presented as one question: "What has been our strategy?" The question applies to the existing strategy, not that to be developed for the new strategic plan. This strategy is a useful starting point. We can ask these questions:

> *Which parts of our strategy are still effective?*
>
> *Which ones are still appropriate?*
>
> *Which ones must be changed and how?*
>
> *Which ones should be dropped?*

Table 7-1. Some Activities That a Company Can Undertake

Technology

* Change the R & D budget.
* Move into new areas of research and development.
* Cancel certain projects and programs.
* Shift emphasis among existing research projects and engineering programs.
* Acquire outside technologies.
* Transfer projects from Research to Development.
* Purchase new equipment and machinery.

Products and markets

* Improve existing products, by increasing speed, lowering cost, increasing reliability, adding features, etc.
* Develop new products in existing product lines.
* Develop new product lines.
* Withdraw certain products.
* Expand market share.
* Seek new or associated markets, in terms of product applications or geography.

Manufacturing

* Transfer programs from Development to Manufacturing.
* Expand existing facilities.
* Buy new equipment.
* Develop new manufacturing techniques.
* Decrease manufacturing costs.

Marketing and sales

* Undertake new or revised market studies.
* Change sales and advertising budgets.
* Change pricing structure.
* Modify distribution system.
* Add or drop geographical areas of sales.

Service

* Change procedures used for servicing.
* Change the service budget.

Table 7-1. *(continued)*

Manpower

* Hire employees with needed skills and experience.
* Improve training programs.
* Improve compensation and benefit programs.

Finances

* Acquire new capital facilities.
* Undertake new financing.
* Pay off a portion of company debt.
* Sell an unprofitable or poorly operating division.

High-technology equipment

* Develop a plan for the acquisition and integration of such equipment.
* Introduce advanced office equipment.
* Purchase new equipment for increasing worker productivity.

Organization

* Change from product-line organization to function organization, or vice versa.
* Otherwise reorganize the company.
* Change the degree of divisions' autonomy.

Management

* Change style of management.
* Hire key managers with particularly needed skills.
* Implement policy shifts regarding profits, investments, technology acquisition, etc.

The planning process

* Implement a more formal (or less formal) system of planning.
* Change the procedures used in planning.

Socioeconomic areas

* Change public positions on issues.
* Modify lobbying approach.

General

* Shift resources among company functions (R & D, Manufacturing, Sales, etc.).

These questions may not be answerable simply by an examination of the current strategy. More likely, it will be necessary for management to examine corporate strengths and weaknesses, threats and opportunities, and other factors as well.

Preplanning Analysis Report

The preplanning analysis report, developed through the information gathering and analysis process, contains a number of items that are useful in setting strategy. They include major problems, decisions, and sensitivities; company strengths and weaknesses; and opportunities and threats that are present.

Major problems, decisions, and sensitivities

What steps can and should be taken to address the identified major problems, decisions, and sensitivities of our company?

Strengths and weaknesses

How can company strengths be made even stronger?

How can company weaknesses be eliminated or diminished?

What would it cost to accomplish such improvements?

What benefits would result?

Opportunities and threats

How can our company capitalize on its strengths and take actions that minimize the effects of its weaknesses?

Answers to these questions offer guidance in developing a strategy. They direct attention to key points that should form a major part of the developed strategy. Each should evoke several responses, so that alternatives can be identified.

Critical Success Factors

One useful approach to identifying issues for management to address in strategy setting is the concept of the *critical success factor* (CSF). Robert Anthony and John Deardon use this term to refer to those areas of concern to a company in which satisfactory results will insure successful performance [7]. Some CSF's apply to all companies; these include financial actions, earnings, and return on investment. Technology-oriented CSF's are technology development, invention, creativity, competitive surveillance, and product improvement by technology advances. Management should determine the CSF's for its own company as a source of ideas for identifying activities to be undertaken.

Product Analysis

Product plans drive technology development, and an examination of a company's present and planned products offers guidelines in identification of important possibilities for technology projects. James Quinn points out that management should look at present products, foreseeable new products, and entirely new applications [8]. This categorization parallels the options described in Section 7.1.

Present products. One begins with an assessment of the technology needed to support present product lines in the years ahead. First, one predicts the company's potential market for each product line. This includes determining what technologies will keep products attractive to customers, despite competitive threats and changing needs. Present plans for technology are then compared with needed technology and any gaps are identified. If enough is known to fill these gaps, development programs can be identified to fulfill needs. If not, research investigations will be needed to support the development work. Whether or not research is needed, technology for existing products proceeds from well-identified needs to development programs.

New products. In a dynamic technological environment, present products almost certainly will not fulfill all company goals. Management should therefore try to find new market applications for its present or planned technologies and to identify any other technologies or technology advances needed to supplement these to fulfill the applications. Once again, development programs and, possibly, research activities are needed to support required technology development.

New applications. A company may require technologies beyond those for present and planned products. Its corporate objectives may not be met by those products. It may need technology that develops entirely new applications, for which new research work may have to be undertaken. Here, the planning approach is opposite to that for the two cases above. Technical management should first identify scientific areas which may provide the bases for products compatible with company objectives. Individuals in Research should be encouraged to pursue their interests, since they know the technologies best, and technical management should insure that these have relevance to company goals.

Product Niches

The families of products in a given market that all competitors collectively sell can be plotted on a two-dimensional graph. For example, we can plot the capacity of computer memory versus its access time, as in Fig. 7-2. The graph shows that there are "niches" or "holes", areas of the graph in which no products exist. We look for the places where the largest circles can be placed without encircling any plotted points; two are shown in the figure. Presumably, products inside them have a better chance of selling than others. In any event, such charts serve to define markets and to indicate how they are being addressed.

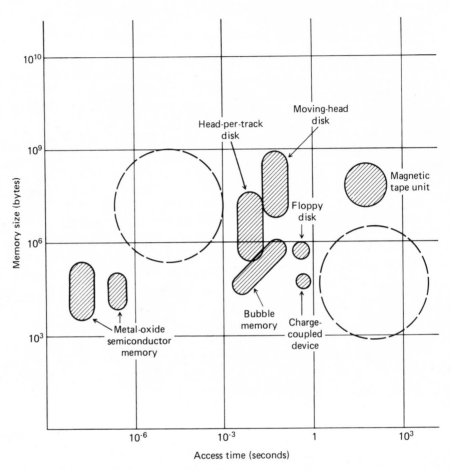

Fig. 7-2. Product niches for computer memory devices.

The Difference in the Futures

A company, at any given time, pursues a course of action whose progress and direction are determined by decisions made in the past and by forces in its environment. A company's future, as noted in Chapter 4, is determined by an examination of its status today, with due consideration of expected future external changes.

There is another, equally important future that has to be considered. That is the future that management would like to see for its company. That future is, of course, expressed in the objectives and goals it has set for the firm.

A company's strategy-setting process is in part driven by the differences between these two projected futures. An analogy can be made with a feedback control system.   In such a system, the output parameter — be it velocity, temperature, position, or something else — is compared to a predetermined value. If there is a discrepancy, a correction is applied. This is similar to what is done in strategy setting. When the company's projected future differs from that which management would like to see, a correction is necessary. The correction consists of the implementation of new decisions. The analogy is limited, however, because the strategy required in a company is much more complex than the control system, but the basic principle is the same.

The differences in the futures can be measured in the same terms as the corporate objectives. If an objective is to grow profits at 20% each year from the present value, the difference between the projected and desired profits can be expressed as a series of percentage points of profit, one value per year, by which the projected future falls short of the objective.   If an objective is the development of a new product line, the difference is the discrepancy between the specifications of the planned products and those that would result by actions of past decisions.

In general, the differences comprise a collection of information, such as financial data, product specifications, and philosophical ideas. It is not important that they form a neat, concise set of facts and ideas. The purpose in identifying them is to develop one basis for setting a strategy. This approach is termed *gap analysis*.   The gap referred to is the difference in the futures.

A disadvantage of this approach is that it relies on forecasts of future events and the expected effects of these events on the company. If there is reason to doubt the validity of the forecasts, there is reason to doubt the utility of the approach. Management should rely on gap analysis only to the extent that the forecast accuracies warrant it.

The Product Matrix

A useful device in developing strategy is the *product matrix*, which also goes by other names. It takes several forms, but basically it is a matrix showing how a company's businesses and products relate to markets in the industry. Fig. 7-3 shows a matrix that plots company business strength versus industry attractiveness; it is widely used by planners. The products of a company are placed in appropriate squares of the matrix. For example, if a product or product line is located in a "grow" square, the company should presumably increase its investment in that product line. The company can, for that product line, increase its R & D budget, increase its advertising budget, or increase its sales force. The matrix does not indicate which choice is the wisest; it is not that detailed a mechanism.   Rather, it indicates general directions for product emphasis.

The matrix is more useful if the sales or profits of products are shown on the matrix by circles of appropriate diameters. The chart is more useful yet if it includes both old and current products. Historic trends can then be illustrated.

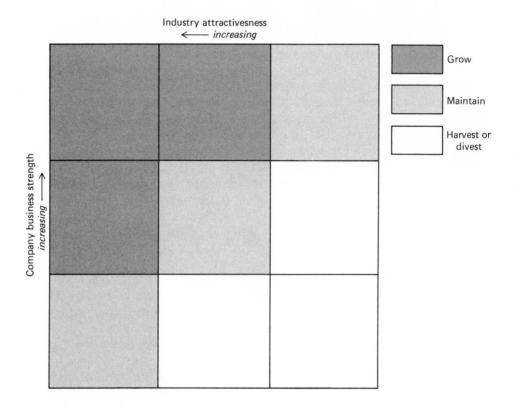

Fig. 7-3. Product matrix.

Strategic issues addressed by the use of this matrix are actually more complex than its structure suggests. There are many aspects to both business strength and industry attractiveness, and all of these should be considered. Some of the factors in business strength are technological expertise and position, marketing ability, and market share. Some of the factors in industry attractiveness are potential market size, profitability, ease of product entry, and regulatory aspects.

Another type of matrix that is used plots a company's relative market share against the growth rate of a market in which the company competes. This is depicted in Fig. 7-4; the coordinates shown are arbitrary. *Relative market share* is the ratio of the company's market share (for the product) to the share of the largest competitor (for a competing product). The location in this matrix, termed a *market share matrix,* of a company's product determines the strategic alternatives available for that product. A market leader in a fast-growing market will require large amounts of cash to achieve its growth. Strategies must protect the existing market share by price reductions, product improvements, and better market coverage. Market non-leaders require different strategies. In a fast-growing market, much cash is needed, but in a slow-growing market, R & D and other support should be cut back to maximize whatever profitability is left.

About half of the companies responding to the author's survey on strategic planning use a product matrix of some kind as an aid to strategy setting. One company adds a third dimension, indicating technologies needed for the products.

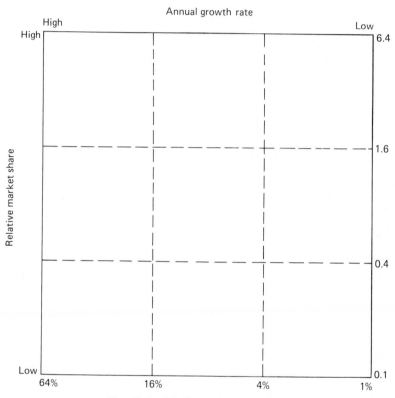

Fig. 7-4. Market share matrix.

Trade-offs

As products are developed or modified, management often has to make trade-offs among goals or product specifications. For example, assume that a management decision has been made to develop an improved version of an existing product. The decision was driven by a desire to remain competitive, not by any particular defect in the existing product. Improving product price (or manufacturing cost) and speed of operation are two approaches that management feels will meet that goal. For budgetary reasons, only one goal can be sought. The choice will depend upon (a) the relative advantages as perceived by customers and (b) the relative engineering costs of achieving the goals, when quantitatively specified.

Many other similar trade-offs always exist. Choices come down to relative benefits and relative costs. Table 7-2 gives a number of product characteristics among which trade-offs can be made.

Table 7-2. Product characteristics for trade-offs

Reliability

Cost of manufacturing

Speed of operation

Quality (by some measure)

Service cost

Size (or volume)

Cost of operation

Product features

For a particular product, the best "formula" for trading off among these parameters is usually hard to determine. It is difficult to establish benefit-to-cost ratios among them, so guesses have to be made. Further, with many parameters to be considered, the pairwise comparisons can be very numerous. It may be best to go after several parameters perceived to be most important, and analyze them. Some goals will be more expensive, relative to their benefits, than others and may have to be abandoned. In any event, strategy for product development can be based in part on such trade-off decisions.

A trade-off analysis is often performed by surveying prospective customers. There are three stages to this process. First, interviews are conducted with these customers, at which they are asked to rate several product features or characteristics in order of importance to them. Second, an analysis is done of the responses, which are weighted or ranked. Third, a determination is made of the set of features or characteristics that give the product the highest ratings. This approach is useful, though the costs of the proposed traits are ignored by it.

Less Formal Procedures

Several formal procedures for identifying possible activities have been described. There are less formal methods that may prove as valuable. For example, all managers within the company can be solicited for ideas that their experiences may suggest. In a technology-based company, technical management is often an especially fertile source. Various reports written on particular industries suggest product trends and may offer ideas of use to a company. All outside developments in a company's markets and businesses have the potential of stimulating ideas for new activities.

The Influences on Strategy

The many influences on the selection of activities for strategy-setting are illustrated in Fig. 7-5. No attempt has been made either to order these influences as they occur over time or to rank their importance.

Fig. 7-5. Influences in strategy setting.

7.4 SELECTING ACTIVITIES

At this point in the strategic planning process, management must select the activities to be undertaken to meet corporate objectives, thus formulating a strategy. This process can begin by answering question 2 in Section 7.2, which is the following:

What should we do and where should we go during the plan period?

This question can be expanded into a series of questions paralleling those given in Appendix for Chapter 7, which address all the issues discussed in early chapters. A simple substitution of the word *should* for *can* provides the necessary questions. We look at some considerations and some methods for making the selection.

The R & D Budget

Prior to the selection of any activities is the need to establish how much money will be spent on the total R & D program and how much will be spent on each of its major elements. There are several approaches to determining the total R & D budget: (a) the amount needed to fund the R & D work to realize corporate objectives; (b) the amount needed to accomplish a particular set of R & D tasks; (c) a value related to certain external trends such as competitive R & D spending or government regulations; (d) a certain percentage of revenues, profits, or other financial value; and (e) a particular rate of growth, such as 10% increase annually.

Theoretically, it should be possible to allocate "whatever is needed to realize corporate objectives", and no more or less. In practice, this cannot generally be done, because there is usually no way to determine this value. So management often falls back on the simpler methods listed, that is, methods (d) and (e). It is interesting to observe, however, that most companies claim that their R & D budgets are determined by the need for a particular amount of money, according to the author's survey on strategic planning. Such phrases as these were used by corporations: ". . . as needed to satisfy business goals;" ". . . as required to maintain leadership and market share;" and ". . . as needed to satisfy needs and to respond to opportunities, yet be affordable." A survey made many years ago, reported by Stacey and Wilson, yielded similar results; 62% of the respondents stated that an analysis of project needs determined the budget [9].

Whatever the method chosen, the amount that management decides to spend for R & D should be determined in part by the following factors:

a) Extent of the role of technology in the company's products;

b) Rate of advancement of technology in the company's fields;

c) Product market share and the extend to which management wants this to grow or to shrink; and

d) Total revenue of the company.

The allocation of R & D resources to its major elements should reflect top management's views on how corporate resources as a whole should be allocated to corporate objectives. In other words, top management's priorities for corporate objectives should be reflected in allocations for R & D elements.

Priorities for Research

A company must minimize threats to its technologies and to its product line. Selection of projects for research must first address this issue. Its management should identify technology positions that must be defended under any circumstances. These are usually its main-line technologies that have been the focus of R & D efforts over many years. Those positions should be defended by significant investments in research. To remain the leader in a particular technology field, it may be necessary for a company to have a larger research effort in that field than any of its competitors.

The next priority for research projects should be a consideration of opportunities for technology advances, based on an analysis of company strengths and weaknesses. The strategy for research must also ensure that external scientific and technology advances are not sudden, damaging surprises. Further, it must ensure that opportunities for exploitation of advances are not overlooked. It must be responsive to technological needs as perceived by customers.

Other factors in the selection of activities in a particular field include the rapidity with which technology advances occur, the anticipated amount of information yet to be discovered, and the relative pertinence of the area's knowledge to company objectives. One other consideration usually made by research management is that of "unconstrained" research, which is research that is totally science or technology driven, i.e., is supply-pushed. Most R & D organizations permit a certain portion of such research, which is driven by the technical promise inherent in the research itself. Management must decide what that portion ought to be.

Matching Objectives and Goals

Since the purpose of a strategy is to achieve corporate objectives and goals, management must look to these guides. Each proposed activity should be weighed against them, determining to what extent they are likely to help in achieving them.

In practice, it may be difficult to determine directly whether a particular activity supports a corporate objective or not. For example, does the undertaking of a particular new exploratory research activity support the corporate objective to provide a new line of electronic office products? An examination of subobjectives or divisional objectives may be needed to make the determination.

Activity Selection

There are several methods that companies use to evaluate R & D programs and other corporate activities for planning purposes. The goal for each of these methods is to optimize the use of resources in carrying out these programs and activities. *Optimization* may mean something different to different companies, so that the first task of management in this process is to decide what *optimal* means to its firm.

Generally, in order to optimize, a company utilizes its present resources and plans a program so as to maximize the probability of success by some measure. That measure might be profitability, market share, revenue growth, etc., or a combination of some of these. A technology-based company must begin its resource optimization plans around its R & D resources because of the major role that R & D plays in such companies. in other words, out of the many research projects and development programs it can choose to undertake, it must select those that collectively yield the best expected results as determined by the company's own measure of success.

The several factors that a method of optimizing activity selection has to consider are *timing, cost, benefits,* and *probability of success.*

Timing means the period of time over which the activity is carried out and the date that the product is made available to customers. For example, if a research project is at issue, the times for development, manufacturing, and distribution must all be included. The project may have exciting prospects, but if these other periods of time are excessive, it may be best to drop the project.

The *cost* of the activity is obviously important. The cost of individual phases of the activity should also be identified. Often, particularly in the case of research, total costs are hard to quantify. Total costs must be considered; these include both *one-time* costs, such as R & D, and *ongoing* costs such as manufacturing, sales, and service.

The *benefits* expected to accrue from the investment in the activity constitute the other side of the coin. Quite simply, management hopes to have a favorable ratio of costs and benefits. The *cost − benefit ratio* or an equivalent value is usually the measure. Benefits are even harder to estimate than costs, largely because the readily identifiable benefits, usually such factors as improved reliability, greater speed, and new features, are hard to evaluate quantitatively. Only the workings of the marketplace, the interaction of customers' desires, their budgets, and products can put a value on such product improvements. This occurs only long after the time when management must make project and program decisions.

The *probability of success* can only be approximated. If a development program is expected to be successful with only a 50% probability, then management may have far greater doubts in funding it than if it had been estimated to be 90% successful. Another point to note is that while expected results may have a modest probability of success (say, 50%), lesser yet still acceptable results may be more probable (say, 75%). For example, a program goal may be to operate a machine at 0.98 reliability (i.e., with the machine running 98% of its scheduled time), while expectations for 0.96 reliability may be far more likely and still be acceptable. In such a case, the estimation of probability of success becomes more complex. There is really a set of probabilities, to be jointly considered. As noted in Chapter 6, undertaking R & D activities involves risk. That is in fact true of all activities in a corporation. Thus, when various activities are considered for inclusion in the strategy, their risk and probability of success should be assessed.

In summary, each of the several factors that management must consider in selection or rejection of a candidate for a research project or a development program are difficult to quantify. Estimates of their values should nonetheless be made, with a recognition of the limitations in the procedure.

Present-Value Considerations

In quantifying the expected value of particular technology advancements and products, it is important to consider the *present value* of such benefits, which is the value in the future translated back to today's dollars, with the time value of money taken into account. This accounts for the fact that a dollar is worth more today than it will in the future, since it may be invested and yield a return. (Inflation adds to the shrinkage of money's value.) Present value is determined by estimating the benefits at future dates and then projecting these values backward in time. As an example, $1000 invested today at 15% interest per year would be worth $1150 in one year and $2010 in five years. Consequently, a benefit having a value of $2010 in five years should only be sought if its cost is no more than $1000 today. In actuality, the cost (here, $1000) would be spread over several years, so the calculations are more complex. Such calculations should be carried out wherever possible in making current decisions on investments in R & D.

Recent Decisions

Management should also look at decisions made in the recent past on selected activities and determine whether each is still valid for the future. Such decisions have brought the company to its present state, so an examination of that state (as identified in the self-analysis) is a logical place to begin. Management should determine which current activities should remain ongoing, which should be halted, and which should be modified in some way. The decisions that led to these should then be examined, to see why they were made and to determine if they still apply. It is probably not possible, nor is it necessary, that final conclusions be reached about all such decisions; that is not important at this stage. The effect of this thorough analysis is to start from scratch, to do "zero-base planning", wherein every past assumption and decision is questioned anew and strategy setting starts with a clean slate. Decisions on every major aspect of the company's operations are reviewed.

Business Factors

There are many business factors that companies consider in selecting their strategies. The most prominent of these are the following:

Company's competitive position or market share

Revenue growth rate of the market

Market opportunity or attractiveness

Industry maturity

Potential profitability in the product line

Potential for improved performance in market

Outlook for the business (or product line)

Market growth possibilities

Specific Methods

Much has been written on methods for selecting activities for a strategy from a portfolio of possible activities. The methods range from simple scoring systems to elaborate statistical analyses. We briefly review three simple approaches and one computer-based approach.

Th. Bemelmans describes a method for evaluating research projects, so that some can be selected for a strategy [10]. He indicates that there are two parts to the evaluation. First is a technical evaluation, comprising these steps: (a) making an inventory of all relevant technologies, (b) identifying technology parameters, so that the state of the art of each technology can be described, and (c) identifying technical bottlenecks by comparing values wanted and actual values of the technological parameters. In (c), the larger the discrepancy, the greater the technology development required. Second is an economic evaluation with these steps: (a) selecting criteria, (b) doing a cost–benefit analysis, and (c) determining economic bottlenecks. He uses a scoring model that can be applied to project evaluation. The model is given in Table 7-3; dollar amounts would be adjusted to individual situations. To determine the score for a project, the individual scores are added. There is no explicit reference to benefits, but the item "strategic need" is close. For example, if the project is essential to current markets (with a score of 3), then it follows that expected benefits are high. The item "net revenues" also relates to benefits.

Table 7-3. A Scoring Schedule for Projects

Evaluation	Possible answer	Score
Probability of success	Unforeseeable	1
	Fair	2
	High	3
Time to completion	Greater than 3 years	1
	1 – 3 years	2
	Less than 1 year	3
Total research costs	Greater than $1,000,000	1
	$100,000 – $1,000,000	2
	Less than $100,000	3
Strategic need	No apparent market	1
	Desirable for market position	2
	Essential for market position	3
Net revenues	Less than $1,000,000 per year	1
	$1,000,000 – $10,000,000 per year	2
	Greater than $10,000,000 per year	3

Another method for selecting successful R & D programs is described by Bruce Merrifield [11]. He defines six *business attractiveness* factors: sales/profit potential, growth rate, competitor analysis, risk distribution, industry restructure opportunities, and special factors. These address the question: "Is this a good business for *anyone* to be in?" He also defines six *company strength* factors: capital needs availability, in-house marketing capability, in-house manufacturing capability, strength of the technology base, raw materials availability, and management and other skills. These address the question: "Is this a good business for *us* to be in?" Each of the 12 factors is scored from 0 to 10, and the scores are added. Merrifield states that if a program scores less than 70 points, it is very unlikely to be successful. If it scores over 80 points, it is very likely to be successful. The method clearly addresses many aspects of a company's environment and of the company itself.

It is possible in principle to derive a formula that utilizes the factors discussed earlier for optimization:

$$\text{desirability index} = \frac{\text{benefits (if successful)} \times \text{probability of success}}{\text{cost} \times \text{timing}}$$

Numerical values attached to the factors going into this index have no intrinsic significance; they only have meaning in relation to one another.

A quite different approach to strategy development is provided by the Strategic Planning Institute (SPI) of Cambridge, Massachusetts. The Institute, a nonprofit membership organization, has developed a program called "Profit Impact of Marketing Strategies" (PIMS). The goal of PIMS is to provide insight and information on expected corporate performance, by industry and under specific conditions [12]. Questions such as the following are answered: "If the company continues on its present course, what are its future operating results likely to be?" "What changes of strategy promise to improve these results?"

Some of the noteworthy findings by PIMS are these:

1. Business situations — competitive interactions among buyers and sellers in a given market — generally behave in a regular and predictable manner.

2. The laws of the marketplace determine about 80% of the observed variance in operating results across different businesses.

3. The generally more profitable businesses are those that

   a) Are not mechanized, automated, or inventory-intensive;
   b) Produce higher value added per employee;
   c) Have large shares of their markets;
   d) Have products in growth markets;
   e) Have products judged to be of high quality by customers;
   f) Are heavily involved in product innovation and differentiation;
   g) Are vertically integrated in stable markets and are not vertically integrated in growing markets.

SPI offers information to member clients only. These companies contribute data on their businesses, such as their key decisions, characteristics of their environments, their manner of operation, their strategy, and their operating results. SPI has developed a model to predict return on investment (ROI). It issues a computer-generated report that specifies the ROI that is "normal" for a corporation, given the choices of its markets, its competition, its technology, and its manner of operation. This report is useful in helping a firm forecast its profits under particular and varying conditions.

Comments on Methods

Care should be taken with scoring methods for project selection, such as those described. Though they force a consideration of quantitative values on project and program evaluation and provide an easy measure of worth, they may imply a precision that is higher than the one that truly exists. While the dependence of certain parameters on others may be readily identifiable, the precise relationships among them may not be. For example, it is obvious that the sales volume of a magnetic tape deck will increase as its purchase price drops, all other things being equal, but the precise volume as a function of price is usually unknown. The actual volume for a particular proposed price is, of course, also unknown.

It is important that the algorithm management uses for scoring and evaluation of activities be flexible and represent rules that are reasonable for the company to use. The precision of the process and its manner of use must be acceptable to management with respect to the way it manages the firm.

Despite the limitation of quantitative selection methods, they serve a useful purpose. They allow managers to organize and clarify relationships among parameters and to understand which are most important. The methods undoubtedly improve the selection process; they are not guaranteed to make it precise.

The Selection Process

Management next reviews the activities to select the ones it will adapt in its strategy. In making the selection, one of the scoring methods described may be of value; other methods may be more appropriate in particular situations. In reviewing the activities, management may wish to give special consideration to certain of them, for any of a variety of reasons. Management's goal is to select a set of activities that both fully and optimally utilizes all resources available during the plan period. As the selection is made, the fiscal constraints of a budget must be considered. The formulation of strategy and the development of a budget, at least at a gross level, cannot be done independently of one another.

A strategy should not be based upon the corporation's organizational structure as it currently exists. The structure often acts as a barrier to the identification and pursuit of new initiatives. The structure reflects the firm's product lines as of today, which may be different from those of the future. It should be assumed, in planning, that the organizational structure is fluid and will be made to fit the strategy for the future.

Activities to be Canceled

Decisions to drop activities under way are part of the strategy formulation process. Some may be dropped prior to the plan period; others may be canceled sometime during the plan period, and management should include decisions to do so in the plan. The conditions that would lead to making such decisions should be specified.

There can be several reasons why R & D programs should be canceled; they include the following:

a) <u>The program fails for technological reasons.</u> The technology may not provide the technical capabilities sought or needed for product programs. For example, a particular desired level of reliability or a planned reduction in size by a factor of ten may not be possible technically.

b) <u>The technology or the product using it is too expensive.</u> The planned product may cost too much for market feasibility. The technology may fail to meet specifications at an affordable cost or the capabilities sought may come at too high a price to be competitive.

c) <u>The program is too costly.</u> The development cost for the product may be too expensive for the company to recoup over the lifetime of the product.

d) <u>Competitive technology moves too rapidly.</u> The pace of the company's technology advances may be too slow, compared to outside developments. The result is that by the time the company offers the product, there is too much competition.

e) <u>There is a re-prioritization of product plans.</u> The company may, for any of a number of reasons, shift priorities among its product plans. As a result, some R & D programs may no longer be as important as others under way or to be instituted. They may have to be dropped even though they were not inherently inadequate.

It should be noted that, although reasons are given here for canceling programs, an alternative in many cases is to cut them back partially, keeping the activity going at a slower pace.

R. Balachandra and Joseph Raelin have developed a model to identify R & D programs that should be dropped [13]. They point out that there is relatively little research in the area of project-termination analysis.

ConTronics Corporation prepared the following material for their strategic plan strategy: (a) decisions for R & D and for the Company's businesses, (b) a tabulation of the activities selected for the strategy, and (c) the projections for future revenues and profits and the budget for the 1982–1986 strategic plan period. This material follows below. Reasons for the decisions made are included, and these reasons also support the choice of activities selected. Several contingency plans are included as well.

Decisions on R & D

ConTronics management decided to increase the R & D budget significantly in the future, compared to the current plan. The annual year-to-year rise in the early years (1982–1984) will be very large, tripling the current value (for 1981) by 1984. Management's reason for doing so is to strengthen technology development in the face of greater competition than was previously expected. The materials research efforts, holding more promise than a year ago, will be increased well beyond the current plans. This is also true of materials development in the later years of the plan.

The level of risk varies among the R & D programs. In research, the materials work has very high risk and is expensive, but it has a very high potential payoff. Management feels it must accept this risk because of the possible very positive impact on future products. The other research activities, software development and automated circuit design, have medium risk and less projected cost, but the payoff is not as high as for the materials activity. The work is, however, very important for extending the product line and improving existing products.

The development work on product improvements, adding new features, and developing new products at the low end of the markets all involve less risk than do the research activities. Of these activities, management rates risk as follows: product improvement, low; adding new features, low to medium; and developing new products, medium to high.

Decisions on Businesses

With respect to its businesses, the Company plans to do the following:

* Remain in the OEM business, supplying electronic controllers to manufacturers for a variety of applications. In so remaining, (a) extend the product line downward, to less expensive models, and (b) develop improvements in current products, including improved reliability, lower cost, smaller size, etc.

* Remain in and grow the retail business, selling electronic controllers through retail outlets. In so remaining, undertake the two approaches for the OEM business and, in addition, add new features to all models.

* Expand into new markets closely allied to present ones, considering the home electronics market in particular. Develop plans for defining products in these markets.

* Expand in new markets, considering the small, stand-alone office electronics product area, such as electronic message systems for telephones. Develop plans for defining products in these markets.

* Undertake actions to improve engineering and manufacturing productivity, where the benefits are very high compared to costs.

Specific Actions to be Undertaken

The budgeting actions below were taken with due consideration of available funds.   Top management set the total R & D budget.

Research and Development

* Increase the R & D budget from its 1981 level of $1,700,000 to $9,600,000 for 1986.   Increase the budget more rapidly in the early years.   This is viewed as essential, if the plans for the new materials and other basic technologies are to be realized.

* Increase greatly the funds for materials research reaching a peak of $500,000 in 1984.   This is the first technology identified as broadly applicable across product lines.   Much research work remains to be done on materials.   Because of the high risk involved in this work, plans must be reviewed periodically very carefully.   A semiannual review will be held, and funding will be adjusted up or down accordingly.

* Increase somewhat the funds for the other projects to high levels of $200,000 each in the middle years of the plan period.   Key breakthroughs in the software and circuit design activities are still needed.

* Include greater resources for projects yet unidentified: $400,000 in 1985 and $800,000 for 1986.   Prior to those years, new research work is expected to be identified.   These items are included because of uncertainties in the budget in later years of the plan period.

* Keep the budget for current product improvement development at $300,000 for two years, and then phase it out, as the current products are replaced by newer ones.

* Gradually increase the budget for new features development from $300,000 in 1982 to $500,000 in 1986, supporting the evergrowing product base.

* Development costs for the new products (Model 110 and System N4) are to be set high in the early part of the plan ($1,500,000 in 1982) and fall off rapidly by 1984 to a low level.   A great deal of engineering is necessary in those years if these products are to reach the marketplace when planned.

* Develop detailed plans for home electronics controllers, for office products controllers, and for office systems.   These plans should be completed by mid-1983.   These products represent the bulk of the Company's future revenues; all are new businesses.   Plans in all areas must be completed in a short period, so that R & D work can progress.

* Begin development work in these new development programs:
  * Miniaturized products, in 1983
  * New materials technology, in 1983

- Home electronics controllers, in 1983
- Office products controllers, in 1984
- Office systems, in 1985

All of these programs are to be funded at $300,000 to $400,000 in their first year and are to reach spending levels of $1,200,000 to $1,800,000 two to four years later. Funding five new product programs over a three-year period is a major undertaking for the Company. This approach will be carefully reviewed in late 1983, and there is a good chance that only three of the five will actually be undertaken in a serious manner from 1984 on. Very significant R & D investments are required for these new products.

* Study the feasibility of a central group to develop certain technologies for general use across product lines. Budget a modest amount ($100,000) for this activity in 1983 and increase it gradually over the plan period. If the concept proves feasible, increase its funding according to its projected success and cut back on specific product programs.

Other Activities

* Increase staffing and budget for competitive analysis, market studies, and technology forecasting. These activities must all be strengthened to meet greater competitive threats.

* Plan, design, and construct new physical facilities for staffing and manufacturing. Space is already insufficient, and much growth is planned.

* Study automatic drafting machine and automatic manufacturing systems and, if economically feasible, acquire one or both of these.

* Acquire Popeye Manufacturing Company and the circuit design and fabrication system of Auto-Electronics. Studies indicate that these investments are cost-effective.

7.5 SPECIALIZED TYPES OF PLANNING

Several specialized planning activities are practiced by corporations. These are described here.

Business Planning

Business planning addresses the businesses that a company is in or plans to be in. The term *strategic business unit* (SBU) is used to identify organizations within a corporation that address specific business markets of interest to the company. Examples of such markets are those for small appliances, desktop copiers, and video recorders. The concept best applies to corporations that are organized along product lines. SBU performance must be measurable in profit and loss.

Business planning addresses business areas rather than products and is an activity that precedes product planning, discussed below, if indeed a company undertakes both types of planning. A small company is more likely to address product planning and ignore business planning, since it has relatively few products and is less likely to think in terms of areas of business. If a company is considering significant diversification, then it would be well advised to think of business areas that it can address. As noted in Chapter 5, a corporation should probably consider itself as being in certain businesses rather than making products.

Business planning is in actuality a part of strategic planning which addresses the markets that a company is in or intends to be in. We have identified questions on products and markets; these are addressed in this arena of planning. The outcome of this task is the identification of SBU's, against which technology planning and product concepts can be matched.

The SBU concept recognizes the existence of two distinct levels of strategy: a strategy that affects the status and direction of the corporation as a whole, and business-unit strategies that each affect only specific SBU's. As management develops its strategy, it may be necessary to address each unit by itself, since planning horizons, types of products, nature of markets and customers, and other factors may vary widely among the units. If that is the case, the concepts of strategy development described in this chapter must be applied to each strategic business unit in turn.

There are limitations to the SBU approach to planning; it is not universally applicable. Sometimes, a company cannot be divided into strategic business units, as when it is organized by function or is vertically integrated. Sometimes, a strategy may require the sharing of several units' resources to meet an objective, and separate strategies would be inappropriate. As noted, the organizational structure of a company is a factor in the usefulness of SBU's.

An example of a company that uses the planning unit approach is Monsanto Company, as described by Ralph Neubert [14]. It uses the term *strategic planning unit* (SPU). SPU's are units of the corporation for which discrete strategies can be written and which warrant visibility at the corporate level. Some SPU's cover single products; others address entire divisions. Considerable effort goes into properly identifying these units, which are key elements of corporate strategy. Monsanto uses about 50 SPU's to describe the company.

A *business direction paper* on each SPU is prepared. It covers these points: position of the company in the business, the position the company can realistically expect to achieve in the future, a course of action recommended to achieve this position, and a means of measurement of progress. These papers represent the principal tool used for developing strategies for the units. A consensus between corporate management and operational management is achieved via this document.

Planning begins with corporate objectives; Monsanto's three major corporate objectives were given in Chapter 5. These lead to the business direction papers for the SPU's. The next stage of planning calls for the preparation of summary long-term plans, which provide estimates of the costs and consequences of implementing the approved business direction papers. They answer the question, "Where are we going in the future environment?" Finally, operational plans and annual budgets are prepared.

Product Planning

A related and equally important type of planning for a corporation is *product planning*. This is an activity wherein products to be offered by the company in the future are defined; i.e., these products are given specifications. Generally, major functions for products are defined, with some identified as "necessary", others as "highly desirable", and still others as "nice to have". The manufacturing costs or sales prices are specified, usually in today's dollars. Certain goals in cost, speed, quality, efficiency, and reliability are among those usually stated. In addition, the dates when the products are to become available in the marketplace are probably identified as a way of defining objectives quantitatively.

Product planners draw upon the following information to make decisions on what product specifications should be and when the products should be introduced: (a) corporate objectives and goals that relate to the businesses the company is in and plans to be in; (b) studies that identify what customers want and/or need; (c) studies that identify markets as to nature and size; (d) analyses and forecasts of technologies, both within and outside the company; (e) assessments of corporate resources available for manufacturing products; and (f) estimates of the costs of manufacturing certain products and of the probabilities of success (i.e., meeting product specifications in the given time period).

It is important for Product Planning to interact with Research and Development in the definition of product goals and specifications. Such interaction is essential with respect to Development, since that organization will be aiming for these goals and specifications. However, such interaction with Research is also important, although the time frame is different; research work is generally aimed further into the future.

The activity of product planning parallels the activity of setting a strategy in that much information must be gathered, analyzed, and certain choices out of the many possible must be made on some rational basis. Product planning is, in one sense, an outcome of strategy setting, in that by selection of a set of activities to be undertaken, a company defines the products it plans to design and build. One can, however, look at this from the opposite point of view. Management can define products and, from those specifications, develop a strategy for developing those products.

The distinction between business planning and product planning is important. Product planning yields the specifications for actual end products, the ultimate goal of the company. It centers about specific products and families of such products. Business planning focuses on businesses, which are really markets. It does not address specific products. Once the businesses that a company wishes to be active in are defined, product planning can be used to define the products in each of those businesses.

Frederick Gluck, Stephen Kaufman, and Steven Walleck describe five distinct planning levels for a corporation [15]. The levels are the following:

1. Product and market planning. This is the lowest level of planning, where products, prices, and services are planned.

2. Business-unit planning. Most planning efforts occur here The largely self-contained businesses control their own market position and cost structure.

3. Shared-resource planning. Sometimes, several business units share resources for various reasons Strategy is developed for these groupings.

4. Shared-concern planning. Sometimes, strategies must be developed to meet the unique needs of certain industry or geographic customer groups or to plan for technologies used by a number of business units.

5. Corporate-level planning. This planning covers identification of worldwide technical and market trends, setting corporate objectives, and allocating resources to meet these objectives.

Resource Planning

The many different types of resources that a corporation must address in planning were reviewed in Chapter 2. These include technology, markets and products, manufacturing, raw materials and supplies, manpower, facilities, and finances. Resource planning addresses each of these, and terms such as *technology planning, manpower planning, market planning, product planning, financial planning*, etc., are in common use. Although many authors spell these out individually as separate tasks, the generalized planning approach described here encompasses them all. Taken as a whole, the several types of resource planning address several key questions, which are the following:

What is needed?

What are the various ways of obtaining it?

What is the cost?

How long will it take to obtain it, once ordered?

This view of planning has the advantage that activities involving resources are brought together.

Project Planning

The term *project planning* refers to planning at a project or program level, the lowest organizational level that lends itself to strategic planning. The scope of such planning is very limited. This planning proceeds as has been described for divisional planning, and so it need not be singled out as particularly distinct. Coordination with allied organizations is usually critical.   For example, if a research project is at issue, coordination with the development organization is important.

7.6 *CONTINGENCY PLANNING*

Some of the assumptions made at the start of the planning process may turn out to be invalid or seriously under- or overestimated. If this is discovered after the plan is in use, replanning may be required. The extent to which this is done will depend upon the extent to which the assumptions prove invalid. If they are greatly in error, management may have to take action and replan some portion of the strategy. The expected impact of the change in the projected future and the extent of replanning must be determined.

In order to allow for the possibility that replanning may be needed prior to the next planning cycle, *contingency planning* should be undertaken. This is planning that yields a set of alternatives to the decisions made for the strategic plan, to allow for assumptions that turn out to be wrong. The alternatives are different strategies, or portions of strategies, to be called upon if required.

If events and trends turn out differently than projected, a strategic plan may not lead to desired results, unless it is redone. As an example, the price of a raw material may have been projected to grow at 8% per year but instead grew at 18%. This might mean that the manufacturing cost of a product planned for 1983 might have to be raised from $650 to $750, resulting in a correspondingly higher sale price. This could have a serious effect on the sales volume of that product in a very competitive market.

A company must, in its strategic plan, allow for the possibility that its projections and assumptions may be wrong. The best approach is to determine the deviation that can be tolerated and then to decide what to do if it went beyond that point. For example, management might decide that a deviation of up to 15% either way from an expected trend line is acceptable. Any change beyond that would call for a strategy change. The alternative plans for such cases are the *contingency plans* associated with that factor.

Contingency plans should not be as extensive as the basic plans.   The decisions and activities that would be modified in replanning should be identified with some quantification. Details can be omitted. For example, management might state that if *Event X* took place in 1982 instead of 1984 as expected, the research budget for *Project Y* for next year should be raised from $2,500,000 to the $4,000,000 – $5,000,000 range.

Another, very useful approach in contingency planning is to ask these "What if . . . ?" questions: "What if the assumption is wrong?"   "What if some unexpected event occurs?" "What if an expected event occurs two years earlier than thought?" Management can pose many such questions and then develop contingency plans, identifying what must be replanned if the answers to these questions are "Yes".

Despite the strong presence of uncertainty, particularly in the later years of a strategic plan, budgets and plans are generally written to imply no uncertainty. Management is more comfortable with this approach, but there is a weakness in it, for it implies certainty. On the other hand, there may be little harm in it, since plans are usually reviewed and rewritten annually, and adjustments can be made as uncertainty for a particular calendar year diminishes over time.

To the extent that it is feasible, uncertainty should be incorporated into the strategy formulation and budgeting process. When done, this highlights uncertainty for future reference, so that management's attention can be focused on it later, particularly during the next planning cycle. Management can seek out information needed to resolve the uncertainty and make decisions where possible.

Uncertainty can be incorporated into a strategy as follows: (a) by developing contingency plans; (b) by developing an interim strategy or a strategy with interim portions, to be followed until enough is known to reduce the uncertainty; and (c) by developing a strategy which uses a decision-tree approach that shows alternative paths to be taken, pending the outcome of certain alternative events. This latter approach is useful when the alternatives are close to being equal in probability, so that selecting one path over another has a fair chance of being the wrong decision. Probabilities of the alternatives should be included. In Chapter 8, *Writing and Using the Plan*, the way in which these approaches are incorporated in the budget process is discussed.

7.7 REVIEW OF THE STRATEGY

It is very important to review the strategy that was developed. This should be done before the plan is implemented. As a starting point for technology-based companies, top management should take an objective overall look at the set of R & D programs selected. It should be certain that the proper emphasis is given to each of the following points, identified by James Quinn, so that an appropriate balance of resources among them is achieved [16]:

* <u>Phases of effort</u>: whether there is the proper balance among research (fundamental, applied, and developmental) and development.

* <u>Scientific areas</u>: whether all scientific areas presenting major long-range scientific threats or opportunities are included.

* <u>Offensive versus defensive R & D</u>: whether there is enough growth activity and maintenance of present businesses.

* <u>Product lines supported</u>: whether each present and potential product line is getting sufficient technical support.

*   <u>Support for operating divisions</u>:   whether each division's needs receive adequate technical attention.

*   <u>Types of results sought</u>:   whether goals are supported properly by various types of technology activity.

Quinn's entries in this list have been modified to extend them to development as well as research activities.

There is no precise method to determine the proper balance of technical resources for a given company. What is right for one may be wrong for another. The proper balance for a company depends on its goals, strategies, capacities, and its management style. Moreover, a selected balance cannot be considered inflexible. If certain programs show important results, they should be emphasized. Others may become less attractive and should be diminished. The result is constant dynamic balancing; one sure sign of weakness is a static balance of emphasis over time.

Top management must ensure that R & D program selection is adequately tested against company objectives and that all relevant business considerations are weighed in selection decisions. The considerations should include marketing, production, finance, legal, personnel, and management factors. These are business considerations, and management must subject projects to several tests. Technical management must test each project in terms of its technical merit, its fit with company goals, and its economic potential. As technologies move closer to product commercialization, their business implications must be increasingly examined.

General questions about the proposed strategy should next be asked, as follows:

1. *Does it address all corporate objectives?*

2. *Does it address each of the major problems identified at the start?*

3. *Does it address each of the identified strengths and weaknesses of the corporation?*

4. *Does it address each of the identified opportunities for and the threats to the corporation?*

5. *Does it fully address the projected future of the company and its environment?*

6. *Does it take into account the key influences in the industry or industries addressed?*

7. *Does it address all areas of concern discussed in the preplanning analysis report?*

8. *Are the levels of risk and the schedule in the strategy acceptable?*

9. *Does it call for utilization of all the available resources? Or, rather, does it omit some resources or call for more resources than are available?*

10. *Is it self-consistent with regard to its major provisions?*

If the selected activities yield any unsatisfactory answers to the questions above, the selection process must be repeated, probably with some previously chosen activities rejected and others selected. The procedure is repeated until all the questions have been satisfactorily answered.

7.8 · STRATEGY FOR DIVISIONS

As the corporation's strategy is being developed, it is necessary for management to develop strategies for each of the divisions. Divisional strategies are strongly tied to corporate strategies, just as divisional objectives are tied to corporate objectives. But the parallel between strategies and objectives is not total, because divisional strategies may evolve somewhat at the same time as corporate strategies, or even before them, whereas divisional objectives are usually developed after corporate objectives.

An alternate approach is for management to set corporate strategy first and then to derive divisional strategies from them. In doing so, management essentially divides up the set of selected activities among the divisions.

In truth, neither approach is as straightforward as it sounds. First, it should be noted that each division's strategy must match its objectives as well as its own resource constraints. Second, some activities identified at the corporate level will be carried out jointly by two or more divisions. Third, the steps of developing both corporate and divisional strategies are probably best handled somewhat simultaneously, with more emphasis on the bottom-up approach.

The methodology for doing divisional strategy depends to a large extent on whether the company is organized by product line or by function. In product-line structures, the approach is essentially the same as for the corporation as a whole, which consists of executing, for each product-line division, the steps described in this chapter. Once that is done, all divisional strategies are coordinated by top management and the planning staff into a coherent strategy for the corporation.

If a company is functionally organized, the top-down approach, where corporate strategy leads to divisional strategies, usually is the better method. An activity that is defined at corporate level may have to be shared among functional divisions and so become part of several divisional strategies. Personnel functions, capital improvement planning, and R & D are examples of activities often centralized at the corporate level.

7.9   THE SCHEDULE

The task of identifying feasible activities for a strategy can begin even before corporate and divisional objectives and goals have been completed. It is wise to start them early. Actual strategy formulation, i.e., selection of activities to be undertaken, must follow objectives and goals setting, but they can overlap the identification process.   The development of divisional strategy is likely to start ahead of corporate strategy formulation, in a tentative way, but it must be completed subsequently.   All strategy setting activities take place in the second quarter of the year.   A schedule is given in Fig. 7-6.

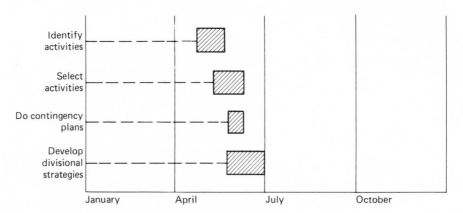

Fig. 7-6. A schedule for setting strategy.

7.10 PROBLEMS IN STRATEGY SETTING

The activity selection process is the key to strategy setting, yet doing it optimally is a very difficult job.   Selection methods have been discussed, and their limitations have been noted.   Because of these limitations, the methods can only provide approximate rating systems.   Some of them are time-consuming to use, and often management can do as well with much less effort.   However the selection of activities may be undertaken, it remains a difficult yet crucial task in strategy development.

There is a tendency, among managers, to avoid investing in high-risk ventures.   While a certain amount of prudence in this regard is commendable, caution is often excessive.   The most significant advances often result from investments in R & D for high-risk technology development.   Management must guard against this kind of thinking which can often lead to cutting one's options too sharply and losing out on important opportunities.   Some part of a company's strategy should be of high risk.

Another problem in setting strategy is that too often there is little encouragement of imaginative thinking; sometimes managers have too much inertia to do such thinking.   The result is a strategy too heavily dominated by existing conditions, current products, present organizational structure, and the like.

SUMMARY

The strategy in a strategic plan is the means whereby corporate objectives and goals are to be attained. The development of strategy involves these steps: (a) identification of all feasible activities for a strategy, (b) selection of activities to be undertaken, (c) allocation of resources, (d) determination of how resources are to be used, and (e) identification of measures of progress toward objectives.

Strategies are based on combinations of the options of harvesting, growing, extending present businesses, and creating new businesses. Strategies are driven by different forces; among them are: "First to market", "Catch up" or "Me too", "Have technology; must find use", "Have need; must find technology", and "Customer defines the product". Strategy development addresses two key questions: "What can we do?" and "What should we do?" The process is completed when the question "What will we do?" is answered.

The task of identifying possible activities can be approached from several points of view, all of which should be considered. First, management can analyze the current strategy, determining what is still applicable. Second, it can study the preplanning analysis report, which identifies major issues, strengths, weaknesses, opportunities, and threats. Third, it can analyze current, planned, and possible new products. Fourth, it can look for product niches in the marketplace. Fifth, it can do gap analysis, which studies the difference between the desired future of the company and the future that is projected from the current situation. Sixth, management can study product matrices, which show the relationships between a company's businesses and its products. Finally, a consideration of trade-offs among product goals provides a useful point of view. There are also informal methods for gathering data.

The task of selecting activities follows their identification. Again, there are several approaches. An initial consideration is the setting of the R & D budget, i.e., determining how much money will be allocated to it over the plan period. Priorities for research can be identified. An attempt to select activities to match corporate objectives and goals should be made. Management should also attempt to optimize the use of resources, considering activity timing, cost, benefits, and probability of success. Then, recent decisions that have been made should be reviewed for current and future validity.

There are several scoring methods for evaluating R & D programs. The goal of these approaches is to yield an optimal selection of programs for the company's strategy. A "desirability index" can be calculated. Because it is hard to quantify most factors involved, the process can only be approximate at best.

Management must also determine which activities, if any, should be dropped.

There are several specialized types of planning, including business planning, product planning, resource planning, and project planning. They are useful tasks for focusing attention, but a generalized approach to strategic planning encompasses them all.

Contingency planning, allowing for deviations from any assumptions that management initially made, must be undertaken. A company must allow for the possibility that its projections into the future are wrong. A useful way to consider contingency planning is to ask questions that begin with "What if . . . ?"

It is important to evaluate the selection process by asking questions about the set of activities selected for the strategy. Questions should be asked about objectives, major problems, resources, strengths and weaknesses, and opportunities and threats. These questions are about consistency, the addressing of objectives and the futures gap, the use of resources, and the limitations of company divisions.

Strategy setting for divisions generally follows that for corporations; both bottom-up and top-down approaches have their merits in this task.

REFERENCES

1. Lindblom, Charles, "The Science of Muddling Through", *Public Administrative Review*, Spring 1959.

2. Quinn, James Brian, "Strategic Change: Logical Incrementalism", *Sloan Management Review*, Fall 1978, vol. 20, no. 1, pp. 7–19.

3. Quinn, James Brian, "Long-Range Planning of Industrial Research", *Harvard Business Review*, July/August 1961, vol. 39, no. 4, p. 94.

4. Steele, Lowell W., *Innovation in Big Business*, Elsevier North Holland, Inc., New York, 1975, Chapter 6.

5. Allio, Robert J., and Malcolm W. Pennington, *Corporate Planning*, Amacom, New York, 1979, pp. 12–14.

6. Shepherd, Mark, Jr., and J. Fred Bucy, "Innovation at Texas Instruments", *Computer*, IEEE Computer Society, September 1979, vol. 12, no. 9, pp. 82–90.

7. Anthony, Robert N., and John Deardon, *Management Control Systems*, Richard D. Irwin, Inc., Homewood, Illinois, 1976.

8. Quinn, James Brian, *op cit*, pp. 97–98.

9. Stacey, N. A., and A. Wilson, *Industrial Marketing Research: Management and Techniques*, Clowes, London, 1963.

10. Bemelmans, Th., "Strategic Planning for Research and Development", *Long Range Planning*, April 1979, vol. 12, no. 4, pp. 33–44. (This paper also provides formulas for evaluating development programs.)

11. Merrifield, D. Bruce, "How to Select Successful R & D Projects", *Management Review*, December 1978, vol. 67, no. 12, pp. 25–28, 37–39.

12. Schoeffler, Sydney, Robert D. Buzzell, and Donald F. Meany, "Impact of Strategic Planning on Profit Performance", *Harvard Business Review*, March-April 1974, vol. 52, no. 2, pp. 137–145.

13. Balachandra, R., and Joseph A. Raelin, "How to Decide When to Abandon a Project", *Research Management*, July 1980, vol. 23, no. 4, pp. 24–29.

14. Neubert, Ralph L., "Strategic Management the Monsanto Way", *Planning Review*, January 1980, vol. 8, no. 1, pp. 3-6, 44–48.

15. Gluck, Frederick W., Stephen P. Kaufman, and A. Steven Walleck, "Strategic Management for Competitive Advantage", *Harvard Business Review*, July-August 1980, vol. 58, no. 4, pp. 154–161.

16. Quinn, James Brian, *op cit*, p. 100.

Additional References

Weston, Fred J., and Eugene F. Brigham, *Essentials of Managerial Finance*, The Dryden Press, Hinsdale, Illinois, 1977. (This is suggested as a reference on financial planning.)

Merrifield, D. Bruce, *Strategic Analysis, Selection, and Management of R & D Projects*, Amacom, New York, 1977. (This book is an expansion of the ideas expressed in the reference by this author cited in the chapter. Case histories are given.)

Royce, William S., *Generating Strategic Alternatives*, Business Intelligence Program, Research Report 620, SRI International, Menlo Park, Calif., November 1979. (This report is very useful in helping management generate alternatives for use in setting strategy; cited in this chapter.)

Chapman, Beverly Jean, "Practice of Consulting Firms in Corporate Strategic Planning", M. S. Dissertation, Sloan School of Management, Massachusetts Institute of Technology, 1978. (This dissertation describes the approaches to corporate strategic planning of ten of the major U. S. management consulting firms.)

Boschi, R. A. A., H. U. Balthasar, and M. M. Menke, "Quantifying and Forecasting Exploratory Research Success", *Research Management*, September 1979, vol. 22, no. 5, pp. 14–21. (This paper discusses a quantitative way of forecasting research success.)

Patel, Peter, and Michael Younger, "A Frame of Reference for Strategy Development", *Long Range Planning*, April 1978, vol. 11, no. 2, pp. 6–12. (The authors describe the key factors that management should use to describe SBU's. They offer guidelines for strategy, as a function of these factors.)

Day, George S., "A Strategic Perspective of Product Planning", *Journal of Contemporary Business*, Spring 1975.

IEEE Transactions on Engineering Management, November 1974, vol. EM-21, no. 4. (The entire issue is devoted to R & D program selection. Of special interest, since it assesses selection models, is: Norman R. Baker, "R & D Project Selection Models: An Assessment", pp. 165–171.)

Allen, D. H., "Credibility and the Assessment of R & D Projects", *Long Range Planning*, June 1972, vol. 5, no. 2, pp. 53–64. (This paper offers a methodology assessing the future of R & D programs.)

8

WRITING AND USING THE PLAN

INTRODUCTION

Strategic plans are developed to be used. They cannot be used in a meaningful way unless there is a way to translate a strategy developed for such plans into actions to be taken and into decisions to be made. The translation is best accomplished by the development of specific, detailed plans. This step involves preparing a tabulation of specific actions, resource allocations, timing of events, and budgets, as well as a rationale for the actions selected.

The plan document is useful in providing guidance for decision making during the plan period; changes in strategy may be required. It is necessary, with a plan in place, to include a means whereby the act of carrying them out can be monitored and controlled. Finally, it is important to evaluate the plan as time passes, so that future plans can be built upon the successes of their predecessors.

8.1   RESOURCES, OPERATIONAL PLANS, AND BUDGETS

Allocation of Resources

The first step in allocating resources for a strategy is to establish projections for revenues, total expenses, and earnings over the plan period. Revenue projections represent, of course, a combination of management's hopes and expectations for the future. They are based on what management expects from current operations and what it hopes will result from future operations. Management must choose any approach it deems appropriate for making those projections: extrapolation of past revenues, consideration of new forces both inside and outside the company, and consideration of any planned changes in operations. The many questions on the future addressed in Chapter 4 will be of value in doing this task.

The projections of total expenses can be derived in a manner resembling the approaches suggested for establishing an R & D budget. There are differences, though. A company's plan for its operations is more readily determinable than for R & D. Many expenses of the future are established by plans already in place. If, for example, a decision has been made to introduce a product in 1983, the development, manufacturing, sales, and service costs are easier to project than were the R & D costs alone back in 1978 when the original research was begun.

The determination of these two sets of numbers — revenues and expenses — is, in effect, a part of the strategy-setting process. For example, a company may have as its main objective increasing the market share for its primary product. This may be a new objective, a change from those established the year before. Its management may believe that the only way to do that is to (a) improve a key product's reliability through additional investment in R & D and (b) increase the company's sales force. This may have the effect of cutting its profit margin over the next two years to half that would otherwise be expected. If that is management's decision, then it clearly has set a strategy that will result in reduced profits for those years.

Next, management must extend the expense projections to individual activities, i.e., it must allocate resources to them. Part of the resource allocation task has already been accomplished. The identification and selection processes included evaluations of each proposal, which covered estimates of the costs and resource requirements of each activity, as well as expected benefits.

The job now at hand is to complete this allocation procedure. The resources identified must be very specific at this point; they include the size of staffing and requisite skills, equipment and capital improvements needed, and costs. The allocation of resources must be made among functional operations and purposes such as research, development, manufacturing, marketing, sales, distribution, and service, and to the several programs in each of these. The allocation must also be planned over a period of time, year by year and perhaps quarter by quarter, with times identified when new resources will be required. The allocation must take place on all organizational levels for which there is a specific responsibility for spending.

In projecting expenses into the future, a company would be well-advised to review the Boston Consulting Group's Experience Curve Effect [1]. According to this hypothesis, product unit costs of manufacturing decrease at about 20 to 30% every time product experience doubles, either for a company or within an industry. That is, when a company has doubled its production over an earlier point, its costs per unit are 20 to 30% less than at that point. The Group has developed many graphs of costs over time to support this hypothesis. As a corporation does its budgeting, it should take into account the drop in costs of established products, whether by this rule or by a rule of its own.

Operational Plans

The next task is to generate detailed plans, termed *operational plans,* for all activities, which will indicate how allocated resources will be used. These plans show all activities selected in the strategy-setting process as tasks assigned to R & D programs and other programs within the corporation.

The use of operational plans, as described below, implies a very detailed approach to the process of converting strategy into plans for action. In many companies, such detail is reserved for the operating plan, which usually covers the first one or two years of the plan period. In that event, this description of operational plans would apply to the operating plan process. It is included here to show how the link between the strategic and the operating plans is made. Management should choose whether to include all this detail in the strategic plan. If it chooses not to, then a summary of the operational plans described belongs in the strategic plan.

The approaches used by companies to translate strategy into operational plans vary considerably, but many use forms for developing them. An example of a form for the operational plan for a research project or a development program is given in Fig. 8-1. For each corporate operational element (research project, product program, manufacturing program, etc.), information on objectives, approach, rationale, resources, schedule, and milestones for the activity should be included.

Under "Objectives", the particular objectives of the operational element should be stated. For example, if a research project is at issue, a statement of what the research is to accomplish would be appropriate. If the work is being done for a particular product line, that should be mentioned.

Under "Approach", a description should be given of the method by which the work will be undertaken and the objectives will be sought. This is, in effect, the strategy of the program. The particular studies and investigations to be made, the conditions under which they are to be made, the information sought, stages in the work and other details of this type should be included, as appropriate.

Under "Rationale", there should be an explanation of how the activities relate to corporate objectives and goals. Their relationship to corporate strengths, weaknesses, opportunities, and threats can also be included. Such information explains why the activity was chosen for selection as part of the strategy, i.e., why it is important to the company and what positive results can be expected as a result.

Under "Resources", a listing of all associated costs should be included, along with information on staffing. The details of the costs may be present, covering such items as labor, materials, and depreciation. Because inflation is a significant factor in costs, data are often given in both *period economics* (actual dollar costs in the years involved) or in *constant economics* (dollars costs for all years in today's dollars).

RESEARCH AND DEVELOPMENT DIVISION 1982 – 1986 strategic plan						
Program:						
Objectives:						
Approach:						
Rationale:						
Resources:						
Costs Manpower	1982	1983	1984	1985	1986	Total
Schedule:						
Date:			**Manager:**			

Fig. 8-1. Operational-plans form.

Under "Schedule" it is necessary to provide the sequence of events to be carried out and decisions to be made over the plan period. Information on events (completion of programs, purchases of equipment, transfer of product prototypes from engineering to manufacturing, introduction of products, etc.) must include times at which they are scheduled. It is useful to identify specific assumptions and planned activities that determine the dates at which events are scheduled. Such linkage allows management and planners to follow events and monitor progress towards those events.

Other, optional entries can be made to operational plans. Among these items are "Product Programs Impacted", "Relation to Other Programs", "Organizations Responsible" (directly and Indirectly), "Billables to Other Organizations". Many other special items may be appropriate. Needs vary considerably among divisions of a company.

It is valuable to summarize the detailed operational plans by using schedules of activities that encompass many or all of the activities within a division. Fig. 8-2 shows such a schedule, covering all R & D activities in a company. It is common for all R & D programs to be identified as passing through a series of stages. These stages may be called *Early Concept, Exploratory Development, Advanced Development, Prototype Engineering, Product Program, Manufacturing,* and *Product Introduction.* The markings along horizontal lines in Fig. 8-2 indicate the times at which such stages occur. The last of these, *Product Introduction*, is an event rather than a stage. This kind of schedule chart ties together the scheduling of operational plans. Similar charts or tables are frequently used to tie together activity resources.

As in earlier stages of planning, functional plans must be made at division and department levels. They must be integrated across all organizational units, particularly where such units strongly interact, as do Engineering and Manufacturing or Marketing and Sales.

Future Decisions

The plan must include decisions to be made in the future. Because of uncertainties in the future, some decisions may have to be deferred until additional required information is available. In general, decisions should be made by using as much accurate information as is available for making them, deferring them as long as is reasonable for that purpose, yet making them as soon as possible when all needed information is at hand. The plan should include statements of such deferred decisions, including the required missing information needed, the circumstances they will be based upon, and the dates when this information is expected to be available. For example, some future decisions that a company may address in its strategic plan are those concerning future acquisition of external technology. Such decisions would depend upon the nature and timing of outside developments in technologies of interest, as well as internal developments.

RESEARCH AND DEVELOPMENT SCHEDULE 1982 – 1986 strategic plan					
Program	1982	1983	1984	1985	1986

Format: | EC | ED | AD | PE | PP | M | ▲

EC: Early concept
ED: Exploratory development
AD: Advanced development
PE: Prototype engineering
PP: Product program
M: Manufacturing
▲ Product introduction

Fig. 8-2. Research and development schedule.

Budgets

Budgets represent the means whereby strategy is translated into a specific guide for future actions. They provide a quantitative means for expressing objectives, goals, and strategy, as well as the means for measuring progress against the operational plans. By setting a standard for performance against which actual progress can be measured, they provide a basis for controlling that performance. The actions that management takes when progress deviates from plans represent its control over operations.

It should be noted that budget allocations beyond the first year or two of the plan are at best approximations and serve to indicate qualitatively where money is allocated. Adjustments will be made in future years.

A schedule in the format of Fig. 8-2 can be prepared to show a budget for the plan period. It would give only a brief overview of company budgeting for expenditures. Each line item would be expanded into a full budget; each item might represent a division of the company or a product line. The several specific research projects, current product development programs, market research areas, etc., each require a line of data across the several years of the plans.

One approach to the process of converting plans to budgets is addressed by David Novick [2]. His method is termed *program budgeting*; he also uses the term *planning-programming-budget* (PPB) system. The approach focuses on the matter of using the company's resources in the way that will be most effective in meeting its objectives.

Program budgeting groups a company's activities into programs that are related to end products rather than to functions, which is more traditional. This allows management to look at *what* is produced in addition to *how* it is produced or what resources are consumed. The program budget presents resources and costs categorized by end product. This approach focuses attention on competition for resources among programs and on the effectiveness of resource use within programs. *Programs* are the sets of activities undertaken to accomplish objectives; *programming* is the determination of the manpower, equipment, and facilities necessary for accomplishing program feasibility in terms of specific resources and time.

Uncertainty

In Chapter 7, the suggestion was made that uncertainty be incorporated into a budget. There are several ways of doing this. First, entries such as *Other research, Other product improvement programs*, etc., can be included in the budget document. These indicate that money is planned for such activities, but that the exact nature of the work is currently unknown.

Second, specific decisions to be made during the plan period can be identified and included. The budget portions in question can simply be not allocated to specific programs, but the unallocated amounts should be indicated.

An example in shown in Table 8-1. In that instance, the future decision is to select two programs of the three, Programs Q, R, and S. At the end of 1984, a decision will be made and the unallocated funds will be assigned to the two programs selected. Management has decided that the two that remain in 1985 will be more heavily funded than the three are collectively to that point.

Table 8-1. Unallocated Budget (dollars in millions)

Product line XYZ	1982	1983	1984	1985	1986
Pdt Q development	1.5	1.8	2.1	---	---
Pdt R development	0.6	0.9	1.6	---	---
Pdt S development	0.9	0.8	0.6	---	---
Unallocated	---	---	---	5.5	7.0

Third, the anticipation of certain events may be included where the approximate probabilities of several alternatives can be determined. This is practical only when there are but a few (two to four) events of approximately equal probability. Table 8-2 illustrates this approach, with three possibilities.

Table 8-2. Probabilistic Budgeting (dollars in millions)

Product line ABC	1982	1983	1984		1985	1986
Pdt W development	0.8	1.2	(a)	1.8	1.8	1.5
			(b)	2.1	2.5	2.2
			(c)	0.0	0.0	0.0

Decide in December 1983:

(a) Successful, per plan
(b) Successful, but delayed one year
(c) Unsuccessful within two years of plan

ConTronics major projections and budgets for the 1982–1986 strategic plan period follow:

(Dollar amounts in millions; units in thousands)

Projections	1982	1983	1984	1985	1986
Revenues	$35	45	65	95	130
Net profit	$ 1.9	2.1	3.0	4.8	7.5
Margin	5.4%	4.7%	4.6%	5.1%	5.8%
Units sold	30	45	75	125	225

Revenue by divisions					
OEM	$22	25	30	40	45
Business	$13	18	27	35	40
Office	$ 0	0	3	10	25
Home	$ 0	2	5	10	20
Budget					
Research	$0.4	0.7	0.8	0.9	1.1
Materials	$0.1	0.3	0.5	0.3	0.1
Software	$0.2	0.2	0.1	0.1	0.1
Circuit design	$0.1	0.2	0.2	0.1	0.1
Other	$0	0	0	0.4	0.8
Development	$2.2	3.1	4.6	6.6	8.5
Current pdts	$0.3	0.3	0.2	0	0
New features	$0.3	0.4	0.5	0.6	0.8
New pdts (110, N4)	$1.6	1.3	0.5	0.3	0.2
Miniaturized pdts	$0	0.4	1.3	1.5	1.4
New matls tech	$0	0.3	0.6	1.3	1.8
Office cntlrs	$0	0	0.3	0.8	1.2
Office systems	$0	0	0	0.3	0.9
Home cntlrs	$0	0.3	1.0	1.5	1.8
Central develop.	$0	0.1	0.2	0.3	0.4
Total R & D	$2.6	3.8	5.4	7.5	9.6

These projected revenues and profits represent 34 and 42% compounded annual rates, respectively.

ConTronics developed a series of operational plans for its R & D activities. The plans for the software research project and the product miniaturization program are given here.

SOFTWARE RESEARCH PROJECT

<u>Objective</u>. To conduct research into new computer software methodology for the operation of controllers for home electronic products.

<u>Approach</u>. The functions to be performed by the software include information encoding and decoding, information storage and retrieval, and the management of data traffic. Consequently, in-depth investigations of work done in these fields will be undertaken. New coding techniques will be studied, applicable to the controller environments. High-speed, limited-memory information processing methods will be developed.

Rationale. In order to achieve goals of very short response time and low manufacturing costs, new methods of information handling must be developed. Existing methods do not meet the stringent needs of the planned controllers. (Note: A rationale for undertaking the development of the controllers is needed in the plan. Such rationale appears elsewhere.)

Resources (manpower)

    1982–1983:   four persons

    1984–1986:   two persons

Schedule

    1982:   investigations completed

    1983:   early prototype developed

    1984:   final prototype developed

PRODUCT MINIATURIZATION PROGRAM

Objective. To develop miniaturized versions of the Company's current product lines.

Approach. The goal is miniaturization in volume and weight of the products. New technologies that use less power will be developed. Semiconductor circuits and switches will be investigated. New materials, having greater structural strength than materials now in use, will be studied; these should allow reduced size. VLSI (very large scale integration) circuitry will be incorporated into the product wherever feasible.

Rationale. Smaller devices are required in order that more markets – such as small offices and homes – can be penetrated. Size requirements are more stringent in those environments than present requirements.

Resources (manpower)

1982:   0   1983:   8   1984:   25   1985:   30   1986:   28

Schedule

    1984:   early prototype for first product

    1985:   early prototypes for all products

    1986:   final prototype for first product

8.2 MILESTONES

A strategic plan calls for the completion of certain tasks in some definite period of time. This enables management to have standards against which to measure progress. Some activities are well defined, so that completion dates and dates of intermediate phases can be determined reasonably well. The completion dates of other activities are less certain, because the extent of the required effort is uncertain or even unknown. Some activities are identified by the accomplishment of certain tasks, while others have their progress best measured by improvements in operation to be effected over set time intervals. In all these cases, however, one can identify measures of progress, which we call *milestones*.

Milestones identify accomplishments toward objectives and goals. To be useful, they must contain measures of performance and times of occurrence of events. The following are examples of valid milestones:

* Completion of the first engineering prototype of Program Delta, with full documentation, delivered to Advanced Engineering — by March 1982.

* Proposal completed for the establishment of new sales offices in ten North Atlantic Region cities — by May 31, 1982.

* Reduction in the manufacturing cost of subassembly H-38 of Program Charlie by 10% in each of the next four years (1982–1985).

Note that each of these milestones includes a well-defined task and a completion date. (In the third example, there are really four milestones, with completion dates of December 31 in 1981, 1982, 1983, and 1984.)

Sometimes stated milestones have little meaning or value, such as these:

* Improve productivity of all factory workers by 1983.

* Cut spending in office supplies by an average of 15%.

The first milestone omits a specific target, and as such offers no means of measurement. It might, for example, imply 2%, 20%, or other improvement. The second milestone omits a date for completion, and so it fails to indicate whether there is urgency (e.g., "completion in 1981") or not ("completion in 1984").

Milestones are really short-range goals. They are established to allow evaluation of progress toward objectives and long-range goals. For that reason, they should have the characteristics of objectives and goals. The milestones selected should be realistic yet represent significant achievements for the periods involved; they should not be easy to achieve. They should also be consistent, such that a sequence of them follows logically, one to the next. Finally, they should be specific.

Milestones should represent points of completion of activities or portions of activities and thus be natural measuring points. They should represent relatively frequently occurring points over time, e.g., every three months. If a particular activity does not have natural measuring points more frequently than every ten or fifteen months or so, intermediate points should be forced. A milestone might read: "Completion of 50% of testing of System 35 — by January 15, 1981", provided the 50% point can be determined. The quarterly guideline given is only a suggestion. In some cases, either monthly milestones or semiannual milestones may be more suitable.

It is appropriate for milestones to be identified at a corporate level (or divisional level in product-line corporations), for top management to measure progress. Milestones are also valuable at the operational plan level, where they define progress within specific activities. They are shown as part of functional plans in Fig. 8-1.

ConTronics management has established the following milestones for its new product programs and for one of its miniaturized product programs:

New products

* Complete early engineering prototypes of System 110 and Model N4 by January 1981 and June 1981, respectively.
* Complete final engineering prototypes by August 1981 and January 1982.
* Introduce the products commercially in July 1982 and December 1982.
* Introduce Version II (more features, lower price) in July 1983 and November 1983.

Miniaturized products   (first product in line)

* Complete early concept proposal in March 1984.
* Complete early engineering prototype in November 1984.
* Complete final engineering prototype in April 1985.
* Introduce the product commercially in February 1986.

8.3 THE STRATEGIC PLAN DOCUMENT

Necessary Material

As noted earlier, the strategic planning process is more important than the strategic plan document. The document has value too, of course, in that its development requires accomplishment of the process and that it serves as reference for monitoring and for development of the following year's plan. The latter tasks are discussed in Sections 8.5 and 8.7.

The plan should be *concise* to insure its being read, *coherent* to insure its understanding, and *comprehensive* to insure its effectiveness. Many strategic plans are very lengthy, containing too much detail and numerous, extensive tables of numeric data. The writers of the plan should remember that a short-range document, an operating plan, will be written to elucidate the details of operation for the next year or two. There is no need, in the strategic plan, to provide all the detail one may eventually need. (Comments to that effect regarding the operational plans were made earlier.)

The plan should contain the following information for the planning period, at a minimum:

* Corporate objectives
* Corporate goals
* Divisional objectives
* Highlights of a self-analysis
* Highlights of the environment analysis
* Tabulation of forecasts
* Tabulation of assumptions
* Major technology alternatives likely to emerge
* A strategy: major activities to be undertaken, each to include approach, rationale, resources, and schedule
* Corporate milestones
* Contingency plans

The physical size of the plan will depend on a number of factors, including the size of the corporation, the extent of its product line diversity, and the degree of its technological activity. The greater each of these factors is, the larger the plan should be. Beyond these qualitative guidelines, one cannot specify the specific size of a strategic plan. There are too many different styles of management and specific situations within companies to allow such a specification.

Optional Material

In addition to the essential material listed above, the plan may include more details. It may be best to place such information in appendices, to indicate its lesser importance and to avoid having the main body of the document become too large. Optional material includes the following:

* Corporate mission and philosophy of operation
* Corporate objectives beyond the plan period
* Divisional and subdivisional objectives
* Details of self-analysis, environment analysis, forecasts, and assumptions
* Added technology alternatives, less important than the major ones
* More detail on activities selected for the strategy
* A list of "What if . . . ?" questions

Very often, the various organizations in a corporation issue their own strategic plan documents. Consider, for example, a research strategic plan. Such a plan should be related to the corporation's business as a whole, and information that establishes that linkage should be present. A tabulation can be included of the roles that Research has played in the products the company has already on the market or that are planned for introduction in the future. A tabulation of advanced technologies that are currently under development in Research can also be included.   This list ought to stress those technologies that have the highest likelihood of incorporation into products as well as those that have the potential for the greatest impact.

8.4   USING THE PLAN

Decision Making

As we noted early in the book, the purpose of strategic planning is to set corporate objectives for the future in response to perceived opportunities and threats and develop a strategy to meet these objectives.   The process involves making decisions about activities and resource allocations and making plans for future decisions.

The planning process and the strategic plan itself create a framework that serves as a standard to determine if decisions, as they are proposed, are consistent with the company's strategy.   As decisions are made during the plan period, they should be weighed against the backdrop of the plan strategy, to verify whether they do indeed support it.   Some of these decisions are planned, but most probably arise without such prior scheduling.   For each proposed decision, these questions can be asked:

> Is this decision consistent with the plan strategy?

> If it is not, is there a rational reason why it should be made anyway?

Clearly, not all decisions can or should be so queried.   The major decisions are the ones to test this way.   Managers of divisions and lower organizations should look at their particular strategies in answering the questions, while top management looks at corporate strategy.   Management may decide that a decision should be made despite disagreement with the strategy.   In that case, it may be that the strategy warrants being modified.   Very likely, decisions involving major new R & D programs, acquisitions, new product lines, diversifications, reorganization, and new plant sites or expansions of existing sites should be guided by or weighed against corporate strategy.

Changes in Strategy

A change in corporate strategy may be necessary if decisions force it, as discussed earlier.   Most likely, top management will decide on a change in strategy for an external reason.   For example, a competitor may introduce a product that threatens the firm's own product, or there may be a gradual saturation of the firm's market in a product line.

In the first case, assume that the competitor announces a new, unexpected product, one the company thought would not become available for at least 18 months. Top management might decide that its own R & D programs must be modified by tripling the development effort in that product line area. The strategy must be changed to give higher priority to that product program.

In the second case, assume that the company wishes to extend its product line into new markets, where the same technology will be used but where new features are needed and where different, more stringent reliability criteria apply. This is to be done to strengthen profitability for applications of the technology that is used in the old product. The management may decide to strengthen its development activity in those areas that will improve reliability. (Presumably, it will also have to develop technologies to provide the new features.) Perhaps the goals of lower cost or faster operating speed, planned for the product line, will have to be postponed or dropped in favor of improving reliability. This also is a change in strategy.

In both of these cases, where strategy is changed, management should examine its corporate objectives to see if the new strategy contributes toward meeting them. Again, the strategic plan provides guidelines for decision making, here at the strategy level.

Verifying Assumptions

During the information analysis phase of strategic planning, certain assumptions about the future were made. These were based on management's assessments of where the environment was heading, i.e., what events were expected to take place in the future.

As time proceeds, those assumptions must be reviewed at reasonably regular intervals for continued validity. They represent one of the bases for the setting of objectives and the formulation of strategy. Certain assumptions are bound to be in error, some slightly so and some greatly so. The significant discrepancies must be noted and assumptions reviewed and, possibly, replaced by others. Some assumptions can be replaced by facts, of course, since the passage of time confirms or denies them. Management must look to see what impact, if any, these changes have on the developed strategy.

As part of strategy setting, management should have developed contingency plans, which were to be invoked if certain assumptions proved wrong. It may thus be appropriate to call upon some of these plans and implement them.

8.5 MONITORING PROGRESS

Control

Control refers to the actions taken by management to insure that the performance of a company conforms to plans. There are three phases to this task: (a) setting standards and measures that define expected performance, (b) determining when there is nonconformance or deviation from these standards and measures, i.e., from the plans, and (c) taking corrective action when nonconformance occurs. This set of actions corresponds to that of a feedback control system. A control system, in some form, should be available in the company as an aid to management in this task.

The standards that are set to define expected company performance may be the milestones, the budget, a decision methodology, or a combination of these.

To determine nonconformance (or deviation), measures of performance must be defined. The measures may include rate of sales growth, rate of spending, growth of certain markets, rate of technology breakthroughs in particular technology areas, etc. The measures must then be used to make comparisons between actual and expected performance.

Reports showing deviations from plans must be prepared and conveyed to those in a position to recommend or take corrective actions. It is necessary to determine how much deviation from plans must occur before any corrective action is warranted. The systems generating these reports should monitor appropriate aspects of performance so as to enable managers to respond properly. It is important that the reasons for the deviations are understood, so that future planning can be improved.

The reports issued by the reporting system must be tailored to their users' needs. The CEO of a corporation, the controller, the head of a product division, and the chief planner all have different needs. For example, the CEO will be concerned with whether corporate objectives remain viable, the controller will want to know whether spending is within satisfactory limits, the head of a product division will be interested in whether sales of its products are as expected, and the chief planner will be concerned with the general adequacy of the strategic plan.

A control system should be able to predict future trends and events. Managers are generally more concerned with what is likely to happen than with what has already taken place, as far as exerting control is concerned. Though the past is a useful indicator of the future, it is only over the future that managers can exert control by taking actions today.

Computer-based information systems, discussed in Chapter 9, *Computers in Planning*, can be of help in yielding information to managers for control purposes, provided the models and data bases can be effectively designed. Often such design tasks are quite difficult.

Checks on Milestones

Milestones, as noted, are useful in identifying deviations from the strategic plan during its execution. Progress of the company, as indicated by occurring events, is compared with the milestones. The comparison, done periodically or whenever circumstances warrant it, takes one of the following forms:

1. A check is made at the date a milestone was due:

   Was the milestone achieved?

   That is, did the planned event or state of things yet occur?

   If not, when is it now expected to occur?

   If it is late, why is it late?

2. A check is made when a milestone is achieved:

   Did the achievement of the event take place when it was planned?

   If not, by how much is it early or will it be late?

   If it is late, why is it late?

The results of these checks, as mentioned above, should be properly reported to responsible managers.

Handling Deviations for the Plan

Once management has determined why a milestone was not achieved or that some other standard of performance was not met and that something must be done, it must either bring the activity back on schedule or modify the plan. These are the two basic alternatives. Management can respond by attempting to force activities back to the schedule. This can possibly be achieved by expending more resources, which may or may not be a reasonable alternative. It may be essential, however, to do so. Specific corrective actions that can be taken are too numerous in kind to be elucidated here. The main requirement is that they be appropriate to the potential impact of the deviation.

Management can also respond by modifying the plan, adjusting it to follow the actual sequence of transpired events more closely. This will likely be necessary if a decision is made not to increase the budget. As a third approach, the two kinds of responses can be combined.

In any event, a response is necessary. A deviation from plan can be permitted to remain for a while, as, for example, when management believes it is a temporary aberration that will correct itself shortly. There must, however, be a management response before very long if the deviation persists. To allow a deviation to exist without correction beyond a reasonable period is usually unwise. It serves little purpose and weakens the monitoring process, allows unreality to invade the management and planning processes, and makes future planning more difficult. Fig. 8-3 indicates the monitoring process and associated corrective actions. Reference should be made to Fig. 1-1 for a comparison.

If a milestone is achieved ahead of schedule, then it is appropriate to adjust the plan to take advantage of this situation. Management may choose not to do anything about the early achievement of a milestone, thereby gaining some slack to allow for later slippage. This is reasonable, but if such early achievements continue, it is important here too to adjust the schedule. If this is not done, some reality in planning is lost, and optimal use of resources becomes less likely.

The contingency plans drawn up for the strategic plan can be used when deviations from the plan occur. If, for example, a program developed serious technical difficulties and is far behind schedule, it may be necessary to abandon it. In that event, it may be appropriate to undertake an alternative program, defined in the contingency plans.

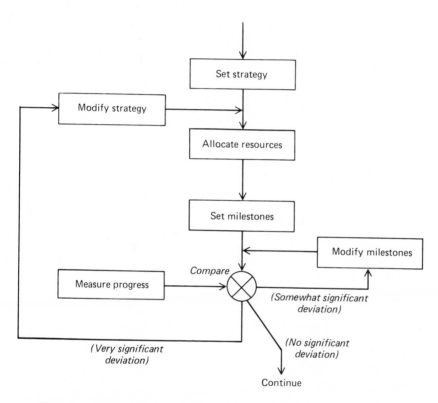

Fig. 8-3. Monitoring progess and modifying plan as needed.

Evaluation of Monitoring Process

How effective is the monitoring of our company's performance?

It is useful to evaluate the monitoring process itself. That process should be optimally done, so that its benefits outweigh its costs. It is important to determine whether the monitoring has been successful in identifying problems early enough. One must also determine whether the necessary information for measuring performance is readily available. Finally, the cost of monitoring must be determined. If it has been less than optimal, it must be improved.

8.6 EVALUATION OF THE PLAN

It is important for a company to review the strategic plan it has undertaken, to determine whether it was optimally developed. The planning for a given five-year period is completed somewhat in advance of that period, yet its quality cannot be judged until it has been in use for a while. It cannot be effectively judged by the time the next cycle of planning gets under way, for the next plan period. A strategic plan can only be evaluated about two to three years after work on it began. Some aspects of it can, of course, be evaluated sooner. For example, the assumptions made for the early part of the plan can be judged sooner. The first year's performance can be judged sooner. But most aspects of the plan must be evaluated later on.

What characterizes a "good" plan? What characterizes a "good" planning process? How can both the planning process and the plan developed by using that process be improved? The following questions can be used to evaluate a strategic plan.

Analysis of company and the environment:

> *Was the information gathered accurate and complete enough for the planning process?*
>
> *Was sufficient information of value gathered?*
>
> *Was it gathered quickly enough?*
>
> *How can information in the future be gathered more efficiently, more accurately, more completely, and more cheaply?*

Setting objectives and goals:

> *Were the objectives and goals appropriate?*
>
> *Were any keys ones omitted?*
>
> *Where they the right kind of objectives and goals?*
>
> *Were they enduring enough to be useful?*

Projecting the future and making assumptions:

> *How accurate were the projections and the assumptions?*
>
> *If they were seriously inaccurate, why is this so?*
>
> *Can better methods be devised for these tasks?*

Setting strategy:

> *Was the decision process used in setting strategy reasonable?*
>
> *What were the "best" and "worst" decisions, and how were they made?*
>
> *What was the impact of these decisions?*
>
> *Were there many changes in strategy necessitated by subsequent events?*

Milestones:

Were any milestones unrealistically set?

Why was this so?

How reasonable, generally speaking, were the milestones?

Were many changes necessitated in the plan, as evidenced by milestone slippages?

Once these questions, and others that management may devise, have been answered, Planning should review the results and make recommendations as to how the planning procedure should be improved. It may be that improvements are possible only by the expenditure of more money for more information gathering and analysis, for better forecasting, and for more effort in strategy formulation. As a possible alternative approach, no additional funds need be expended but a more efficient set of procedures might be used. Some of the time, effort, and money spent on information gathering may be unnecessary; an excess amount of information may have been gathered and an excess amount of effort expended on its analysis. The planning organization should review the work to assess the situation. There is a great deal of uncertainty in strategic planning, and management can readily expend too much effort and money on planning, more than can be justified by the overall general level of accuracy of the process.

8.7 DOING A NEW PLAN

Use of the Old Plan

Strategic plans should be prepared and written on a regular basis, usually once a year. That is the frequency most commonly used by corporations. Since the plan covers several years, generally five, it follows that the "new plan" being done currently must be strongly related to the "old plan" of last year. For a company that is in a highly volatile environment, the relationship between the two plans may be slight; such a company clearly can only plan over a relatively short range, perhaps two years. Such a company probably should do a new strategic plan every six months. For other companies, the relationship between the two plans should be close.

Because of this connection between the two plans, the best starting point for doing new strategic planning is the old plan. The two plan periods overlap for all but one year, or 80% of the total period of a five-year plan. Decisions made for the old plan for most of the period will to some extent be repeated in the new plan. Thus a good beginning to the new planning process is to review the old plan, discarding its first year, since that has become history. One year is added at the end to complete the new five-year period.

The methods for evaluating a strategic plan were discussed in the last section. The evaluation that results should be carefully considered in developing the new plan. Both the methodology used and the resultant plans should be reviewed.

Factors to Consider in New Plan

Management should review the old plan and the information gathered for its preparation and determine what is valid for current use, possibly with modification, in the new plan. Each batch of information should be looked at critically.

Objectives. Corporate and divisional objectives may not change every year, so it is possible that the new objectives are the same as the old ones. More likely, however, some changes are required. Reasons for the changes might include a desire to modify the product line, surprise competitive product introductions, a worsening of the economic climate, and technology breakthroughs in Research. Any significant event that was unexpected can cause management to seek new or modified corporate objectives. Even many that are expected may evoke this response.

Goals. Clearly, if objectives are changed, goals must be also, since they represent the means whereby objectives are achieved. If objectives are not changed, it may still be appropriate to change goals, since the means of achieving objectives may have to be replanned.

Company analysis information. The self-analysis information should be reviewed, since it can form a basis for new data gathering, but because it is a year old, much of it no longer applies. However, it identifies the kind of information previously gathered.

Environment analysis information. The environment analysis information to be gathered now is largely new, but it will most likely include some repetition of last year's data. This is true because parts of the environment do not change rapidly. Nonetheless, it must all be reviewed, since it is unsafe to assume that any information remains unchanged for a year.

Forecast information. Forecasts were made over the plan period and so will usually retain much of their validity, especially for the short-term period. The forecasts for the first year of the old plan period (now partially history) should be checked for their accuracy. Any errors made should be noted and studied.

Assumptions. Each of the assumptions must be reviewed to determine whether it is still valid one year later. Unless the environment is especially volatile, many assumptions will remain valid.

Technology issues. The several acquisition possibilities of last year that were not acted upon should be reviewed, and others should now be considered. The technology alternatives may still be valid, except that some may be dropped as no

longer feasible, others will have emerged in the past year, and others will have
been developed into product programs or actual products.   Each must be
reviewed for current applicability. Technology assessments should be examined
for current validity. Technology transfers planned but not executed should also
be reviewed to determine if their timetables still apply.

Strategy. The old strategy forms a basis for the new strategy. Most activities in
a company continue from year to year, and during their lifetimes their
components (objectives, approaches, rationale, resources, etc.) can often be
predicted at an early stage. It is necessary to review these and determine if they
are currently applicable.

Milestones Old milestones should be reviewed and form the basis of a new set.
Milestones that occurred in the first year of the old plan must be discarded.

Changes in Planning

As the new planning proceeds through its several stages, the changes in objectives
and goals, in the company and the environment, in forecasts, in technology
alternatives, in the strategy, and in the milestones should all be noted and
documented. They will serve as a useful reference for future strategic planning
activities. In some cases, it is appropriate that commentary on the changes be
included in the plan, either in the main body or in an appendix.

   A by-product of the process of developing a new plan from the old is a
check on the ability of the company to forecast the future of both the company
and the environment. Such a study may lead to improvement of that ability this
time around. The means by which forecasting was done last year should be
carefully reviewed, so that management can learn from any errors of the past.

8.8   THE SCHEDULE

The final tasks of developing operational plans (including the budget), setting
milestones, and writing the plan are shown in the schedule in Fig. 8-4. As
pointed out early in the book, a completion date of August 1 is assumed.

8.9   PROBLEMS IN WRITING AND USING THE PLAN

Monitoring a company's performance to determine that it is heading for trouble
is sometimes difficult. Not all deviations from planned performance should
evoke responses, and among those that do not all are serious enough to warrant a
change in strategy, though they may appear to be on the surface. Management
must exercise judgment in knowing if, when, and how to respond.   Both
overreaction and underreaction are to be avoided if possible.

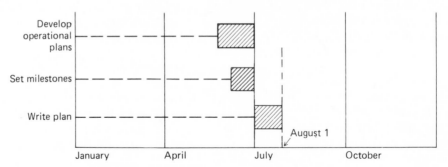

Fig. 8-4. A schedule for writing the plan.

Although it is highly desirable that major decision making be linked to strategic plan strategy, it is difficult for top management to be certain that this is always done. Too many short-range problems arise that demand quick responses, leading to actions that are taken in spite of the guidelines of the strategy. This can result in a loss of effectiveness of the strategy.

There is a tendency among managers not to question assumptions made for a strategic plan, once the plan has been in effect for awhile. This is a serious mistake, for the result can be that the company moves towards objectives and goals that are at odds with the true nature of the environment.

8.10   AN APPROACH TO STRATEGIC PLANNING

We briefly describe the approach to strategic planning taken by a high-technology corporation.

International Business Machines

IBM uses two distinct but interacting kinds of planning: program planning and period planning [3]. A *program plan* generally has a single objective but may involve several functional elements. Its time span is determined by its specific objective and the tasks required to achieve it and by the inherent dynamics of the program. Such programs, for example, may be planned to develop a product or to improve the productivity of a function. A *period plan* balances program objectives with other objectives, so as to achieve profit targets assigned. Its time span is fixed by corporate management at five years for a strategic plan. Review and decision making is tied to the calendar to assure the availability of an operating budget for each unit at the start of each year. Clearly, each type of planning affects the other.

Program planning is directed toward a product, an industry (i.e., a specific class of customers), or a functional objective. IBM relies upon in-house econometric models to forecast both the U.S. economy and the demand for the company's products. An annual income and expenditure model provides input for use in the strategic plan. The company also uses an input−output model to project industry supply and demand patterns. Many forecasting methods are used, including analyses of growth and replacement patterns for new products and systems; extrapolation from case studies selected to represent industry, size, and application distributions; interviews or questionnaires for new products; and projections based on sales or backlog analyses for products already announced.

Period planning corresponds to what we have called strategic planning. Key elements in strategic planning are corporate targets, operating unit goals, product and functional strategies, and a strategic plan. The strategic process is as follows:

a) <u>Corporate targets and operating unit goals</u>. Corporate management assigns profit targets to each operating unit. In response, each unit develops and assigns goals to managers to guide their strategy development.

b) <u>Strategies</u>. Operating units with development responsibilities prepare and maintain product strategies to serve as the foundation for their marketplace offerings. All units prepare functional strategies to assure that the most effective organization and business approaches are used to achieve increasing productivity of resources.

c) <u>Strategic plan</u>. The strategic plans of the operating units integrate the several product and functional strategies of the units, present the financial results over the plan period, and compare planned results with corporate targets. These plans are submitted to the Corporate Management Committee (CMC) by the units. Assessments of these plans are made by corporate staffs prior to the CMC review.

To support this planning work, the operating units with product development responsibility generate product assumptions. Corporate economists provide economic assumptions. Using the product and economic assumptions, the forecasting department of each operating unit produces an overall set of business volume projections. These are reviewed by corporate management and distributed to the units as the basis for their final plans. Each function then uses its own planning factors and models to translate these volumes into workload, resource, and expense data.

SUMMARY

The final steps in writing a strategic plan involve translating the strategy into a set of actions and decisions, embodied as operational plans and budgets. Developing operational plans begins with making projections of future revenues and expenses. From these data, information is available for allocating resources. Management should develop operational plans, which are written for all activities, such as research projects, product programs, manufacturing programs. Information on objectives, approach, rationale, resources, schedule, and milestones for all activities should be included. Decisions to be made in the future should also be present in these plans. Detailed operational plans may be put into an operating plan.

Finally, budgets should be drawn up. Budgets represent the means whereby strategy is translated into a specific guide for future actions. Spending plans by year and by line item are necessary. Similar data on manpower requirements are also to be included.

Uncertainty can be included in plans, by several means. Since planning intrinsically involves uncertainty, such information is useful.

The final step in the writing of the plan is the development of milestones, which are standards for measuring progress. They should contain measures of performance and times of occurrences of events.

The strategic plan document should contain certain narrative information, including corporate objectives, corporate goals, highlights of the company's self-analysis and its environment analysis, forecasts, assumptions, technology alternatives, a strategy, milestones, and contingency plans. In addition, the plan may contain corporate objectives beyond the plan period, divisional charters, divisional objectives, and other details.

The strategic plan is a guide to actions and decision making. The plan provides a means whereby decisions, as proposed, can be determined to be consistent with corporate strategy. Sometimes, a change in strategy may be necessary if decisions force it. Assumptions made early in the planning process must be verified during its execution.

Monitoring the progress of the company's operation is essential. Milestones should be checked regularly against performance. When deviations from the plan occur, management may have to take action in response. Either the plan or the performance must be modified. Deviations must be carefully analyzed, so that the reasons for their occurrence are understood, before actions are taken in response.

It is important, once the plan is in operation, that it be evaluated by management. This can only be done after it has been in use for a while, perhaps a year or so. Each stage in the process should be questioned to determine its validity. Errors made in planning provide information for an improved approach the following year.

A new strategic plan can be based in part on its immediate predecessor. However, to a large extent, new information has to be gathered and strategy carefully reviewed for current and future applicability.

REFERENCES

1. Boston Consulting Group, *Perspectives on Experience*, Boston, 1970.

2. Novick, David, "Long-Range Planning through Program Budgeting", from *Long-Range Planning for Management*, 2nd edition, ed. by David Ewing, Harper & Row, New York, 1972, Chapter 28.

3. Katz, Abraham, "There's No Room for Guesswork at IBM", in *Corporate Planning: Techniques and Applications*, ed. by Robert J. Allio and Malcolm W. Pennington, AMACOM, New York, 1979, pp. 221–230.

9

COMPUTERS IN PLANNING

INTRODUCTION

Computers have very significant capabilities in calculation and in information storage and retrieval, and these traits can be exploited in the planning process. There are two major areas in planning that make valuable use of computers: modeling and information systems.

Models, to a large extent, involve the solution of a great many equations and formulas that interrelate various parameters relevant to planning, e.g., revenue, expenses, market size, and inflation. Through the use of such analytical models, planning staffs can better predict the projected future states of a company in an environment.

Planning also involves the collection and analysis of a great deal of information. Such information must be retained by the company in a logically organized fashion for use in the future. Additionally, a great deal of external information stored by commercial vendors on their computers is of values to companies.

9.1 MODELING

The Application

Many computer-based systems have been developed to allow companies to model their operations and their environments. The mathematical equations that interrelate various parameters can be incorporated into computer programs, to allow calculations to be made that involve such items as sales, market growth, the economy, return on investment, and many others.   Calculations on projected future results are especially valuable for forecasting change.   In such cases, since actual operating data are not available, they must be estimated.   Used with equations that describe the operation of the company and the environment, such data can aid in projecting future results. Thomas Naylor defines *modeling* as the process of creating a small, controllable system which responds in the same manner as a large, less controllable system [1].   In corporate modeling, the small system (the model) normally consists of a set of logical relationships which simulate the behavior of the large system, the company, one of its divisions, or a part of its environment.   Such models are used to determine the effects of management decisions, changes in company policy, or changes in the environment before they actually occur, thereby allowing management to anticipate change as it carries on the company's business.

Because computer-based models are executed rapidly, a manager can try a lengthy series of different conditions in quick succession and compare the results. He or she can ask a series of "What if . . ?" questions.   For example, several different rates of inflation, several different market growth rates, and several different rates in technology price decreases can be postulated over the plan period, and the responses of a financial model of the company can be noted. This can be done with one parameter varied at a time or with several parameters varied simultaneously. By varying just one parameter at a time we can determine the model's (and the company's) sensitivity to that parameter.   This ability to consider many alternatives in the market or within the company is one of the major benefits of the use of corporate models.

The use of models involves two stages.   First, one must determine the relationship among parameters. This is usually done by writing equations or their equivalent.   This stage requires the identification of all significant parameters and of the relationships that exist among them. If any specialized analytical methods are required, they must be identified.

Second, one must gather data that reflect the values of these parameters. All sources of data to be used must be identified. The reliability and currency of the data must be determined and understood. The ranges of values to be examined must be identified. In short, the full range and extent of all supplied data must be known. During the actual use of the model, the various data values are supplied to it.

The validity of any model and the results it provides can be no more accurate than are the mathematical descriptions of the interrelationship of all parameters and the data supplied about the company and its environment. This is a very important point about modeling, and it must not be overlooked.   It implies, e.g., that it is useless to create a model that implies high precision in its equations while using data that are very inaccurate. All this is not to imply that only with very accurate information can a useful model be constructed and used. Rather, these comments are offered as a warning; users of models should be aware of the limitations in their information, both in the parameters' relationships and the supplied data.

Not all modeling for planning is appropriately performed on a computer. The use of a computer is generally warranted if the model is complex, involving many parameters, if there are large amounts of data, or if the calculations are to be repeated many times. The latter might true where "What if . . . ?" questions are frequently asked. Developing a model may be costly, but once developed, if it is frequently used, its ongoing cost for usage may be quite low.

Types of Models

Models take many forms. There are financial, production, and marketing planning models, to name a few. *Financial models* provide the financial results within a company in response to particular strategies, market states, and competitive actions. They yield the sales and profits that would result. Some financial models are relatively simple, dealing only with the major parameters that are involved with overall company or divisional performance.

An example of a very simple financial model is the following:

$$\text{cost of sales} = 0.30 \times \text{sales}$$

$$\text{selling expenses} = 0.15 \times \text{sales}$$

$$\text{advertising expenses} = 0.03 \times \text{sales}$$

$$\text{debt expenses} = 0.10 \times \text{debt}$$

$$\text{expenses} = \text{cost of sales} + \text{selling expenses} + \text{advertising expenses} + \text{debt expenses}$$

$$\text{pretax earnings} = \text{sales} - \text{expenses}$$

$$\text{taxes} = 0.45 \times \text{pretax earnings}$$

$$\text{net earnings} = \text{pretax earnings} - \text{taxes}$$

This model has two input variables, *sales* and *debt*. Though simple, this model illustrates the concept. In practice, financial models have dozens of variables and equations.

T. Lomas describes a financial model that includes six submodels: Manpower, Income, Current expenditure, Capital expenditure, Depreciation, and Financing [2]. The Manpower submodel supplies the two expenditure submodels, and the next four submodels listed supply the Financing model. This last submodel addresses profit, borrowing, total return, interest, capital requirements, net assets, return on capital, and net cash flow. The purpose of this model is to enable managers to make assumptions about future demands for products, pay rates, productivity, prices, etc., (i.e., inputs) and to determine the likely effects on profit, return on capital, borrowing requirements, interest charges, etc. (i.e., outputs). The model is illustrated in Fig. 9-1.

Production models provide the cost of manufacturing products at a level the company plans to achieve to meet a projected share of the market, for a projected sales forecast. The several factors that determine production costs are considered. These include labor, materials, equipment, and inventory policy. The economies of scale are considered, which address fixed and variable costs.

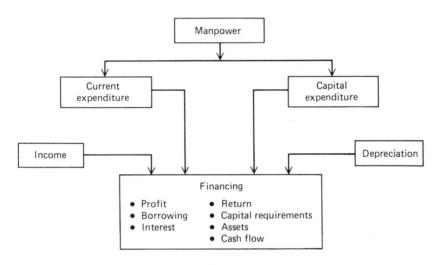

Fig. 9-1. A financial model.

Finally, *marketing models* provide information about the sales of a product for particular practices in advertising, pricing, and promotion. The sizes and price elasticity of the company's markets are considered. The sizes of the markets are dependent upon a number of parameters, such as the state of the economy, the nature of the company's products, the existence of competitive products, and the company's pricing policy. It is necessary to develop a set of equations interrelating all these parameters. Then a series of values can be supplied, so that the model can calculate results.

It is important to integrate these models with one another in simulating a company's performance, since they represent activities that interact with one another. Both the marketing and the production models supply financial data and so should be linked to the financial model. Thomas Naylor describes the several models mentioned and their manner of integration [3].

Models can also include the capability of forecasting. Generally, in this application they are useful primarily over the short term; long-term forecasting involves many uncertainties. Several technological forecasting methods were described in Chapter 4. These methods can be programmed to provide forecasting models.

Product Models

Products and the interrelationship among their characteristics can be modeled, but because of the uncertain nature of the dependence of technological success on various parameters, such as product goals, resource allocation, and technology experience, this may be hard to do. Such a model can be useful in making decisions on the setting of strategy, i.e., which programs to pursue and to what extent. For this to be so, it is necessary to quantify the expected costs and benefits of engineering various features, as well as the impact of technologies on product cost, sales, and profit margin.

Models of products have been built that interrelate product features, manufacturing costs, and customer values. These models are developed in an attempt to quantify the relationship between costs and benefits. Such models are really dual models, for they actually relate (a) features to their costs and (b) features to their values as perceived by customers. Used jointly, the two models relate costs and values (benefits).

The feature–cost model is the easier model to construct. It represents the manufacturing cost of each feature or feature improvement. R & D costs should also be considered; these are generally amortized over the lifetime of the product. In Chapter 7, we discussed the present value of future funds, which should be considered here. The model must allow for the expenditure of funds at different times over the R & D period. One factor that may complicate the model is the interrelationship among features. For example, features A and B may add $500 and $800, respectively, to the manufacturing cost of a product, while included jointly they may add only $1,000. The model must allow for such possibilities as well as others of this type.

A difficulty in the use of the feature–cost model lies in the uncertainty of the data supplied to it. R & D costs can be estimated, but it is often hard to know what they will be a few years out.

The feature–value model is harder to construct. Each such model must, in general, be custom designed for the product (or product line) to which it applies, since its features are likely to be peculiar to it. The interrelationship of features must also be considered, as in the feature–cost model. The trade-off analysis described in Chapter 7 can be used here, to help develop the model. It would be useful both in determining the relationship among product parameters (how one can be traded for another) and in determining numerical values of benefits (how one is rated relative to another).

Obtaining the proper data to supply the product model requires taking customer surveys. These surveys attempt to put a dollar value on proposed new features and combinations of them. Customers cannot always provide such values before they experience the features they are evaluating. That adds difficulty to the problem.

The use of such models can aid in strategy development, for they provide information on the value of pursuing certain courses of action in lieu of others.

Once a product model is built, information from the R & D activity can be supplied to it, as technology advances. This would allow the model to be improved, since better technical data would be available. Additionally, as new products (both a company's and its competitors') come into the market, better data on customer values become available.

An Example

As a simple example of the process of establishing a product model, consider the case of an engineering group that feasibly can provide three different feature improvements for different costs; these are shown in Table 9-1. The first improvement doubles the speed; the second lowers the operating cost by 30%; the last yields a lower manufacturing cost of 20%. Other data are available on the costs of achieving intermediate goals, less ambitious than those in the table, such as a 50% speed increase, 10 and 20% operating cost drops, a 10% purchase price drop, and the like.

Table 9-1 Product Feature Improvements

Feature improvement	Cost	Development time	Value
100% speed increase	$1,500,000	18 months	0.5
30% operating cost drop	$750,000	18 months	0.5
20% purchase price drop	$2,000,000	12 months	1.0

At the same time, a market study indicated that customers rate a 100% speed increase about half as valuable as a 20% purchase price drop and about equal to a 30% operating cost drop. This information is shown in the right-most column of Table 9-1. These relationships among features can only be approximate, even though numeric values appear in the table.

The company must translate "value" into volume of sales. Assume that its management does so, with the result that a value of 0.5 means a volume increase of 50% over present sales and that a value of 1.0 means a 100% increase. If we let the product price be $1000, the net profit be 10% of revenues, current annual volume be 10,000 units, then the current annual profit is $1,000,000. Over a five-year period, the profit is $5,000,000, if no volume change is assumed and inflation is ignored. If each of the three improvements is considered separately, in the order listed, the five-year profit totals become $5,250,000, $6,000,000, and $5,400,000, respectively.

This is, of course, a simplified version of a product model and its use. The model should also consider (a) inflation, (b) the present value of money, (c) other points on the feature—value curve (e.g., the value of a 50% speed increase), and (d) other points on the feature—cost curve (e.g., development cost of a 15% operating cost drop).

Model Generators

Models can be developed through the use of a *computer model generator*. A generator consists of the planning language, the instructions for use of the language and of the model generated, and the programming systems that generate the model. The language of the generator is used to describe parameters of concern and their relationship, data to be supplied, mathematical techniques used in the models, and information on the reports to be created.

A widely used planning modeling system is SIMPLAN, a service of SIMPLAN Systems, Inc. Its language and capabilities are briefly described here by way of illustrating the nature and use of modeling systems. Britton Mayo provides an example of a model written in the SIMPLAN language, as given in Fig. 9-2 [4]. This model is designed to calculate the current assets portion of a typical Comparative Statement of Financial Position. For simplicity, only one type of product is manufactured by using one basic raw material.

In this model, the first five statements (numbers 3–20) represent the constants in the model; each is given a value. Statement 30 sums two of those constants.

The next statement (40) states that each year's production will be the same as the previous year's sales. This dependence on the previous year is shown by the "(-1)" in the statement, reflecting a *lag*. (The suffix "(-3)" would refer to the

```
  3    GROWTHRATE = 7
  5    PRICE = 1.2
 10    MATCOST = .6
 15    REORDER = 3000
 20    LABOR = .285
 30    UNITCOST = LABOR + MATCOST
 40    PRODUCTION = SALES(-1)
 50    MATERIALS = MATERIALS(-1) - PRODUCTION
 60    WAGER = LABOR * PRODUCTION
 70    SALES = SALES(-1) * (1+GROWTHRATE/100)
 80    FIXEDCOST = 50
 90    VARCOST = UNITCOST * SALES
100    COGS = FIXEDCOST + VARCOST
110    DOLLARSALE = SALES * PRICE
120    IF MATERIALS < REORDER
130        PURCHASES = REORDER + 2 * PRODUCTION - MATERIALS
140        MATERIALS = MATERIALS + PURCHASES
145    ELSE
146        PURCHASES = 0
150    END
160    COLLECTION = 3/4 * AR(-1)
170    AR = AR(-1) - COLLECTION + DOLLARSALE
180    PAYMENTS = .6 * AP(-1)
190    AP = AP(-1) - PAYMENTS + (PURCHASES*MATCOST)
200    CASH(-1) + COLLECTION - PAYMENTS - WAGES
210    MATVALUE = MATERIALS * MATCOST
220    CURASSETS = CASH + AR + MATVALUE
```

Fig. 9-2. Example of a financial model.

value of a variable 3 years earlier.) The next several statements (50–110) complete the "production and sales" portion of the model. The variable *COGS* represents the cost of goods sold.

At this point, the raw-material inventory is being depleted with no provision for replenishment. Consequently, provision is made for maintenance of an appropriate inventory level. Statements 120–140 say that if the inventory level is below the reorder point, more raw material should be purchased. Statements 145–146 say that if the level is not below the reorder point, make no purchases. Statement 150 simply ends the IF/ELSE/END sequence. The next several statements (160–220) represent the cash flow calculations. The variables *AR* and *AP* are accounts receivable and accounts payable amounts, respectively.

The results of the use of this model appear in Fig. 9-3. There, the time period covered is 1976 to 1980. The values of the variables each year are listed in alphabetical order. Only 12 of the 22 variables are shown in the figure. The symbol "---" represents an undefined variable value.

This is a simple model. It can readily be extended into many other areas, such as fixed assets and depreciation, liabilities, dividends, and taxes.

TIME	AP	AR	CASH	COGS
1976	1400.00	2000.00	1000.00	---
1977	560.00	1527.20	1432.00	807.56
1978	1644.80	1480.90	1997.44	860.59
1979	657.92	1546.27	1860.20	917.33
1980	1549.58	1644.93	2345.84	978.04

TIME	COLLECTION	CURASSETS	DOLLARSALE	FIXEDCOST
1976	---	---	---	---
1977	1500.00	4879.20	1027.20	50.00
1978	1145.40	6305.54	1099.10	50.00
1979	1110.68	5864.11	1176.04	50.00
1980	1159.70	6966.80	1258.36	50.00

TIME	GROWTHRATE	LABOR	MATCOST	MATERIALS
1976	---	---	---	4000.00
1977	7.00	0.28	0.60	3200.00
1978	7.00	0.28	0.60	4712.00
1979	7.00	0.28	0.60	3796.08
1980	7.00	0.28	0.60	4960.07

Fig. 9-3. Results from use of the model.

Computational Support

Strategic planning requires the analysis of historical data that yield projections for future trends. Computers can provide support for such analyses of the historical data. Models of the environment (particularly the economy and markets of interest) are useful here. There are many economic models maintained by the U.S. Government and a number of universities. Techniques to support data analysis, forecasting the future, and financial analysis include the following (cited by Gordon Davis) [5]:

a) Historical data analysis techniques. Historical data are analyzed to detect patterns that will be useful in projecting future values.

b) Planning data generation techniques. Historical data are analyzed to allow estimates of data required for planning purposes.

c) Financial planning computations. Various computations and analyses are performed for measuring profitability.

Integrating Modeling into Planning

In his book on planning models, Thomas Naylor outlines six steps for integrating modeling into the planning process, the first four of which constitute a planning audit [6]:

1. Review of the planning environment. Review the overall environment in which planning takes place in the company, covering organizational structure, management philosophy and style, business environment, and the planning process.

2. Specification of planning requirements. Review the planning requirements of the corporation, its divisions, and managers; review external factors having impact; and review reports needed.

3. Definition of goals and objectives for planning. Determine management's perception of the planning process and of goals and objectives.

4. Evaluation of existing planning resources. Review existing planning resources of the company, considering collections of information, forecasts, models, reports, programming systems, and human resources.

5. Design of an integrated planning and modeling system. Design the system, which is dependent upon the planning environment, the planning requirements, and the available resources.

6. Formulation of a strategy for integrating the model. Implement the integrated planning and model system, which comprises seven elements:

    a) The strategy must include an *organizational framework* for developing, implementing, and maintaining the model and integrating it into the planning process.

    b) *Changes* in the *existing planning process* may be necessary, as a result of the data gathered in steps 2 and 3.

    c) It may be desirable to *modify* existing *data bases, forecasts, models, reports,* and *computer software* to make them more compatible with the company's planning needs.

d) The *human and technical resource requirements* for an integrated planning and modeling system must be specified.

e) An *educational program* for management on the planning and modeling system must be developed.

f) A *schedule* for implementing the modeling process must be developed.

g) A *budget* for the modeling project must be prepared.

In order to integrate modeling into the planning process, a deliberate, carefully organized effort is essential. Following these steps should facilitate the process of integration.

Problems in the Use of Models

As indicated early in this section, the major problems in using models for planning are the difficulties of obtaining an accurate mathematical representation of that which is to be modeled and of obtaining valid data to supply the model. It is often equally hard to define precisely what problem is to be solved by the creation of a model.

It is sometimes difficult to understand the interrelationships among forces in the environment. There are too many parameters involved, as a rule. It is also difficult, though usually less so, to understand parameters within the company and how they interact. A common mistake is the inclusion of too many details in the model. Careful judgment is required in selecting the proper number of details, all of which are of about equal importance.

Product models present their own problems. We noted that the dependence of technological success on various parameters is generally not well understood. The interrelationships among factors (with respect to costs and customer preferences) is also generally not well understood. Consequently, the model is hard to develop. It is sometimes difficult to do the trade-off analysis accurately because customers often cannot quantify their preferences.

9.2   INFORMATION SYSTEMS

The Application

Another major area where computers can serve the planning process is in the storage and retrieval of information. We have noted that much information must be gathered during a company's self-analysis and its environmental analysis. We have also seen that much information is needed by a firm to monitor its competition. If a company has a variety of products and is in several markets, its collection of such information will be large. A computer may be very useful for the storage of this information. The collection of information that a company retains for its operations can also be handled very conveniently in this manner.

Such information would greatly exceed that used for planning, though much of the latter is derived from the former.

Data Bases

When a collection of related, structured information is stored in a computer's auxiliary memory, it is termed a *data base*. The nature and format of data bases are as varied as their contents and uses. The structure of a particular data base, i.e., the particular manner in which the information it contains is structured, will depend on the nature, extent, and use of the information in it. Usually, a data base consists of a number of *records*, structurally similar to each other. Each record contains information about one of the items stored in the data base. A record, in turn, is comprised of *fields*, each of which holds one element of information about the record's item. As an example, a data base of internal technical reports may have several thousand records in it, one per report. Each record may have six fields, containing the report title, its author, its publication date, its size, the author's organization, and a series of words or phrases that describe the contents of the report. Such a record is termed a document *citation*. The last field, with words or phrases, is a *variable field* of different lengths. These words and phrases are usually called *index terms*; they are used to retrieve documents in a selective manner.

A *data-base system* is a set of programs that allows a user to enter information into data bases, to manipulate the data, and to generate printed results. The system also includes a language to allow such operations as entering and changing data, manipulating files, querying the system for particular information, and printing out desired results.

Companies utilize at least two classes of data bases. One class comprises collections of company records, on personnel, accounts payable and receivable, sales, investments, etc. These are essential for the daily running of the business. Another class comprises collections of outside information that the company uses for information analysis for planning purposes. The information generally consists of citations of books, articles, news stories, reports, and other documents of value in environmental analysis.

These data bases are of value at various stages of the planning process. They are valuable for the company and environmental analyses, since they provide a large part of the needed information, particularly on the environment. The data bases will also be of value in setting strategy, for they can provide answers to many of the questions that arise during that phase of the planning task.

Data base usage comprises several tasks: identifying the information wanted, selecting from among the many documents in the data bases by identifying criteria (as by date, subject, author, etc.), searching the data base, and analyzing the results. The library staff in a company normally aids the user in these tasks, except possibly for the analysis. For a given data base system, the proper formulation of queries is important. In many companies, the library staff is trained to do this job. A user who is familiar with the system may be able to do this task unaided.

Analysis is a personalized task, best done by the user of the information. It involves perusing the document citations that have been identified by the searching process and identifying the information needed for the task at hand.

Commercial services provide all of the tasks described, except for searching and analysis. Again, it is best for the library staff to do the searching for users not familiar with the systems. Commercial data bases are less expensive than internal ones (since their cost is paid for by many companies), but they are less tailored to individual company needs and may not be as current as those developed by a company for its own use. They are useful only for external information.

Management Information Systems

A *management information system* (MIS) is a computer-based, organized collection of information and programming systems. It is used to process information that helps management make decisions. "MIS" is a general term that pertains to many applications and uses of information in management tasks; such systems are especially valuable in planning. An MIS comprises one or more data bases, a data-base system, and a report generator (discussed below). It may also be capable of generating graphs of data. Most MIS systems are utilized in an online mode, with users at terminals that access the MIS and other systems.

Designing a management information system is generally a complex task. The needs of managers (even those doing similar tasks) vary considerably as do their styles of managing. We have noted that the proper type of reporting and information system must be developed for monitoring a company's performance. This is true of such systems for all applications. The design of these systems is complex because it must take into account managers' needs, their knowledge, their preferred methods for retrieving and using information, and so on. The system must be flexible yet not be so customized as to be prohibitively expensive.

A *report generator* provides reports on material stored within an MIS, in a formalized, structured manner. It is used to specify what is to be printed and how it is to be printed. A report generator should be able to provide any type of report that management desires. It provides almost any format desired, with titles, headings, columns of data, and other entries, located just as management wishes.

Management information systems aid managers in making decisions. As noted earlier, decisions can only be made when sufficient applicable information is at hand. In any reasonably complex firm, the information needed is voluminous and far-ranging, so that it is generally impossible for it to be properly collected, stored, analyzed, and presented without a computer-based system that can do these tasks. More specifically, an MIS may provide the following support for management decision making in the planning process:

a) It permits the storage, in a structured manner, of the information gathered for planning purposes about the company and the environment.

b) It processes the information, sorting it, classifying it, checking for redundancies, etc.

c) It can be integrated with models of the company or the environment, supplying data to them and accepting computed results.

d) It supplies responses to queries about information stored in it, which is needed for for decision making.

e) It allows management to ask "What if . . ?" questions by varying parameters in desired ways.

f) It supplies reports, on a regular basis or on demand, on a variety of subjects.

g) It is useful in scheduling, budgeting, and monitoring of operations performance.

This is a lengthy list of capabilities, and not all MIS's have the lot. An MIS developed for use by a company should be designed to meet the company's specific needs in these areas.

An MIS is useful in the decision-making process. Herbert Simon proposed a model for this process [7]. He sees the process as having three phases:

a) <u>Intelligence</u>. Search for conditions that require decisions; gather information and examine it for problems and opportunities.

b) <u>Design</u>. Develop and analyze possible courses of action, which involves trying to understand the problem or opportunity, generating possible responses, and testing them for feasibility.

c) <u>Choice</u>. Select a particular course of action from among those identified.

A review of the list of tasks that an MIS can perform indicates that MIS's are valuable in each of these three phases.

There are limitations to the support that MIS's can provide in aiding strategic planning. Much of the information needed for planning is based on judgment and cannot be well specified and so cannot be placed in the system. Nonetheless, an MIS can be useful in such areas as data summarization for ready analysis; projection into the future by analysis of past data, with adjustments by management on the basis of their knowledge; and storage and retrieval of data, such as competitive information, market trends, and economic indicators.

One particular type of MIS, a *decision support system* (DSS), is widely used. A DSS is a computer-based system that aids decision making by providing information and models. It comprises a data base, a model base (a collection of models), and a software system for interconnecting data and models for making them available to users. Well-designed DSS's support decisions that are both simple and complex, they support all levels of management, and they support all aspects of the decision-making process.

A DSS should most likely be developed by a firm for its own use, rather than be acquired as a commercially available system. The DSS must be built to meet the unique needs of the corporation and so should be built in-house. Outside suppliers may be able to provide software tools, however, from which DSS's can be constructed. Peter Keen and Michael Scott Morton state that three types of decisions can be defined to illustrate where computer-based approaches are likely to be successful; they are *structured, semi-structured,* and *unstructured* decisions [8]. In structured decisions, all rules are understood (and can be programmed in a computer); in semi-structured decisions, some of the rules are understood and human judgment must be used where they are not; and in unstructured decisions, human judgment is required totally. The more nearly structured a decision is, the more the rules that can be programmed and the more likely a decision support system is to be useful.

Query Systems

Query systems are computer-based information systems, which allow users to store information about which questions can be asked. The answers to these questions comprise information selected from the system that meets the criteria stated in the query. The object of such queries is typically a collection of company document citations or records, such as personnel, sales, or manufacturing data.

When a user wishes to retrieve information from a query system with document citations, he or she supplies the system with a *query*, such as the following:

> *DATES: Jan−June 1979;*
>
> *SUBJECTS: sales, California, and home products.*

This query asks for information about all documents in the data base being searched that were issued during the first half of 1979, on the sales of home products in California. It is possible, in most such systems, to ask simultaneously for documents on any *one* of the three subjects given, in which case the "and" of the query would be replaced by an "or". Such a query is representative of those that can normally be used with a data base, although the complexity of the query can be far greater in some data-base systems. The response of the system is a tabulation of all documents meeting the criteria in the query. The user would presumably go to the company library for the necessary documents.

There are many data-base query systems that a company would find useful in planning. Their contents would likely be the many subjects that were addressed in Chapters 2 through 4. Very often, a data base of information on a corporation's competitors is maintained by the firm. Such a data base would cover patents, technical reports, technical disclosures, news items, product announcements, organization notices, and the like. They would be placed in the data base either by the company itself, if it were able to justify the cost, or by a commercial data base firm that sold retrieval services.

A Company's Document Retrieval System

If a company does operate its own document information system, with data bases on internal technical reports, invention proposals, and external reports of a technical and business nature, it will have to provide appropriate resources. The cost of such an undertaking will, of course, depend on the size and scope of the data bases it wishes to maintain. If the company's product line is very broad, it may require extensive data-base coverage. If it uses much advanced technology, it may want to monitor many outside developments in technology. It may want to monitor all of its competitors, who may be quite numerous. For example, a company whose sales are in the one billion dollar range might collect and store about 10,000 to 25,000 document records annually.

To illustrate the level of costs involved, assume that a company wishes to collect and store information on 25,000 documents per year. The staff would perhaps number twelve workers: five indexers, five clerks, and two data-base maintainers. The indexers develop information for entry into the data base. Their primary job is to identify *index terms* that describe the documents. The clerks do the data entry into the computer. The data-base maintainers see that the data bases are accurate and up-to-date and are purged as needed. Purging of old records takes place when those records are no longer needed. With sufficient auxiliary memory available, though, all records can be retained. Computer operating expenses and costs of acquisition of the material to be indexed and stored must also be considered. These costs typically run to about the same as staff costs.

A competitive surveillance system was described in Chapter 4. A computer-based document retrieval system is ideal for the maintenance of such a surveillance system, if a large volume of items is stored. The computer would be valuable in the storage and retrieval steps of such surveillance. It can be used to retrieve selectively from the data base, by company, industry, product line, or technology.

Network Planning

The planning of projects can be aided by the use of computers. A method called *network planning* is commonly used; some approaches are *critical path scheduling*, *PERT*, and *CPM*. These systems provide expected completion dates of projects, the critical paths of events for meeting schedules, and slack time available for other events.

A brief description of PERT (program evaluation and review technique) illustrates the general thrust of these systems. PERT addresses the scheduling of a project that has these traits:

a) It consists of well-defined activities; when all are completed the project is ended;

b) The activities are independent of each other; and

c) The activities are ordered; i.e, they must be performed in a particular order (though some leeway in the order may exist).

To use PERT, one begins by constructing flow diagrams that display graphically the relationships of activities to one another. Specifically, they show which activities must follow other activities and which may proceed simultaneously. The *critical path* is the path in the structure that represents the longest time to traverse. Activities in that path are critical in the sense that, if they are delayed, the entire project is delayed.

Several computer programs for scheduling large projects have been written. They determine critical paths, analyze variations of configurations, and aid in optimal scheduling of activities. Such programs are reviewed by Edward Davis [9].

Problems with Information Systems

Designing an information system that is useful for a variety of needs yet is not too expensive is not an easy task. The motivation to make the system broadly usable tends to increase the programming task and therefore its cost, while the motivation to keep the cost down tends to limit its breadth and general utility.

Data gathering, entering, and verifying is highly labor intensive and expensive, so funding these tasks must be carefully questioned. This cost is often overlooked by those who plan online retrieval systems. Once operational, such systems are often very valuable, but the cost of creating and maintaining them can be considerable. It is essential to determine whether all the data to be gathered are necessary, in the light of their cost and use. Commercial systems, though rather general, may provide reasonable alternatives.

Information systems have limitations. As with all programming systems, their capabilities are limited by what their designers and programmers build into them and by the quality of their data. Managers who undertake planning often need to have questions answered that are beyond the capabilities of such systems. All that the systems can do is supplement management's decision-making responsibilities; they cannot replace them.

SUMMARY

There are two major areas in planning activities for which a computer is particularly valuable. One is the modeling of systems of interest to a company; the other is the creation and use of information systems.

Computer-based models have been built for simulating companies' operations and their environments. Models can be executed rapidly on computers, allowing management to ask a series of "What if . . . ?" questions by varying many parameters of the model over ranges of values. The use of models involves two stages: (a) the relationships among all parameters in the model must be identified, generally as a set of equations; (b) the values of all relevant data must be gathered and supplied to the model during its execution. There are financial, production, marketing planning, and product models. Model generators are available for the construction and use of models. Integrating modeling into planning involves six steps: review of the planning environment, specification of planning requirements, definition of goals and objectives for planning, evaluation of existing planning resources, design of an integrated planning and modeling system, and formulation of a strategy for integrating the model.

Information systems allow companies to store and retrieve information of importance to them. Data base management systems are the vehicle for this activity. Management information systems (MIS's) are information systems designed to aid management in carrying out its responsibilities. Specifically, they store and process information, respond to queries, supply reports, and aid in monitoring operations. They can be integrated with models and allow managers to make conjectures about the company. Decision support decisions (DSS's) are special types of MIS's; they are supportive of decision making.

Query systems are computer-based information systems that allow users to ask questions about stored information, which commonly refers to external matters. A special language is generally available to permit the asking of such questions. Of special value in a company's attempts to monitor the environment is a document retrieval system

REFERENCES

1. Naylor, Thomas H., *Corporate Planning Models*, Addison-Wesley Publishing Company, Reading, Massachusetts, 1979, p. 87.

2. Lomas, T., "A Business Planning Model", Chapter 11 of *Mathematical Modeling*, J. G. Andrews and R. R. McLone, editors, Butterworths, London, 1976.

3. Naylor, Thomas H., *op cit*, pp. 17–21.

4. Mayo, R. Britton, and SIMPLAN Systems, Inc., *Corporate Planning and Modeling with SIMPLAN*, Addison-Wesley Publishing Company, Reading, Mass., pp. 88–107.

5. Davis, Gordon B., *Management Information Systems: Conceptual Foundations, Structure, and Development*, McGraw-Hill, Inc., New York, 1974, pp. 349–352.

6. Naylor, Thomas H., *op cit*, Chapter 3.

7. Simon, Herbert A., *The New Science of Management Decision*, Harper & Brothers, New York, 1960, pp. 54ff.

8. Keen, Peter G. W., and Michael S. Scott Morton, *Decision Support Systems: An Organizational perspective*, Addison-Wesley, Reading, Massachusetts, 1978, pp. 93–96.

9. Davis, Edward W., "Project Scheduling Under Resource Constraints – Historical Review and Categorization of Procedures," *AIIE (American Institute of Industrial Engineers) Transactions*, December 1973, vol. 5, no. 4, pp. 297–313.

Additional References

Naylor, Thomas H., *The Politics of Corporate Planning and Modeling*, published in book with same title, ed. by T. H. Naylor, Planning Executives Institute, 1978. (The paper deals with corporate planning and modeling, with emphasis on the problems involved in implementing models for planning.)

"Computer Support for Managers," *EDP Analyzer*, May 1979, vol. 17, no. 5. (This issue addresses various types of computer-based systems that aid management in decision-making, including MIS's and DSS's.)

Wiest, Jerome D., and Ferdinand K. Levy, *A Management Guide to PERT/CPM*, Prentice-Hall, Inc., Englewood Cliffs, N. J., 1977. (Both PERT and CPM are described, and many applications are offered.)

Davis, Gordon B., *Management Information Systems: Conceptual Foundations, Structure, and Development*, McGraw-Hill, Inc., New York, 1974. (This is a comprehensive book on MIS's, covering all aspects of the subject, including their relationship to planning.)

Benton, William K., *The Use of the Computer in Planning*, Addison-Wesley Publishing Co., Reading, Mass., 1971. (This book surveys applications of computers in solving problems in planning.)

Blanning, Robert W., "How Managers Decide to Use Planning Models," *Long Range Planning*, April 1980, vol. 13, no. 4, pp. 32–35. (The author describes four ways in which companies make decisions to develop planning models.)

Smith, L. A., and P. Mahler, "Comparing Commercially Available CPM/PERT Computer Programs," *Industrial Engineering*, April 1978, vol. 10, no. 4, pp. 37–39. (This paper provides a list and brief evaluation of computer programs.)

Gorry, G. Anthony, and Michael S. Scott Morton, "A Framework for Management Information Systems", *Sloan Management Review*, Fall 1971. (This is an early paper on the subject; it provides a good introduction to it.)

10

THEORY AND PRACTICE

INTRODUCTION

The process of strategic planning, as described in this book, can be considered a framework or a set of guidelines for the planning process in a corporation. Although this book stresses that no single method is applicable to all companies, it is useful here to define that framework as a starting point for a company to develop its own approaches. There are many reasons for a company to deviate from the theoretical framework to meet its needs. Often, corporate executives will want to impose their own style of management, which will have some impact on strategic planning. In the real world, there are many problems in undertaking the strategic planning process. There are many circumstances under which the framework must be modified merely to match reality. There are methods for addressing many of the problems, but not all will work in all situations.

10.1 A THEORETICAL FRAMEWORK

The Framework

The planning method described in this book can be summarized by the following series of steps:

1. Perform analyses
   1.1 Analyze the company. Consider: major problems, technology, products and markets, manufacturing, marketing and sales, service, manpower, finances, organization.

   1.2 <u>Analyze the environment</u>. Consider: major problems, the competition, technology, markets, supply factors, socioeconomic factors.

2. Forecast the future

   2.1 <u>Project the future</u>. Consider: competition and technology, markets, customers, raw materials, supply factors, socioeconomic factors.

   2.2 <u>Predict technology needs</u>. Identify: needed product and technology advances, technology expectations, technology gaps, R & D required to close gaps.

   2.3 <u>Make assumptions</u>. Make assumptions on what the environment is expected to be over the plan period.

   2.4 <u>Determine extrapolated future in the environment</u>.

     a) Project the future of the environment.

     b) Project the future of the company, taking into account the future of the environment.

3. Set objectives and goals

   3.1 <u>Ask key questions</u>. Address business the company is in, what rate of growth is satisfactory, what methods of growth to use.

   3.2 <u>Define mission and philosophy of operation</u>

   3.3 <u>Set corporate objectives</u>. Consider: current objectives, technology alternatives, strengths and weaknesses, opportunities and strengths, constraints, corporate image.

   3.4 <u>Set divisional objectives</u>.

   3.5 <u>Set subobjectives</u>.

   3.6 <u>Set goals</u>.

4. Consider technology issues

   4.1 <u>Consider objectives for technology</u>. Develop linkage between corporate objectives and technology objectives.

   4.2 <u>Address rapid change of technology</u>. Address: proprietary advances, product modularity, need for much R & D investment, maintenance of awareness of outside developments.

   4.3 <u>Consider risks</u>. Assess level of risks of all programs.

   4.4 <u>Consider acquisitions</u>. Alternatives: internal development, external purchase or lease.

   4.5 <u>Send up technology alternatives</u>. Develop alternatives; send to top management; have management respond to them.

   4.6 <u>Perform technology assessments</u>. Consider: historical development, potential, opportunities, status, cost, time, probability of success, competition.

4.7 <u>Plan new technology development</u>. Do a technology assessment; identify products; identify time and resources needed.

4.8 <u>Consider technology maturity</u>. Consider degree of maturity of all technologies.

4.9 <u>Plan technology transfer</u>. Consider: methodology, communications, timing.

5. <u>Set strategy</u>

5.1 <u>Identify feasible activities</u>. Consider: current strategy, preplanning analysis report, critical success factors, product line, product niches, difference in desired and projected futures, current strategies, the product matrix, feature trade-offs.

5.2 <u>Select activities to be undertaken</u>. Consider: R & D budget, priorities for research, research priorities, evaluation procedures, ranking, selection, activities to be canceled.

5.3 <u>Do contingency planning</u>. Develop alternative strategies for the possibility that assumptions may turn out to be wrong; ask "What if . . . ?" questions.

6. <u>Prepare the plan</u>

6.1 <u>Allocate resources</u>. Project financial future, allocate resources

6.2 <u>Develop operational plans</u>. Consider: objectives, approach, rationale, resources, schedule.

6.3 <u>Develop budgets</u>.

7. <u>Set milestones</u>

7.1 <u>Identify specific tasks</u>. Include completion dates.

8. <u>Monitor progress</u>

8.1 <u>Compare progress to plan</u>. Modify as required.

A chart of the planning process, summarizing these steps, is depicted in Fig. 10-1. An important aspect of the process, not shown here, is the flow of information, which is cyclic, iterative, continuous, and bidirectional. Another important aspect of the model is the sequence of events, as described by the calendar of events.

The outline of steps above is what we call the *theoretical framework*, or *model*, of the planning process. In this process, steps are straightforward, information flows as is required, and decisions are made on a schedule that allows the smooth development of a strategic plan. As we shall see, this theoretical approach requires modification and adaptation before it can be used. It requires modification for particular situations as they occur in a variety of companies' management styles.

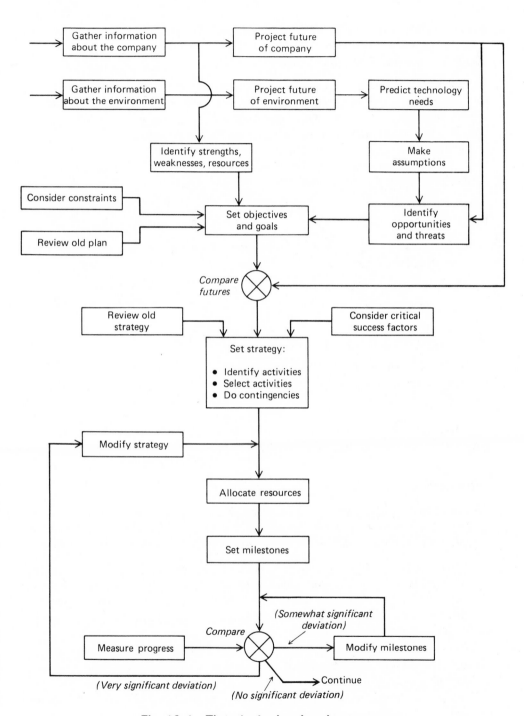

Fig. 10-1. The strategic planning process.

10.2 CHANGES TO THE FRAMEWORK

Modifying the Framework

The theoretical framework can be used as a set of guidelines for carrying out the process of planning. Most likely, it should be modified to meet the needs of individual companies and their managements. If a company so chooses, it can be modified to become that company's own theoretical framework. The purpose of doing this is to allow the company to establish guidelines for its own planning. Even beyond this, there may be deviations from this customized model, as current circumstances warrant them.

Factors in a Company

Some factors within its company that management should examine in developing its own framework are the following:

A. Product development time

B. Type of products

C. Type of markets

D. Degree of uncertainty in environment

E. Style of management

F. Nature of technology

G. Organization of company

These company factors are referred to below, where various planning parameters are considered.

Planning Parameters

We consider the parameters of the planning process that may have to be changed to meet a company's needs and note which factors in the company (given in parentheses) influence each of these parameters:

1. Overall approach to planning. The style of management plays a large role in all aspects of planning done in a company. The more formal or tightly controlled is the style, the more formal and intense must be the planning process. Besides, since competition plays a major role in determining a company's performance, the whole planning process is affected by this factor. Finally, the greater the uncertainty in the environment, the more difficult is the planning. (Factors: C, E.)

2. Planning and plan periods. The strategic planning and plan periods are related to product development times. If the planning period is very short (e.g., six months), it is probably not necessary to repeat each step each

period; objectives setting may still need review but once a year. Another factor that influences the plan period is the volatility of the markets being served. If they change rapidly, long-term planning may not be possible. Finally, the more advanced the technology being planned for products, the longer the plan period ought to be, though there are exceptions to this. (Factors: A, B, C, F.)

3. Degree of environmental monitoring. The effort required in monitoring a company's environment depends on the need to be aware of events in that environment. This need increases with the extent of competition, newness of markets being addressed, the uncertainty in the environment, and the depth of technology orientation. (Factors: B, C, F.)

4. Extent of forecasting into the future. Forecasts, made closer or further into the future, have greater or lesser accuracy. In volatile and uncertain fields, shorter-range, less accurate forecasts must suffice. Products with long development times demand long-term forecasting. (Factors: A, C.)

5. Types of objectives. In a volatile industry, it is difficult to set specific objectives; they must be very general. In a rather quiescent industry, objectives can be specific and are likely to remain relatively static. If technologies are new and untried, setting objectives will be difficult. If a company is diversified along product lines, it may develop different objectives for each division. (Factors: C, F, G.)

6. Methods of setting strategy. In fields with much uncertainty, the choices of activities are relatively very numerous, so that decision making is especially difficult, and contingency planning becomes more critical. In short, the strategy setting process becomes more complex. With products having long development times, strategy setting involves fewer choices but must deal with more details. If a company is diversified, it may develop different strategies for each division. (Factors: A, C, G.)

10.3 PROBLEMS IN PLANNING

In many of the previous chapters, problems that exist in each stage in strategic planning are described. Many of these problems are summarized here, grouped by categories, and suggestions for dealing with them are given. It should be noted, though, that just as the problems vary among companies, so do the proper responses to them.

Management Problems

Lack of sufficient top management support. There is much preoccupation by management with current, short-term problems, and often long-term thinking is given a low priority. The result can be a discrediting of strategic planning.

This situation can be improved by convincing and allowing top management to devote the majority of its time to planning. It is important to establish an organizational structure whereby only the most important short-term issues are sent to top management and whereby a corporate planning staff monitors planning activities so that the CEO need only address major planning issues.

Strategic planning cannot be accomplished and serve its purpose without the support of top management. The CEO of a corporation probably should spend at least half of his or her time in planning. The CEO has to be convinced that doing strategic planning will provide better corporate results than not doing it. Strategic planning has to be integrated within the management's decision-making process. We have seen how strategic planning is linked to decision making, and this link must be maintained.

Attitude of managers. There may be misconceptions about planning, a fear of giving up control, and a resistance to change in general. There may be little perception of the need for strategic planning.

Clearly, the answer here is the proper education of all management about the purpose, the nature, and the methodology of planning. All managers should take part in the process. It isn't enough for only top management to be sold on strategic planning. All managers in the company must see the need and the potential benefits. They must believe that their planning efforts will pay off for them.

Inappropriate reward systems. Typically, the reward system in a company discourages strategic planning while encouraging short range planning and concern over day-to-day operations.

A solution to this problem is to modify the reward system, with a portion of each manager's compensation being based on performance several years in the future. As an example, a portion of a manager's total compensation might be paid in five yearly installments and be based upon the results in the future of a manager's current decisions. Thus, each year the manager's salary is based on each of the past five years. This runs counter to virtually all current systems of compensation, but it is likely to result in better strategic planning.

Improper decision making. Decision making often tends to be reactive rather than be based on plans, as managers react to surprises and base decisions on them.

An approach to changing this situation is to base decisions tentatively on plans and then to modify them if new elements are discovered. The objectives and strategy of the strategic plan can and should serve as a guide to decision making, and this link cannot be ignored.

Entrepreneurs. The entrepreneurial spirit has often proved highly successful in innovation and product design and development, yet it often tends to be ignored or suppressed in large corporations. Management should do its best to stimulate this kind of thinking and action, by providing budget support and freedom of action.   The scale of activity of the entrepreneur is often a few orders of magnitude smaller than most activity in large corporations, and as such is deemed unimportant.   Entrepreneurial thinking can and should be incorporated in the planning process.

Information Gathering

The problems involved in gathering data for analysis are described in two areas: internal and external information.

Company information.   One difficulty in collecting company information is that needed information is not necessarily organized for planning purposes.   Another is that it is difficult to gather information on managers' concerns, since they often do not like to reveal them.   Top management often promotes this attitude by making it clear it does not want to hear about internal problems.

An approach to the first problem is to identify the reports and other sources of information that will be used for company analysis and then have them written and organized as though their primary function was to serve in the planning process.

An approach to the second problem is to have a company policy whereby difficulties, including failures, are not punished by reduced raises, demotions, or comparable actions.   Managers are hired to solve problems, and their inability to do so is not always indicative of their incompetence.   It may be best to engage a management consultant to address this sensitive area.

Competitive information.   Information about competitors is generally available in abundance, but its accuracy is often low.   One must extract the most useful information, and that is not easy to do.   Management must treat all outside data with suspicion, until their accuracy is confirmed.   If the information is very important, extra efforts at confirmation (as from other sources) is essential.

An important way to deal with competitive information is to establish a comprehensive information system about one's competitors, their products, and markets of interest.   This was discussed in Chapter 4.

Markets.   Identifying new products is not easy if they are radically new to the marketplace.   Market studies in such cases are often misleading.   Even identifying markets is a problem.

Management must define markets as carefully as possible and gather data equally carefully.   Market studies must be very well planned and evaluated.   The right questions must be asked of prospective customers.   These questions should relate to their actual experience; this requirement makes surveying in new markets especially troublesome.   Professional market survey firms can be valuable here.

Socioeconomic factors   The relationship of socioeconomic and political factors and company profits is not always clear.

A solution to the dilemma may lie in attempts to relate company performance to external factors. A model of the company's operation within its environment, with all pertinent outside factors considered, is invaluable in judging the effects of changes in those factors. A model comprehensive enough to address all such factors is not easy to construct, however.

Forecasting

Forecasting the future is often very difficult; events occur that are totally unexpected or considered unlikely to occur when they do. Data gathered from outside sources are incomplete and inaccurate. The cost of gathering data is often high. One must contend with competitors' attempts to maintain secrecy. Finally, obtaining the opinions of experts leads to problems due to wishful or biased thinking, ignoring of pertinent factors, and limited perspective.

There is no simple solution for these difficulties. It comes down to a matter of buying what information one needs and can afford and no more. The more accurate and complete the data gathered, the more expensive it will be. Management must decide just what it needs, estimate what the costs will be, judge if the costs are justifiable, and then decide how far to pursue the search for information.

Several forecasting methods were described in Chapter 4. Some may be particularly useful for the problems at hand. Using experts, as by the Delphi method or on a private basis, may be valuable as well.

The best way to deal with the human errors in forecasting is to use as many different and diverse experts as feasible. It is very helpful if the accuracy and reliability of each are known, so appropriate relative weights can be assigned to all opinions.

Setting Objectives

Setting objectives is difficult because (a) managers tend to emphasize the short term over the long term, (b) the linkage between technology needs and corporate objectives is not always made, (c) the forces that drive R & D objectives differ from those that drive corporate objectives, (d) misinterpretations of technology alternatives by top management may exist, and (e) corporate culture is sometimes ignored. The first of these problems has been addressed above. The last is discussed below. The others are discussed in Chapter 6.

Top management, when it attempts to either change direction in a major way or undertake new initiatives, must closely examine the ongoing traditions and values of its company. Among strong cultures that companies may have are financial discipline, technological innovation, company loyalty, overtaking the competition, and a drive for quality service. Management should carefully examine and understand its firm's values, because they sometimes are at odds with proposed new undertakings. It must ensure that there will be no conflict.

Setting Strategy

Selecting the activities that will go to comprise a strategy is a difficult task, because generally there are many candidates, and it is hard to evaluate each of them accurately. Another problem in formulating a strategy is the tendency of managers to be risk-averse and so take a conservative approach, which may be less than optimal. Finally, there is sometimes little encouragement to managers to think imaginatively.

It is easier to judge a strategy that has been proposed, i.e., where activities have been selected, than it is to make the selection. Management can verify that a strategy meets the company's needs. That should be done thoroughly and rigorously, for it provides the best way to insure that a strategy is likely to meet the company's needs. Since strategy formulation is based in part on projections of the future, there is no foolproof methodology for the process.

The best way to minimize risk-averse attitudes is to create an atmosphere whereby risk taking is not threatening. There should be management encouragement of a certain amount of risk and a lack of punishment if a venture is unsuccessful.

On the matter of encouraging imaginative thinking, top management has to provide appropriate rewards for innovative ideas. During the planning process, there must be an opportunity for all staff members to contribute strategic ideas, and there must be a way of providing incentives for them to do so. The key is in the attitude of all managers regarding their perception of top management's views on the subject.

In developing a strategy, a company should not settle for merely planning for the future, attempting only to respond to expected external events. Rather, it should strongly attempt to *create* its own future.

Special Problems in Technology-Based Companies

Chapter 6 addresses a number of technology issues that technology-based companies must address. Each of these issues has problems associated with it, and they are discussed at some length in that chapter. They are not included here, since they relate more to the nature of technology than to the nature of planning.

General Comments on Solutions

Clearly, none of these proposed solutions to the problems associated with strategic planning is guaranteed to provide success. They are, in fact, rather general proposals. Each, however, is likely to improve the process to some extent. The circumstances within each company vary so widely that these proposals can at best act as guidelines to ways of improving planning. Management must take into the account specific needs of its corporation.

Survey on the Quality of Strategic Planning

The survey that the author conducted on strategic planning in technology-based companies revealed views by planning managers and others on what was not done well in their companies in strategic planning. Following are some comments provided by these companies:

1. The planning is not long-range enough; not enough forecasting is done.
2. The process is too time-consuming and involves too much paperwork.
3. Insufficient attention is paid to new business possibilities that either cross division lines or fall outside all divisions' charters.
4. Particularly troublesome are the tasks of identifying key issues early, obtaining enough satisfactory information for making decisions, focusing on the future in the face of current schedules and problems, and attempting to plan with insufficient planning skills among managers.

Pitfalls in Planning

George Steiner has published a list of 50 planning pitfalls, developed from a survey he conducted [1]. These are "traps" that management can and often does fall into. The list includes the most significant pitfalls in such areas as understanding strategic planning practices, in getting planning started, in doing planning, and in using the resultant plans. The ten pitfalls that are most important to avoid, as judged by respondents to the survey, are the following:

1. Top management assumes that it can delegate the planning function to someone else.
2. Top management becomes so engrossed in current problems that it spends insufficient time on strategic planning, and the process becomes discredited in the eyes of other managers.
3. The company fails to develop goals suitable as a basis for formulating strategic plans.
4. Major line personnel fail to assume the necessary involvement in the planning process.
5. Plans are not used as standards for measuring managerial performance.
6. Management fails to create a climate in the company that is congenial and not resistant to planning.
7. Managers assume that planning is separate from the management process.
8. There is so much formality in the planning system that it lacks flexibility, looseness, and simplicity, and restrains creativity.
9. Top management fails to review with divisional and departmental heads the strategic plans which they have developed.

10. Top management rejects the formal planning process by making intuitive decisions which conflict with formal plans.

These ten pitfalls are offered here without comment, since the cures for the errors are generally more or less obvious. Many have been discussed earlier in this section.

Checklist for the CEO

A list of points that a chief executive officer should keep in mind with regard to strategic planning appears in a publication by Business International Corporation [2]. The list is entitled "For the CEO: A Planning Checklist". The points listed are these:

1. Clarify your own predilections and inclinations.

2. Make sure the goals you really care about come to light in the planning process loud and clear.

3. Planning is essentially decision making; either do it yourself or make sure your top executives do it.

4. Make sure your chief line executives understand your commitment to planning.

5. Always think of *plan* as a verb, not a noun.

6. You cannot stress the concepts of *thinking* and *communications* enough.

7. Emphasize simplicity.

8. Make sure planning concentrates on major business problems and issues.

9. De-emphasize financial detail; instead, stress the words the assumptions. that accompany them.

10. Conceptually divorce planning from budgeting.

11. Emphasize actions or action programs in your planning.

12. Consider, on the other hand, only those actions that will occur "between now and the next planning meeting".

13. Pay close attention to the planning schedule or cycle.

14. Look at planning as an integrated process, or as a system.

15. Look at planning also as a kind of telescope onto your future business.

16. Have the planning director report to you personally.

17. Select a top-flight executive as your planning director.

18. Change something, if you find him or her gravitating toward the shelf.

19. Be certain to follow up, but be careful how you do it.

SUMMARY

A theoretical framework for the strategic planning process can be defined which includes all the steps described in this book. The framework can serve as a set of guidelines for the process. in practice, however, companies will modify this model because of special factors in their particular situations. These factors include product development time, product types, market types, degree of environmental uncertainty, style of management, the nature of technology in the company, and the company's organizational structure.

As a result of such factors, there are several parameters in the company that may have to be changed from the framework described. These include the company's overall approach to planning, the planning and plan periods, the degree of environmental monitoring, the extent of forecasting done, the types of objectives set, and the means of setting strategy.

There is another important reason why the theoretical framework will have to be modified. Management will encounter many problems in undertaking strategic planning. These problems cover almost every aspect of the planning process. To solve the many existing problems, companies will have to change the guidelines offered to suit their needs.

REFERENCES

1. Steiner, George A., *Strategic Planning: What Every Manager Must Know*, The Free Press, a division of Macmillan Publishing Co., Inc., New York, 1979, pp. 287–294.

2. *201 Checklists: Decision Making in International Operations*, Business International Corporation, New York, 1980.

Additional references

Gluck, Frederick W., Stephen P. Kaufman, and A. Steven Walleck, "Strategic Management for Competitive Advantage", *Harvard Business Review*, July-August 1980, vol. 58, no. 4, pp. 158–161. (This paper describes four stages of planning that companies progress through, the last of which is strategic management.)

11

THE FUTURE AND
STRATEGIC PLANNING

INTRODUCTION

That the methodology of strategic planning for high-technology companies will change in the future is as certain as that the nature of technology itself will change. Technology will indeed change, and that change will have an impact on planning methodology in at least two ways.

The way in which strategic planning is done by a corporation depends on the nature of the technologies it addresses. Consequently, since technologies in the decade ahead will have a different character from technologies today, planning will also change.

Additionally, certain technologies will enable strategic planning to be done more efficiently and more appropriately. The technologies that will bring this about lie primarily in the information processing fields.

11.1 NEW TECHNOLOGIES

A large portion of new and emerging technologies deal with information, with its gathering, processing, storage, and distribution. The influence on society of microelectronics and large, inexpensive memory stores, major factors in such processes, will be enormous. This technology is seen as a major hope for reviving lagging productivity growth throughout the industrial world. The "post-industrial society" of Daniel Bell will be based on information and its utilization [1]. The number of jobs serving the *information society*, as it is often called, will continue to grow at a fast pace for many years. Today, about half of the work force in the United States is in this "knowledge-based" industry.

Electronics will also have major impact on education, on the health fields, on transportation, on science and engineering, on the entertainment business, and in fact on almost any industry. Electronics products will impact our lives at home and at work. Personal computers, word processors, communicating networks, electronic file systems, and new video recording machines will become commonplace.

The major driving force in this electronics "revolution" is the advent of microelectronics, a technology that allows incorporation of hundreds of thousands of circuit elements on small chips.   The important consequences of this revolution are exemplified by the substitution of energy-efficient communications for energy-consuming transportation. Microelectronics will allow optimization of the use of scarce resources by computation. In other terms, information, rather than machinery, becomes the central commodity. Microelectronics will, in short, revolutionize all phases of society.

In this book, we have discussed the fast pace of technology advancement. The pace is especially fast in electronics. The consequence is that strategic planning will have to be faster paced, will involve more monitoring of the environment, and will be more difficult to do effectively.

There are forces that work in the opposite direction, too. Changes in society in the United States will have impact on technology development. Among the trends that will influence the nature of emerging technologies are these: (a) society is getting older, on the average, and so will become less mobile than at present; (b) fuel costs are rising faster than most other segments of consumer costs, so that transportation will be curtailed or at least modified; (c) the number of young workers (ages 20 to 30), though large now, will be far less in 1990, as a result of the sharp drop in the birth rate in the 1960's. All of these forces strengthen the views that the information industry will be the fastest growing industrial segment of United States society and that planning for technology will change.

11.2 TECHNOLOGIES FOR PLANNING

As discussed in Chapter 9, the computer has become a useful tool in planning, as a base for models, for information systems, and for the utilization of both in combination.

There will be many more packages for financial planning than there are today. Optimization, risk analysis, and graphic output are three developing areas. There will be advances in all phases of computer modeling, as the interrelationship among parameters, both internal and external, become better understood.   Acceptance of such models will grow as they are improved.

The revolution that has been occurring in the computer industry will continue; the following advances will have certain consequences: (a) greater sophistication will be available at lower cost, causing computers to be yet more pervasive; (b) improved languages for user interaction will induce more direct involvement of individuals; (c) the growth of distributed data processing, where computer processors at several locations are interconnected via a network, will allow greater communication among users; and (d) larger, cheaper memories, with improved access time, will allow users to have access and to utilize more information. All of these changes will ease the burdens imposed by tougher challenges in planning.

11.3 FUTURE TRENDS IN PLANNING

Following are some of the trends in strategic planning that are expected in the future. Many of these trends are under way at the present time.

Heightened importance of planning. More emphasis is being put on planning; this trend is expected to continue. Planning organizations report to higher-level corporate executives than previously, and larger planning staffs are being used. This trend is indicative of the recognition of the importance of strategic planning.

More comprehensive planning. More and more firms are integrating many staff functions with product and business planning; these include finance, organization development, acquisitions and divestitures, manpower, and marketing. The result is that the planning process is being applied to more and more segments of a corporation, in an integrated, holistic manner.

Improved planning methods. In general, the planning process as practiced by corporations will improve over the years. In companies that do little or no planning currently and in companies where the process is still evolving, there is probably going to be improvement for some time. The formalism will be better understood and accepted by management. Information gathering and analysis will improve as managers realize what information is required and how they can best use it. Forces in a company's environment will become better understood. Successive attempts at strategy formulation will yield better approaches and better strategies. Companies go through a stage where their planning becomes ever more formal. Once planning is well integrated into their management process, it becomes more flexible, because it becomes more routine.

Improved analytical tools. In addition to the increased use of computer simulation models described above, there will be more sophisticated mathematical methods available. These will allow better understanding of the decision-making process, better technological forecasting, and better evaluation of strategic alternatives than at present.

Growth in specialized planning. A new approach to strategic planning is receiving attention. It comprises long-range studies aimed at specific countries, industries, or issues. The difficulties of scanning the entire environment, coupled with external pressures in particular areas, is forcing companies to concentrate their efforts more narrowly and deeply.

Less use of portfolio concepts. As competition pressures increase in the United States from overseas, management is relying less on the concept of a portfolio of products and more on achieving a greater return on investment in present product lines. Greater emphasis is being placed on each product line individually rather than as part of a diversified whole. The trend towards growing present product lines and extending them, rather than branching into new businesses, is increasing.

Joint participation of business and government. There will be greater joint participation in strategic planning by industry and government, particularly in critical social-problem areas, such as development of energy sources, city planning, productivity improvements, and pollution and environmental controls. This trend will continue because both the private and the public sectors can offer help in these areas in their particular ways and because joint planning will become more critical.

REFERENCES

1. Bell, Daniel, *The Post-Industrial Society,* Basic Books, Inc., New York, 1973.

Additional Reference

Cornelissen, J. A., "Corporate Strategy in the Eighties", *Long Range Planning*, December 1977, vol. 10, no. 12, pp. 2–6. (This paper discusses changes needed in corporate strategy in the 1980's and beyond.)

APPENDIXES

Appendix for Chapter 2

QUESTIONS ON THE COMPANY

INTRODUCTION

The questions here are related to those appearing in Chapter 2, *Analysis of a Company*. Sections are labeled exactly as in that chapter, indicating that the questions here are for those sections in Chapter 2.

Chapter 2 contains a sequence of key questions for management to address while performing an analysis of its company. This appendix contains a much lengthier sequence of questions, *auxiliary questions*, that follow from the key questions. (Key questions from those chapters are repeated here, for convenience.) If management is to undertake a comprehensive analysis, these auxiliary questions should be addressed. The reader is encouraged to add questions that are appropriate to his or her company's needs.

Following most sets of auxiliary questions are tables that list sources of information within a company. Such sources vary considerably among companies, so the lists are necessarily incomplete.

For Section 2.2 MAJOR PROBLEMS AND DECISIONS

Major Problems

Key questions:

> *What major problems are we currently facing?*
> *What major problems are we likely to face over the plan period?*

Auxiliary questions addressed to each current problem:

What are the probable consequences of the problem's existence?

Have we faced the problem before?

What happened?

What was done about it and with what results?

What are the possible solutions to the problem now?

What are the expected costs and benefits?

Auxiliary questions addressed to each future problem:

What would be the problem's probable consequences?

Have we faced the problem before?

What happened?

What was done about it and with what results?

What would be the possible solutions to the problem?

What would be the expected costs and benefits?

Major Decisions

Key question:

What are the major decisions that management must make during the plan period?

Auxiliary questions addressed to each decision:

What is behind the decision, i.e., why is it a major decision?

What are the several alternatives that can be chosen?

What are the possible and probable outcomes of each of these choices?

For Section 2.3   TECHNOLOGY

Technologies

Key question:

What is the status of our technologies?

Auxiliary questions addressed to each technology:

How is it used today?

How are we planning to use it?

What will be the status of each in the future?

Where is it heading?
What capabilities will it have?
When will it have these?
What cost and performance improvements are expected?

Research Projects

Key question:

What are our research projects?

Auxiliary questions addressed to each project:

What are its goals?
Why was it undertaken?
Where is it heading?
What new capabilities are sought?
At what technologies or product programs is it aimed?
If there are no identified needs for it, is the work justified on some other basis?
What are the milestones?
What are the costs?
What plans are there for transfer to Development?

Research Activity

Key question:

What is the quality of the research done in our company?

Auxiliary questions:

How do the rates of our inventions, patents, outside talks, and published papers compare to other companies in our field?
What plans do we have for changing our research projects?
What areas are planned for increased and for decreased resources?

Experience and Applications

Key questions:

What is our experience in various areas of research and technology?
Where is it applicable?

Auxiliary questions:

In which research disciplines are we particularly strong?

Where are we weak?

What unique or unusual technical skills do we have?

What is the type and extent of our experience in each technology?

Is it proprietary?

In what products has it been used?

In what products might it be used in the future?

Is it currently available for use?

Are there potential breakthroughs in using this technology?

How likely are these breakthroughs?

What benefits may accrue from its use?

What problems in our current or planned products can it solve?

What are the development costs?

Development Programs

Key question:

What are our development programs?

Auxiliary questions addressed to each program:

What are its goals?

To what extent is the program relevant to our planned products?

Where is it leading?

How is it related to our planned products?

How is it related to business plans and objectives?

What are the milestones?

What are the costs?

What plans are there for the program to be transferred to Manufacturing for production?

New Programs

Key questions:

What new R & D programs are planned?

Auxiliary questions addressed to each project and program:

What are its goals?

What products are envisioned?
Toward which corporate objectives is it aimed?
What are the projected costs?

R & D Spending

Key questions:

What is the pattern of our R & D spending?

Auxiliary questions:

What has been the pattern?
What are we planning for the future?
Why are we so planning?
How does our spending for R & D, as a fraction of sales (or other measure), compare with others in our field?
If it is different, why is this so?
What is our projected future spending?

Failures

Key question:

Which R & D programs have failed to lead to products?

Auxiliary questions addressed to each program:

What are the reasons for this?
Were some results technologically but not economically feasible?
Why so?
How can we now do the job better?

Technology Transfer

Key question:

How effectively are research projects transferred to the development organizations?

Auxiliary questions:

What provisions and procedures are established to effect the transfer?
How can the transfer process be improved?
Are any improvements currently planned?

Sources of Information on Company Technology

Source	Information available
Laboratory notebooks	Details on technology developments
Technical reports	Status of old and new technologies
Technical memoranda	Status of technologies
Invention proposals	Invention ideas
Technical progress reports	Status of technologies
Technical assessments	Utility of technologies
Test reports	Technical details of programs
R & D plans	Plans for R & D
Manuals	Details on product operation
Company patents	Operational technologies

For Section 2.4 PRODUCTS AND MARKETS

Product Features

Key question:

What new and improved features are being planned for our products by using our technology base?

Auxiliary questions:

What new features are planned for introduction and when?

What technologies are involved?

What are the costs and development times?

Are there any features that might be affected by government regulations, scarcities, or increased cost of raw materials?

New Products

Key question:

What new products are we planning to offer, based on our technology programs?

Auxiliary questions on planned products:

What new product and product improvements are planned?

What are their specifications?

What dates are planned for their market introduction?
Is our technology program designed to meet our needs in these areas?

Auxiliary questions on potential products:

Which of these products are viable, technologically and financially?
What technology advances are required for these products?
What resources would be required?
When could such products be marketed?

Current Products

Key question:

How well are our current products doing in the marketplace?

There are also key questions in subcategories under this heading:

Key question on sales:

What are the sales of each current product?

Auxiliary questions addressed to each product:

What has been the nature of its sales recently?
Why has it been such?
What is projected for the future?
Why is it so projected?

Key question on market share:

What shares of their markets do our products have?

Auxiliary questions:

How have those shares been growing?
What are the factors that determine our share?
By what means could our company conceivably increase its market shares?
What resources would be required to do so?
In what time period can this be done?
What changes do we expect in the market shares our products now hold?
What are the causes for this?

Key question on product costs:

What are the component manufacturing costs of the product?

Auxiliary questions addressed to each product:

What shares of total costs do R & D, manufacturing, sales, distribution, and service each comprise?

What do these costs depend upon?

Which of the costs can be reduced with technology advances?

Which of the costs are excessively high and should be reduced?

How can this be accomplished?

How will these costs rise over the plan period?

Key question on product withdrawals:

Which products now on the market are planned for withdrawal?

Auxiliary questions addressed to each product:

Why are we planning to withdraw it?

When are we planning to withdraw it?

Will it be replaced by other products?

What are those products?

Markets

Key questions:

What are the markets for our products?

What new markets are we planning to enter?

Auxiliary questions addressed to each market:

How is it structured, by product line, customer traits, volume?

What are recent trends of these factors?

How do customers view this market?

Geographic Areas

Key question:

In what parts of the country or the world are our products now marketed?

Auxiliary questions:

What products are marketed in each area?

What are planned for each area?

What technologies apply to these several products?

Sources of Information on Company Products and Markets

Source	Information available
Strategic plans	Various information
Internal reports	Technical details
Product proposals	Plans for new products
Product program specs	Details on plans for new products and product improvements
Product specifications	Information about products
Market studies	Details on markets, customer views and attitudes
Government reports	Regulations on product specs and environmental impacts

For Section 2.5 *CORPORATE RESOURCES*

Manufacturing

Key question on capacity:

What is the capacity of our manufacturing operations?

Auxiliary questions:

What new plants are either under way or are planned for construction?
What are the dates of completion?
What would it cost to increase capacity by 20, 50, and 100%?
How could this be done?
How long would it take?
What locations would be better — with lower operating costs, better access to materials and supplies, and less expensive distribution costs?

Key question on flexibility:

How flexible are our manufacturing operations?

Auxiliary questions:

To what extent is Manufacturing able to manufacture a product with a new technology embodiment?
How can this situation be improved?

Key question on equipment resources:

What is the state of our manufacturing equipment?

Auxiliary questions:

What new equipment is required?
What are the costs?
How long will it take to acquire them?
What equipment, if any, should be scrapped?

Key question on other facilities:

What is the state of our other facilities?

Auxiliary questions:

What facilities have we?
Which are adequate and which are not?
Where is improvement needed?
Where is expansion required?

Key question on communication:

What is the extent of the communication between Development and Manufacturing?

Auxiliary questions:

Do we have formal procedures for this purpose?
What are they?
Can they be improved?
Are such procedures needed?

Sources of Information on Company Manufacturing and Facilities

Source	Information available
Manufacturing data	Costs, schedules, materials lead times, facilities
Facilities documents	Data on facilities' sizes, ages, capacities

Marketing and Sales

Key question on marketing:

What market studies have we done and are currently doing or planning?

Auxiliary questions:

>   *Have the recent studies been useful?*
>
>   *Could they have been better?*
>
>   *What new market studies, in existing or potential markets, are planned?*
>
>   *Are we addressing all the markets we should be?*

Key question on sales:

>   *Are all aspects of our company's markets adequately covered by our sales force?*

Auxiliary questions:

>   *What is our sales effort in each product line?*
>
>   *Which appear to be most successful?*
>
>   *What is the cost of product sales?*
>
>   *What has been the recent trend of these costs?*
>
>   *What plans have we to improve the productivity of our sales force?*

Sources of Information on Company Marketing and Sales

Source	Information available
Market research reports	Nature of markets
Sales reports	Sales data

Service

Key question on quality:

>   *What is the quality of service provided in the maintenance and repair of products, as perceived by customers?*

Auxiliary questions:

>   *Is this satisfactory to customers?*
>
>   *Is this satisfactory to management?*
>
>   *How can it be improved?*

Key question on costs:

>   *What is the cost of maintenance and repair of each product?*

Auxiliary questions:

>   *What are the components of maintenance and repair costs?*
>
>   *What would the additional cost be of improving the service a given amount?*

What would customer reaction be to such improvement?

What is the trend of costs of product maintenance and repair?

What plans do we have to deal with these changes?

Sources of Information on Company Service

Source	Information available
Service reports	Types and costs of service rendered
Customer letters	Perception of service

Manpower

Key question on staffing:

What manpower skills and technical expertise exist now in our company?

Auxiliary questions:

What is the extent of these skills and expertise?

What skills and expertise are insufficient and in excess?

What is our staff turnover rate?

What are our plans for hiring of needed skills?

To what extent do we have a replacement program for staff?

Key question on training:

What training programs do we currently have?

Auxiliary questions:

Are these programs satisfactory?

What programs are planned?

How will these be implemented?

What available outside seminars would be valuable to our staffs?

What is the cost of these various approaches?

Sources of Information on Company Manpower

Source	Information available
Personnel records	Details on current employees
Recruiting records	Information on applicants and on recruiting methods and sources
Training booklets	Courses offered; instructors

Finances

Key question on cash flow:

> *What has been our cash flow in recent years?*

Auxiliary questions:

> *What has our company's record been on profit in recent years?*
> *What have the components of cash flow been in this period?*
> *What are the primary influences on this pattern?*
> *Are these influences likely to persist?*
> *What do we expect our profits to be in the future?*
> *What are individual divisions and product line profits?*
> *What factors have significant impact on our profits?*

Key question on consistency of earnings:

> *How consistent have our earnings been in recent years?*

Auxiliary questions:

> *Where are significant deviations from a generally smooth curve of earnings?*
> *What are the specific causes of such deviations?*
> *Are these causes likely to persist?*

Key question on revenues:

> *What has our record on revenues been in recent years?*

Auxiliary questions:

> *What are individual divisions and product line revenues?*
> *What are the significant trends?*
> *What do we expect our revenues to be in the future?*
> *What are the factors that we know of that will determine these results?*

Key question on fixed charges:

> *What are our fixed charges?*

Auxiliary questions:

> *What are the specific components in our fixed charges?*
> *Which of these can we control and how?*
> *Which are beyond our control?*
> *How will these change in the future?*

Key question on prices:

What is our pricing structure?

Auxiliary questions:

What is the pricing of all of our products?
How was the pricing of each determined?
What is the price sensitivity of each?
How do our prices compare with those of competitive products?
Are significant differences justified?

Key question on debt:

What is our company's long-term and short-term debt?

Auxiliary questions:

What are the current plans for reducing or increasing this debt?
What is our current ability to reduce it?
What sources of funding do we use?

Key question on assets and liabilities:

What are our assets and liabilities?

Auxiliary questions:

What has been the recent pattern in assets and liabilities?
Which are long-term and which are short-term?
Which are tangible and which are nontangible?
What do we expect over the next several years?
What are our current cash reserves?
What are our other assets?

Key question on additional resources:

What are our sources of additional financial resources?

Auxiliary questions:

What is the potential extent of each source?
What are the costs?
What are the terms?

Key question on return on assets:

What return are we getting on our investments and assets?

Auxiliary questions:

What return are we getting from each major component of our corporation, i.e., each division (Research, Development, etc.) or product line?

What is expected in the future?

Key question on investments:

What is our investment policy?

Auxiliary questions:

What determined that policy?

Is it still valid today?

Will it be valid in the future?

What forces are occurring that should cause us to modify the policy?

Key question on credit:

What is our company's credit rating?

Auxiliary questions:

What is the recent history of its rating?

What factors have determined its rating?

What do we expect in the future?

Sources of Information on Company Finances

Source	Information available
Financial records	Various data
Budgets	Finances of current operations

High-Technology Equipment

Key questions:

What is the present state of our internal use of high-technology equipment?

What are our plans in this area?

Auxiliary questions:

What equipment are we using today?

How are we using it?

What are we planning to use?

How are we planning to use it?

What is the basis for future plans?

What are the costs and benefits today and for the planned equipment?

Organization

Key question:

How is the company organized?

Auxiliary questions:

Why is it so organized?

What is the degree of centralization and/or divisional autonomy?

What are the advantages and disadvantages of the present organizational structure?

What changes are reasonable to make?

What changes are planned?

What benefits would result from these changes?

Management

Key question on style:

What type of management does the company have?

Auxiliary questions:

Is it formal, informal, dictatorial, relaxed, aggressive, flexible, risk-averse, daring, or other?

How does it view the R & D function?

What are the educational and experience backgrounds of top management?

How else can top management be characterized?

Key question on strengths and weaknesses:

What are the strengths and weaknesses of the company's management?

Auxiliary questions:

What skills are strongest among our managers?

What skills are weakest?

What hiring plans have we?

What plans have we for replacement of managers in the future?

What training programs have we for managers?

Do we need new ones?

For Section 2.6   THE LAST STRATEGIC PLAN

Objectives and Strategy

Key questions:

> *What are the objectives of the current plan?*
> *What is its strategy?*

Auxiliary questions:

> *What information was gathered?*
> *Is any of it still useful?*
> *On what basis were the objectives set?*
> *To what extent are those objectives still valid?*
> *On what basis was the strategy set?*
> *How much of that strategy is still applicable?*

Budget

Key question:

> *What is the budget in the current plan?*

Auxiliary questions:

> *What is the budget, by years and by major category?*
> *How was the budget determined?*

For Section 2.7   THE PLANNING PROCESS

Management Support

Key question:

> *What kind of support does top management give to strategic planning?*

Auxiliary questions:

> *What is the responsibility of Planning?*
> *Where does it report in the management structure?*
> *How responsive are operating divisions to Planning?*

Organization

Key question:

> *What responsibilities do various organizations have in strategic planning?*

Auxiliary questions:

> *What are their specific duties?*
>
> *What information do they gather and what do they disseminate?*

Planning Successes

Key question:

> *What successes can be attributed to strategic planning within the company?*

Auxiliary questions:

> *How accurate have previous plans' forecasts of the future been, both within the company and outside?*
>
> *Which aspects of the process in the company are done well and which are done poorly?*
>
> *What plans exist to improve or otherwise change the process?*

Sources of Information on Company Planning	
Source	Information available
Strategic plans	Forecasts, decisions, and strategies
Other plan documents	Resource allocations, budgets
Budgets	Financial data, strategies
Financial reports	Financial measures of success

Appendix for Chapter 3

QUESTIONS ON THE ENVIRONMENT

The questions here are related to those appearing in Chapter 3, *Analysis of the Environment*. Sections are labeled exactly as in that chapter. The auxiliary questions here should be treated as described in Appendix for Chapter 2.

The list below provides sources of information on the environment. Most of these cover the environment in general terms; a few deal specifically with indicated areas.

New England Research Application Center (NERAC), University of Connecticut, Storrs, Connecticut. (This service provides data bases on all business and technical subjects from current literature; it offers automatic searching of citations by user interest profile.)

F&S Index, published annually by Predicasts, Inc., Cleveland. (This book provides information from trade journals, covering companies, products, and industries. Subjects include acquisitions, mergers, new products, technology developments, and sociopolitical factors.)

Business Intelligence Program, SRI International, Menlo Park, California. (This program publishes a series of reports on the futures of industries, as well as *TEAM*, an early-warning system of recent developments affecting companies.)

Daniells, Lorna M., *Business Information Sources*, University of California Press, Berkeley, 1976, Chapter 3. (This chapter provides a comprehensive tabulation of directories of companies, industries, associations, foundations, consultants, government organizations, periodicals, and research centers.)

Directory of Online Databases, Cuadra Associates, Inc., Santa Monica, California; published semiannually with quarterly updates. (This provides a listing and descriptions of online, publicly available data bases in all fields.)

Directory of U.S. and Canadian Surveys and Services, ed. by Joan E. Huber, Charles H. Kline & Co., Fairfield, N.J., 1979. (This is a tabulation of market research reports on many subjects.)

Findex, ed. by Diana Degen and Thomas E. Miller, FIND/SVP, The Information Clearinghouse, New York, annual. (This is a tabulation of market research reports on many subjects.)

The Conference Board. (The Board provides a series of reports on planning methodologies, forecasting, business, and related matters.)

A Guide to SEC Corporate Filings: What They Are; What They Tell, Disclosure, Inc., Washington, 1979. (This booklet describes the several reports that public corporations file with the SEC. The information is largely financial, but there is also information on company businesses, key personnel, and other items.)

For Section 3.2   MAJOR PROBLEMS AND SENSITIVITIES

Problems

Key questions:

> *What problems are we currently facing?*
>
> *What major problems are we likely to face over the plan period?*

Auxiliary questions:

> *Have we faced any of these before?*
>
> *If so, what did we do about them?*
>
> *What happened as a result?*

Sensitivities

Key question:

> *To what factors in the environment is our company most sensitive?*

Auxiliary questions:

> *How serious are these sensitivities?*
>
> *What are their consequences?*

For Section 3.3   THE COMPETITION

Companies

Key question:

> *What companies are in competition with us, i.e., offer products that compete in the same markets?*

Auxiliary questions addressed to each company:

> *How can the company be characterized, as to product line, size, financial results, strengths and weaknesses, etc.?*
>
> *What are its market shares?*
>
> *What are the significant differences from our company, in, e.g., R & D spending per unit of sales, pricing policy, and technology acquisition means?*
>
> *What patents has it recently obtained in our technology areas?*
>
> *Has it undertaken any new programs, expansions, acquisitions, or divestments?*
>
> *What is its financial situation?*
>
> *What problems does it have?*
>
> *What seem to be its long-range objectives, goals, and strategy?*

Products

Key question:

> *What are the products that compete with ours?*

Auxiliary questions addressed to each product:

> *What are its features, cost, and geographic availability?*
>
> *What technologies are used?*
>
> *How are they used?*
>
> *How does the product compete with our products?*
>
> *How much like our company's products is it?*
>
> *Is it appropriate to consider adding any of these features to our products that compete with it?*

Other auxiliary questions:

> *Have there been any recent announcement of new products?*
>
> *Where are gaps (niches) in competitors' products, i.e., where, in a set of products that comprise a "family", are places for new products?*

Sources of Information on Competitors

Sources	Information available
Competitive product reports	Product data
Trade journals	Product announcements, articles on competitive companies, organizational changes
Newspapers	Product announcements, personnel changes organizational changes,
Product announcements	Product information
Press releases	Product and personal information
Annual reports	Various information
Reports to the SEC	Business information
Reports on companies, by various firms that assess markets, technologies, etc.	Product information, company resources
Telephone directories	Locations of employees
Government contract announcements	Projects undertaken
Financial reports	Financial information
Product advertisements	Product data
Personnel advertisements	Information on skills needed (and thus work to be done)
Technical reports	Products

Specific sources	Information available
Market research reports	Information on companies and their products; technology

Companies specializing in such reports include:
    Quantum Science Corporation, Dataquest,
    Frost & Sullivan, Gnostic Concepts,
    International Data Corporation,
    Creative Strategies International,
    SBS Publishing, SRI International	

Federal Register	Actions of Federal Government

Online data bases:
    Predicasts
    Information Management	

Sources of Information on Competitors *(continued)*	
Specific sources	Information available
Dataquest	Assessments of industries
Auerbach	Computer-related products
Datapro	Products, by industry
Dun and Bradstreet Reports	General information on companies
Buyers' Laboratory	Office product evaluations
Business Week: Annual R & D Survey	R & D spending, by industry and by company

New York Times:
    "Executive Changes" and
    "Business People"
	Management changes

Wall Street Journal: "Who's News"	Management changes

For Section 3.4   TECHNOLOGY

Competitive Research

Key question:

What research is being undertaken by our competitors that is of concern to us?

Auxiliary questions:

What are the goals of this research?
At what products are they aimed?
What is the overall quality of research in competitive firms?
What are their patent and publication records?
What are their R & D budgets?

Competitive Technology

Key question:

What is the status of technologies under development in competitive firms?

Auxiliary questions:

What is the patent situation for these technologies?
What is their proprietary status?

What are the scope and potential significance of the technologies?

What technology advances expertise do these firms have?

What development programs do they have under way?

Are any of these technologies available for acquisition?

Other Research and Technology

Key question:

What is the status of research and technology at universities and government agencies?

Auxiliary questions:

Where is this work being done?

Would this work be of any value to us?

In what way?

How far along in development are technologies of value to us?

Acquisition

Key question:

Are there any technologies outside the company that we should consider acquiring?

Auxiliary questions:

What are these technologies?

Where are they located?

Can they be acquired?

How can they be acquired?

What is the cost?

What would the benefits of such acquisitions be?

Sources of Information on Technology

Sources	Information available
Product announcements	Product information
Scientific journals: technical papers	Research and technology advances
Conference proceedings: technical talks and papers	Research and technology advances

Sources of Information on Technology *(continued)*

Sources	Information available
Patents	Technology advances
Disclosure journals	Technologies, devices
Reports on companies by firms that assess markets, technologies,etc.	Product information, company resources
Reports by universities	Technologies, devices
Reports by government agencies (ARPA, DOD, etc.)	Technologies, devices
Reports on technologies	Technologies
Personal contacts: acquaintances, universities' staff, etc.	Various information

Specific sources	Information available
National Technical Information Services (Dept. of Commerce)	Research reports, newsletters
Patent Gazette	Technology advances and methodologies
Applied Science Index	Index of technical periodicals
Battelle Memorial Institute: *Technical Inputs to Planning*	Information on emerging technologies and innovations; implications and applications

Market research reports (See Section 3.2.)

Newsletters:
Among the most popular are these:

Technology Forecasts and Technology Surveys	Technology
EDP Industry Report	Data processing
Graphics Communications World	Facsimile, printers
Office Automation Reporting Service	Office automation
Datacomm Advisors	Communications

Online data bases:
Compendex (Engineering Index; all engineering)
ISMEC (chemical engineering & chemistry)
Inspec (mechanical engineering)
U. S. Patents data base

For Section 3.5   MARKETS

Present Markets

Key question:

What are the markets in which our company competes?

Auxiliary questions:

How can these be characterized, as to size, recent changes in size, type of customer, geography, etc.?

How price sensitive are they?

Are the markets changing?

Are they growing?

How?

Are they seasonal or cyclical?

What allied markets exist that are not tapped?

Potential New Markets

Key question:

In what ways can our present markets be extended?

Auxiliary questions:

Can this be done by providing changes in product characteristics — in functional features, size, cost to purchase and operate, etc.?

What markets could be created by our company or its competitors with new products?

Customers

Key question:

Who are the customers for our present products?

Auxiliary questions:

How can they be characterized, by size (i.e., individual, family, company, etc.), geography, frequency and size of acquisition, etc.?

Why do these customers acquire these products?

What new features or other changes would they like to see?

What is the price elasticity of the products?

What needs and desires are unfulfilled, either by product absence or due to product cost?

How do our customers perceive us, with respect to our products, our prices, and our service?

Sources of Information on Markets

Own market studies

Market studies done for company under contract

Market studies published by various firms

Government reports on markets

Trade and professional associations

U. S. Bureau of Census: reports

Conference Board:
    CBDB (data base) — indicators for industrial markets

For Section 3.6 SUPPLY FACTORS

Raw materials

Key question:

What is the availability today of the raw materials upon which we depend?

Auxiliary questions:

What are current costs and recent cost trends?

What are alternative materials and their availability?

Can we use them?

How reliable are our sources of raw materials?

Suppliers

Key question:

What suppliers is our company dependent upon?

Auxiliary questions:

How reliable are our suppliers?

What alternate .suppliers are there?

What do we obtain from each supplier?

Energy

Key question:

Is our company especially vulnerable to energy shortages?

Auxiliary questions:

If so, how are we vulnerable?
What alternatives have we to decrease our dependence on energy?
What are their costs?
What are their benefits?

Sources of Information on Supply Factors

Government reports
Suppliers reports

For Section 3.7   SOCIOECONOMIC FACTORS

Economic Factors

Key question:

What is the current state of the economy in the geographical areas in which our company operates?

Auxiliary questions:

What is the employment situation?
What is the inflation situation?
What aspects of the economy are particularly important to us?
How susceptible are we to economic cycles?

Social Factors

Key question:

What social factors today have impact on our company?

Auxiliary questions:

What public attitudes towards business have significance for our company?
In what way does public attitude toward technology play a significant role in our business?

Demographic Factors

Key question:

What is the distribution of population that is of concern in our markets?

Auxiliary questions:

What is the current age and wealth distribution?
What affect does this have on our markets?
What is the geographic distribution?
What is the effect of these distributions on our company?

Legal Factors

Key question:

What laws and regulations today affect our company?

Auxiliary questions:

What affects do they have?
What factors drive these laws and regulations?
Are we monitoring all appropriate sources?

Political Factors

Key question:

What are the political conditions in the states and countries in which we operate?

Auxiliary questions:

What affect do they have on us?
Are we properly monitoring the situations?

Sources of Information on Socioeconomic Factors

Factors	Sources
Economic	Government economic reports
	Newspapers
	Business school projections
	Business periodicals:
	Business Week, Forbes, Fortune, Business Economics, etc.

Sources of Information on Socioeconomic Factors
(continued)

Factors	Sources
Social	Government and other reports
	Newspapers
	Special newsletters
Demographic	Government reports
Legal	Published laws and regulations
	Court decisions
Political	Newspapers
	Government studies
General	*Business Periodicals Index*

Appendix for Chapter 4

QUESTIONS ON THE FUTURE

The questions here are related to those appearing in Chapter 4, *Forecasting the Future*. Sections are labeled exactly as in that chapter. The auxiliary questions here should be treated as described in the Appendix for Chapter 2.

There are many sources of information about the future in general terms and about specific aspects of the environment's future. The table below lists several such sources. Additionally, there are two directories of information on the future:

World Future Society, *The Future: A Guide to Information Sources*, Washington, D.C., 1977. (This directory provides a detailed list of organizations, individuals, books, educational programs, films, and other resources dealing with the future. Details on specific areas of work, publications, etc. are included.)

McHale, John, and Magda C. McHale, *The Futures Directory*, IPC Science and Technology Press, London, 1977. (This directory provides a detailed list of organizations and individuals. Details are included.)

It should further be noted that almost any book, periodiclal, or paper published on strategic planning deals with the future. Such sources address the methodology of projecting the future rather than what the future itself may comprise. Most of the material in the two directories and in the sources given in the table are concerned with the latter.

Sources of Information on the Future

Sources	Information available
Purchasing (magazine)	One-year forecasts on economic and key industry factors
National Planning Association:	
National Economic Projection Service	Economic forecasts
Regional Economic Projection Service	Economic forecasts
Predicasts	Projections in many fields
U. S. Dept. of Commerce:	
U. S. Industrial Outlook	Economic forecasts
Conference Board:	Various booklets
Statistical Bulletin	
Economic Outlook USA	
Stanford Research Institute:	
Business Intelligence Program	Reports on future events in various industries
Datalog	New research information
Market research reports	Future of various industries and technologies
Arthur D. Little, Inc:	
Impact	Business forecasts

For Section 4.3   COMPETITION AND TECHNOLOGY

Competition

Key question:

Which companies will compete in our company's markets?

Auxiliary questions:

Which new companies will compete in our present markets?
Which companies will compete in our planned new markets?
How can each of these companies be characterized?
In what ways will our current competitors change: in product line, strengths and weaknesses, R & D spending, technology acquisition, and so on?

Competitive Products

Key question:

What new products will be introduced that will compete with us?

Auxiliary questions:

What features will they have?

What new product modifications and improvements will be introduced?

What trends in competitive products can be projected from a study of competitive patents and other technical literature?

Future Technologies

Key question:

What is the expected future progress of the technologies of concern to our company?

Auxiliary questions:

What new development activities in these technologies are expected?

What new technologies are expected?

What advantages will they provide to both competitors and to our company?

Technology Acquisition

Key question:

What new technologies will be available for our acquisition?

Auxiliary questions:

From what source can each be acquired?

What will the cost be to acquire them?

What are the benefits likely to be?

In what products are they potentially useful?

For Section 4.4   PREDICTING TECHNOLOGY NEEDS

Markets

Key question:

How are our company's markets going to change?

Auxiliary questions:

How will they change in size, nature, and geography?

What new markets of interest to us are likely to be opened up?

Will any be spawned by the competition?

Will any be created by changing customer demands?

Will any be seriously affected by new government regulations?

What will their characteristics be?

What will the causes of these changes be?

Customers

Key question:

Who will be the customers for our future products?

Auxiliary questions:

How will this customer population grow and change?

How will they be characterized?

What new demands and desires will they have?

How will customers respond to changes in prices of the company's products?

Raw materials

Key question:

What will the availability be of raw materials we require?

Auxiliary questions:

What are the future cost trends going to be?

What are alternative materials that can be developed or acquired for use?

Economic Factors

Key question:

What will the state of the economy be in the geographical areas in which our company will be doing business in the future?

Auxiliary questions:

What will employment and inflation trends be?

How influential will business cycles be on the company?

Social Factors

Key question:

What social factors will be critical in determining our future markets and products?

Auxiliary questions:

What will be the impact of changes in social factors on our company?
What changes in public attitudes concerning business and technology can we expect?

Demographic Factors

Key question:

What will the distribution of population be that will be of concern to us?

Auxiliary questions:

What will be the age and wealth distribution?
What affect will this have on our markets?
What will be the geographic distribution?
What will be the effect of these distributions on our company?
What are long-term demographic trends that are of concern to us?

Legal Factors

Key question:

What new laws and regulations will take place that have impact on our company?

Auxiliary questions:

What will the impact be of those laws and regulations?
What factors will drive these laws and regulations?

Political Factors

Key question:

What changes will occur in the political situation in states and countries of interest to our company?

Auxiliary question:

What effect will these have on the company?

For Section 4.5 *ANALYSIS OF FORECASTS*

Key question:

What has been the record of our company in making forecasts in the past?

Auxiliary questions:

How accurate have the forecasts been?
Where have they been accurate?
Where have they been inaccurate?
Are there any patterns?
What has been the consequences of the inaccurate forecasts?
What methods of forecasting has the company used?
How can we improve our approach?
Which sources of information have proven useful?
Which have not?

Appendix for Chapter 7

QUESTIONS ON STRATEGY

INTRODUCTION

The questions here are based upon those given in Chapter 2, which provided an in-depth analysis of the company. Here, the questions collectively represent an expansion of the following question:

What can we do and where can we go during the plan period?

In other words, we are now attempting to develop a strategy that is, in part, based on the responses to those earlier questions. Now we ask what *can* be done? Because these questions are so closely related to those in Chapter 2, the material here is numbered to match that chapter.

In the earlier appendixes, key questions are accompanied by auxiliary questions. This structure can be applied to the questions in this appendix in most instances. The reader is referred to those appendixes for auxiliary questions that can be applied here.

For Section 2.2   MAJOR PROBLEMS AND DECISIONS

Major Problems

What can we do about the major problems currently facing the company?

What can we do about the major problems we are likely to face over the plan period?

Major Decisions

How can we make the major decisions that we must make?
What are the several alternatives in each case?

For Section 2.3   TECHNOLOGY

Research Projects

What new research projects can we undertake?
What research projects can we drop without serious impact?

Research Activity

How can we improve the quality of our research program?

Experience and Applications

In what areas can we strengthen our technology experience?
Where is it applicable?

Development Programs

How can we cause our development programs to become more relevant to our planned products?

New Projects and Programs

What new research projects can we undertake during the plan period?
What new development programs can we undertake?

Technology Transfer

How can we improve our technology transfer process?

For Section 2.4   PRODUCTS AND MARKETS

Product Features

What new features can be added to our products?
What features can be improved by using our technology base?

New Products

What new products can we offer, in present and in new lines, based on our technology projects?

Current Products

How can we improve the sale of our current products?

How can we improve their market shares?

How can we cut the cost of manufacturing them?

Geographic Areas

In what parts of the country or the world, if any, where products are not now marketed could they be?

Markets

What new markets can we enter?

Which of our present markets should we abandon?

For Section 2.5   CORPORATE RESOURCES

Manufacturing

Capacity

How can we increase the capacity of our manufacturing operations?

Flexibility and Change

How can we make our manufacturing operations more flexible?

Costs

How can we improve the manufacturing costs for our products?

Equipment Resources and Other Facilities

How can we improve the state of our manufacturing equipment and our other facilities?

Communication

How can we improve the communication between Development and Manufacturing?

Marketing and Sales

Marketing

What new market studies can we do that would be of value to us?

Sales

How can we improve our approach to sales and our sales force?

Service

Quality

How can we improve the quality of the service provided by the company?

Costs

How can we decrease the cost of maintenance and repair of our products?

Manpower

Staffing

How can we improve our staffing capabilities?

Training

How can we improve our manpower skills and technical expertise?
What new courses and other aids to training can we offer?

Finances

How can we improve our cash flow, consistency of earnings, and revenues?
How can we better our positions in fixed charges, pricing, debt, assets and liabilities, sources of additional funds, return on assets, investments, and credit?

High-Technology Equipment

What new high-technology equipment available today or in the future can we use to improve our operations further?

Organization

How can the company be reorganized to improve its utility and efficiency of operation?

Management

Style

> *In what ways can our management approach change, so as to result in overall improvement of operation?*

Strengths and Weaknesses

> *How can we capitalize on the strengths and minimize the impact of the weaknesses of the company's management?*

For Section 2.7   THE PLANNING PROCESS

Management Support

> *Can we improve the support that top management gives strategic planning?*

Organization

> *How can be develop a better organization for planning purposes?*

Planning Successes

> *How can we take actions to improve the success of our strategic planning?*

GLOSSARY

Following are definitions of the key terms used in this book. The chapters in which the terms are defined are indicated.

Bottom-up planning   Planning where all levels of management submit plans upwards, starting with the lowest feasible units (Chapter 1, page 13).

Business planning   Planning that addresses the businesses that a company is in or plans to be in (Chapter 7, page 172).

Competitive surveillance   The careful monitoring of all public information about companies that are, or have prospects of becoming, competitors in the marketplace (Chapter 3, page 61).

Contingency planning   Planning that yields a set of alternatives (different strategies or portions of strategies) to the decisions made for the strategic plan, to allow for assumptions that turn out to be wrong (Chapter 4, page 91).

Control   The actions taken by management to insure that the performance of a company conforms to plans (Chapter 8, page 198).

Critical success factors   The areas of concern to a company in which satisfactory results will insure successful performance (Chapter 7, page 154).

Data base   A collection of related, structured information stored in a computer's auxiliary memory (Chapter 9, page 220).

Data-base system   A set of programs that allows a user to enter information into data bases, to manipulate the data, and to generate printed results (Chapter 9, page 220).

Decision support system   A computer system that aids decision making, comprising a data base, a model base, and a software system for interconnecting data and models for making them available (Chapter 9, page 222).

Delphi method   A method where experts in a field are questioned individually (usually by questionnaire) about their expectations for a number of possible future events; their collective responses provide the basis for forecasting (Chapter 4, page 80).

Demand-induced innovation   Innovation that results from forces outside the R & D organizations, whereby a need is perceived by someone in the firm and a demand is placed on R & D to develop a technological solution (Chapter 4, page 77).

Environment of a company   External factors that have had, now have, or may in the future have some measurable effect on the company (Chapter 3, page 58).

Environmental analysis (scanning)   An analysis of the company's environment, which addresses events and developments in such areas as technology, the competition, politics, economics, sociology, demography, law, and regulation (Chapter 3, page 59).

Event   An action that occurs at a definite point in time (Chapter 2, page 36).

Exploratory view (of technological change)   The view that invention and innovation are self-generating activities with lives of their own, that technology evolves in response to technological opportunities and challenges, and that technological change occurs without consideration of the marketplace (Chapter 4, page 76).

Forecasting   The construction of models of possible futures, possible activities occurring within those futures, and probabilistic assessments of their taking place (Chapter 4, page 75).

Framework for planning   An outline of the steps involved in planning; a model of the process (Chapter 10, page 232).

Futures gap   The difference in the futures defined by where a company wants to go (its objectives) and where it is projected to go, the latter being determined by consideration of present plans and future expected environmental events (Chapter 7, page 157).

Gap analysis   An approach to strategy setting which addresses a corporation's futures gap (Chapter 7, page 157).

Goal   The means by which an objective is attained (Chapter 5, page 114).

High-technology company   See **Technology-based company**

Intuitive methods of forecasting   Methods using an expert in a technology field, who is well-versed in its underlying scientific and engineering principles, to predict future events and trends in that field (Chapter 4, page 80).

Long-range planning   See **Strategic planning**

Management information system   A computer-based, organized collection of information and programming systems used to process information that management utilizes to help in making decisions (Chapter 9, page 221).

Market share matrix   A matrix that shows annual growth rate of a market against relative market share of a company's product (Chapter 7, page 158).

Milestone   A measure of progress of company activities (Chapter 8, page 194).

Mission   The responsibility that an organization is assigned or assumes, which provides guidance on the general rationale for its existence (Chapter 5, page 103).

Model generator   A computer-based system used for developing models, comprising the planning language, the instructions for use of the language and of the model generated, and the programming systems that generate the model (Chapter 9, page 216).

Modeling   The process of creating a small, controllable system which responds in the same manner as a large, less controllable system (Chapter 9, page 211).

Normative view (of technological change)   The view that invention and innovation are processes determined by existing needs or by economic demand (Chapter 4, page 77).

Objective   A description of what a corporation wishes to strive for and achieve in the future, which generally defines the intended future state of the corporation over the plan period and, possibly, the manner by which the company attains that future state (Chapter 5, page 100).

Operating plan   A "short range" plan, usually covering the upcoming year or two, which includes the tactics needed to implement a strategy, with more details and specifics for operating the company on a daily, weekly, or monthly basis (Chapter 1, page 13).

Operational plans   Descriptions of activities to be undertaken during a plan period which include tabulations of resource allocations made to these activities, as well as a budget (Chapter 8, page 186).

Philosophy of operation   A statement about why the company is in business and the way in which it plans to operate, possibly addressing such matters as product quality, efficiency of internal operations, treatment of employees, and a code of conduct − in short, a company's creed (Chapter 5, page 103).

Plan period   The time period for which strategic planning is done. In this book, a five-year plan period is assumed (Chapter 1, page 12).

Planning period   The time during which planning is done; if this period is a year, it is termed *the planning year* (Chapter 1, page 11).

Preplanning analysis report   A report that contains the results of the company's self-analysis. It includes major problems, major decisions, major sensitivities, strengths, weaknesses, opportunities, threats, responses to internal issues, and responses to external issues (Chapter 2, page 52).

Present value   A value in the future translated back to today's dollars, taking the time value of money into account (Chapter 7, page 164).

Product-market matrix   A matrix that relates the extent of product lines and markets (Chapter 7, page 147).

Product matrix   A matrix that shows how a company's businesses and products relate to markets in the industry (Chapter 7, page 157).

Product model   Models that interrelate product features, manufacturing costs, and customer values (Chapter 9, page 214).

Product niche   A gap in a market where no products exist, as defined by an open space in a graph that plots two product traits against each other (Chapter 7, page 155).

Product planning   Planning wherein products to be offered by the company in the future are defined (Chapter 7, page 174).

Query system   A computer information system that allows users to store information about which questions can be asked (Chapter 9, page 223).

Relative market share   The ratio of the company's market share for a product to the share of the largest competitor for a competing product (Chapter 7, page 158).

Report generator   A computer system that provides reports on material stored within an MIS, in a formalized, structured manner (Chapter 9, page 221).

Risk   A measure of the uncertainty of the successful completion of activities and of the accuracy of estimates made on the cost of and time to completion (Chapter 6, page 125).

Self-analysis   An analysis of a company's major problems, its strengths, its weaknesses, and its resources (Chapter 2, page 36).

Socioeconomic factors in environment   Economic, social, demographic, legal, and political factors (Chapter 3, page 67).

Strategic business unit (SBU)   Organizations within a corporation that address specific business markets of interest to the company (Chapter 7, page 172).

Strategic planning   A process whereby corporate objectives for the future are identified in response to perceived opportunities and threats and whereby activities are selected and resources are allocated to meet these objectives (Chapter 1, page 6).

Strategy   The method whereby corporate objectives and goals are to be attained by the allocation of resources to activities (Chapter 7, page 145).

Subobjective   A more specific achievement to be attained to meet an objective, following from the latter (Chapter 5, page 114).

Supply-pushed innovation Innovation that results from inventions and developments within the R & D organization and does not depend on the existence of any needs for the new capabilities (Chapter 4, page 77).

Technological forecasting Forecasting the future of technologies (see **Forecasting**). The term is also used to refer to examination of nontechnological elements in the environment for information on demands for future technology needs (Chapter 4, page 75).

Technology The systematic application of fundamental, scientific phenomena and principles in a device, process, or concept that performs a function useful to mankind or having commercial value (Chapter 1, page 2).

Technology alternative Choices of current and future technologies that can be used in a company's products, representing technological capabilities and limitations to be considered as new products are conceived and developed (Chapter 6, page 130).

Technology assessment A detailed examination of the state of the art in a technology, with particular emphasis on (a) the possible utility of the technology to the company and (b) the impacts of the technology on the company or on the outside world. The terms *technology utility assessment* and *technology impact assessment* can be used, respectively, to describe these two tasks (Chapter 6, page 132).

Technology-based company A company that puts to practice inventions described in patents, spends a significant proportion of their budget on research and development of new technologies, has a large staff of scientifically trained personnel, and sells products that are relatively new to the marketplace (Chapter 1, page 2).

Technology industry The group of companies that are technology based (Chapter 1, page 2).

Technology transfer The transfer of developed technologies from Research to Development, as the term is used in this book. The term is also used in other senses, referring to the transition of technology from Development to Manufacturing, from one application to another, from one company to another, from government to industry, and from more developed to less developed countries (Chapter 6, page 136).

Top-down planning Planning where the chief executive officer or other top-level managers set guidelines (Chapter 1, page 13).

Trend The sequence of values that some measurable entity experiences over time (Chapter 2, page 36).

Trend extrapolation The simplest type of forecast, where the assumption is made that the environment does not change or changes very little and that whatever has occurred in the recent past will continue in the future (Chapter 4, page 78).

INDEX

Page references in *italics* indicate definitions.